Local Content Requirements: A Global Problem

Gary Clyde Hufbauer and Jeffrey J. Schott
Cathleen Cimino, Martin Vieiro, and Erika Wada

MIX
Paper from
responsible sources
FSC® C010236
FSC
www.fsc.org

Local Content Requirements: A Global Problem

Gary Clyde Hufbauer and Jeffrey J. Schott
Cathleen Cimino, Martin Vieiro, and Erika Wada

PETERSON INSTITUTE FOR INTERNATIONAL ECONOMICS
Washington, DC
September 2013

Gary Clyde Hufbauer, Reginald Jones Senior Fellow at the Peterson Institute for International Economics since 1992, was formerly the Maurice Greenberg Chair and Director of Studies at the Council on Foreign Relations (1996–98), the Marcus Wallenberg Professor of International Finance Diplomacy at Georgetown University (1985–92), senior fellow at the Institute (1981–85), deputy director of the International Law Institute at Georgetown University (1979–81), deputy assistant secretary for international trade and investment policy of the US Treasury (1977–79), and director of the international tax staff at the Treasury (1974–76). Among his numerous books are *Figuring Out the Doha Round* (2010), *Economic Sanctions Reconsidered, 3rd edition* (2007), *US Taxation of Foreign Income* (2007), *NAFTA Revisited: Achievements and Challenges* (2005), and *Reforming the US Corporate Tax* (2005).

Jeffrey J. Schott, senior fellow at the Peterson Institute for International Economics, has been with the Institute since 1983. He was a senior associate at the Carnegie Endowment for International Peace (1982–83) and an official of the US Treasury Department (1974–82) in international trade and energy policy. He is a member of the Trade and Environment Policy Advisory Committee of the Office of the US Trade Representative and the Advisory Committee on International Economic Policy of the US State Department. Among his numerous books are *Understanding the Trans-Pacific Partnership* (2012), *NAFTA and Climate Change* (2011), *Figuring Out the Doha Round* (2010), *Economic Sanctions Reconsidered, 3rd edition* (2007), *NAFTA Revisited: Achievements and Challenges* (2005), and *Free Trade Agreements: US Strategies and Priorities* (2004).

Cathleen Cimino has been a research analyst at the Peterson Institute since August 2012. She obtained a master's degree focused on international economics from the School of International Relations and Pacific Studies (IR/PS) at the University of California, San Diego and a bachelor's degree from Columbia University. She previously worked on development and economic security issues at the Asia Society and the Center for Strategic and International Studies.

Martin Vieiro is an analyst at the Economist Intelligence Unit. He was a research analyst at the Peterson Institute from June 2011 to March 2013. His past experience also includes stints at Ernst & Young, the US Department of the Treasury, and the National Labor Relations Board.

Erika Wada, former visiting fellow at the Peterson Institute, is a PhD candidate at Michigan State University. She is coauthor of *The Benefits of Price Convergence: Speculative Calculations* (2002) and coeditor of *Unfinished Business: Telecommunications after the Uruguay Round* (1997).

PETERSON INSTITUTE FOR INTERNATIONAL ECONOMICS
1750 Massachusetts Avenue, NW
Washington, DC 20036-1903
(202) 328-9000   FAX: (202) 659-3225
www.piie.com

Adam S. Posen, *President*
Steven R. Weisman, *Editorial and Publications Director*

Typesetting by BMWW
Printing by United Book Press, Inc.

Printed in the United States of America
15   14   13   5   4   3   2   1

Library of Congress Cataloging-in-Publication Data
Hufbauer, Gary Clyde.
  Local content requirements : a global problem / Gary Clyde Hufbauer and Jeffrey J. Schott ; assisted by Cathleen Cimino, Martin Vieiro, and Erika Wada.
     pages cm
  Includes bibliographical references.
  ISBN 978-0-88132-680-2
  1. Commercial policy—Case studies.   2. Buy national policy—Case studies.   I. Schott, Jeffrey J., 1949-   II. Title.
  HF1411.H838 2013
  382'.5—dc23
                                          2013027010

This publication has been subjected to a prepublication peer review intended to ensure analytical quality. The views expressed are those of the authors. This publication is part of the overall program of the Peterson Institute for International Economics, as endorsed by its Board of Directors, but it does not necessarily reflect the views of individual members of the Board or of the Institute's staff or management. The Institute is an independent, private, nonprofit institution for rigorous, intellectually honest study and open discussion of international economic policy. Its work is made possible by financial support from a highly diverse group of philanthropic foundations, private corporations, and interested individuals, as well as by income on its capital fund. For a list of Institute supporters, please see www.piie.com/supporters.cfm.

Contents

Tables

Figures

Boxes

Preface

Over the past century, economic downturns generally have increased demand for protectionism, almost always with adverse results. The Great Recession of 2008-09 began with the major economic powers determined to learn from history and disavow barriers to trade. Unfortunately, the commonly held view that countries eschewed protectionism this time turned out to be sadly mistaken. Most of the Group of 20 countries avoided new explicit tariffs and quotas. But many applied more opaque measures, especially behind the border nontariff barriers (NTBs). Among these were local content requirements (LCRs), often accompanying stimulus spending, renewable energy programs, and other industrial policies aimed at creating local jobs and building industries at home.

Local Content Requirements: A Global Problem provides an indepth assessment of this component of protectionism arising from the Great Recession of 2008-09. Gary Clyde Hufbauer, Jeffrey J. Schott, and a team of scholars evaluated LCRs introduced worldwide since 2008. Their comprehensive study identified 117 LCRs imposed or considered. Accurately measuring both the cost and effectiveness of LCRs is a difficult task. Noting these limitations, the authors estimate that these measures potentially could have affected 5 percent of total global commerce in 2010. To be sure, the amount of trade actually impeded by these recent LCRs likely is a fraction of that total; even so, the authors estimate that the actual reduction of world trade on account of new LCRs still amounts to $93 billion annually. Perhaps 3.7 million jobs in targeted import-competing sectors worldwide might have benefited from LCRs, but millions of jobs elsewhere in all these national economies were lost. In short, LCRs, which supposedly aim to shield countries from economic harm, often compound problems at home and end up damaging the global economy as a whole.

Certain WTO obligations in theory limit the use of LCRs, but the rulebook in practice allows many LCRs to flourish. While this study found more than 100 cases of these barriers, only three have been challenged in the World Trade Organization (WTO). As the world economy gradually recovers, political pressures for new LCRs may abate, but there is no evidence that the potential caseload is shrinking.

In addition to the comprehensive survey, this book looks at six case studies of LCRs adopted and their impact in depth. The case studies illustrate the use and impact of LCR measures, ranging from explicit and transparent to implicit and opaque, imposed by both advanced and developing economies. The cases were drawn from the experience of Brazil, Canada, China, India, Nigeria, and the United States. In each case, the authors describe and roughly assess the scope of the LCR costs in terms of higher prices and lost trade.

As for alternatives, the authors propose measures to promote a business-friendly environment; encourage corporate social responsibility; provide better worker training programs; improve logistics; invest in additional infrastructure; and as a last resort, but more effective and transparent than LCRs, use new tariffs and subsidies. They argue that such measures would better foster job creation and industrial growth and entail fewer overall costs to domestic and foreign economies.

Since the financial crisis broke in 2008, the Global Trade Alert and the WTO have issued periodic reports on the incidence of new protectionism but did not fully appreciate the scope of the LCR problem. Our new study brightens the spotlight on the increasing use of these measures, even five years after the crisis. Government officials now seem to be taking note. In April 2013, the United States Trade Representative (USTR) flagged the proliferation of LCRs as a growing problem at the Asia Pacific Economic Cooperation (APEC) Senior Officials Meeting. APEC leaders have chosen to elevate the issue in the future. In June 2013, the United Nations Conference on Trade and Development (UNCTAD) gathered global experts to assess the economic and environmental effectiveness of LCRs in so-called green industries. In October 2013, the World Bank will hold a conference in Vienna to examine LCRs in the extractive industries. We hope this study will further focus attention on the threat from this form of protection.

This study, which evaluates LCRs as one form of trade protectionism, builds on the series of Peterson Institute studies on the cost of protection in major economies published over the past two decades. It demonstrates how protectionism is now more deeply ingrained in domestic policies than the trade restrictions of the past. In that regard, it serves as a companion to the Institute's more recent publications that examine how international negotiations could mitigate global trade and investment problems. They include *Payoff from the World Trade Agenda, 2013* (Gary Clyde Hufbauer and Jeffrey J. Schott), *Global Trade in Services: Fear, Facts, and Offshoring* (J. Bradford Jensen),

Outward Foreign Direct Investment and US Exports, Jobs, and R&D: Implications for US Policy (Hufbauer, Theodore Moran, and Lindsay Oldenski), and *Understanding the Trans-Pacific Partnership* (Schott, Barbara Kotschwar, and Julia Muir).

The Peterson Institute for International Economics is a private, nonprofit institution for rigorous, intellectually open, and honest study and discussion of international economic policy. Its purpose is to identify and analyze important issues to making globalization beneficial and sustainable for the people of the United States and the world and then to develop and communicate practical new approaches for dealing with them. The Institute is completely nonpartisan.

The Institute's work is funded by a highly diverse group of philanthropic foundations, private corporations, and interested individuals, as well as income on its capital fund. About 35 percent of the Institute's resources in our latest fiscal year were provided by contributors from outside the United States. The GE Ecomagination Program provided generous support for part of this study.

The Executive Committee of the Institute's Board of Directors bears overall responsibility for the Institute's direction, gives general guidance and approval to its research program, and evaluates its performance in pursuit of its mission. The Institute's President is responsible for the identification of topics that are likely to become important over the medium term (one to three years) that should be addressed by Institute scholars. This rolling agenda is set in close consultation with the Institute's research staff, Board of Directors, and other stakeholders.

The President makes the final decision to publish any individual Institute study, following independent internal and external review of the work.

The Institute hopes that its research and other activities will contribute to building a stronger foundation for international economic policy around the world. We invite readers of these publications to let us know how they think we can best accomplish this objective.

ADAM S. POSEN
President
August 2013

Acknowledgments

This Policy Analysis was supported by the GE Ecomagination Program. Peterson Institute Research Fellow Barbara Kotschwar and former Peterson Institute research analysts Allie Bagnall, Sean Lowry, Julia Muir, and Alex Selowsky all made substantial contributions to this study. Meera Fickling, former Institute research analyst, drafted chapter 7 on India's solar policies. Ronald Steenblick, senior trade policy analyst at the Organization for Economic Cooperation and Development, gave valuable suggestions on an earlier draft. Several referees provided useful comments.

Abbreviations

AHWP	Asian Harmonization Working Party
ALMP	active labor market program
ANVISA	Agência Nacional de Vigilância Sanitária (National Health Surveillance Agency)
APEC	Asia Pacific Economic Cooperation forum
ARRA	American Recovery and Reinvestment Act
ASCM	Agreement on Subsidies and Countervailing Measures
CDA	Content Development Act (Nigeria)
CEBRI	Centro Brasileiro de Relações Internacionais
CERC	Central Electricity Regulatory Commission
CNOOC	China National Offshore Oil Company
CSi	crystalline silicon
CSR	corporate social responsibility
CWSRF	Clean Water State Revolving Fund
DWSRF	Drinking Water State Revolving Fund
EPA	US Environmental Protection Agency
FDI	foreign direct investment
FEED	Front-End Engineering Design
FEER	fundamental equilibrium exchange rate
FEL	front-end loading
FIT	feed-in tariff
FTA	free trade agreement
FY	fiscal year
GATS	General Agreement on Trade in Services
GATT	General Agreement on Tariffs and Trade

GHTF	Global Harmonization Task Force
GMP	Good Manufacturing and Control Practices
GPA	Government Procurement Agreement
GSP	Generalized System of Preferences
GW	gigawatts
HS	Harmonized System
ICT	information and communications technology
IEA	International Energy Agency
IMDRF	International Medical Device Regulators Forum
IOC	international oil company
IT	information technology
JNNSM	Jawaharlal Nehru National Solar Mission
kW	kilowatts
kWh	kilowatt hour
LAHWP	Latin America Harmonization Working Party
LCR	local content requirement
LPI	Logistics Performance Index
MW	megawatts
NAFTA	North American Free Trade Agreement
NCDMB	Nigerian Content Development and Monitoring Board
NEV	New Energy Vehicle
NNPC	Nigerian National Petroleum Corporation
NTB	nontariff barrier
OECD	Organization for Economic Cooperation and Development
PIB	Petroleum Industry Bill
PV	photovoltaic
R&D	research and development
RFP	request for proposal
SOE	state-owned enterprise
SPDC	Shell Petroleum Development Company
SUS	Sistema Único de Saúde (Brazil's Unified Health System)
TDI	trade defense instrument
TPP	Trans-Pacific Partnership
TPRM	Trade Policy Review Mechanism
TRIMs	Trade-Related Investment Measures
TRIPS	Agreement on Trade Related Aspects of Intellectual Property Rights
TTC	trade transaction cost
TTIP	Transatlantic Trade and Investment Partnership
TWh	terawatt hour
USTR	US Trade Representative
WTO	World Trade Organization

Executive Summary

Local content requirements (LCRs) are a protective device with two simple but powerful appeals: They create jobs at home rather than abroad, and they channel business to domestic rather than foreign firms. Historically, LCRs have been associated primarily with government procurement and mandates imposed on publicly funded projects.

Political leaders who champion LCRs often seek to achieve multiple objectives. First, they seek to create jobs and channel business to domestic firms—the primary goal since the onset of the Great Recession. Second, they may harbor aspirations of building a world-class industry, following the logic of infant industry analysis. Third, they may believe that LCRs offer a promising path to economic development. Fourth, they want taxpayer money spent subsidizing ethanol, solar panels, or other renewables to feed back into the domestic economy.

In practice, however, LCRs have many drawbacks. Most LCR measures use quantity rather than price signals to influence market outcomes, and the economic cost of quantity signals is notoriously difficult to establish. Accordingly, public officials usually have little knowledge of how much their LCR policies cost. Moreover, they may not know what they are getting, as the LCRs may mandate what the market would have achieved on its own. In addition, LCRs are usually opaque, thereby lending themselves to corrupt application. Finally, once in place, LCRs seldom "sunset." As a result, market distortions may last a very long time.

In principle, many LCRs are inconsistent with the rules of the World Trade Organization (WTO) and regional free trade agreements. In practice, the rulebooks have many gaps. Moreover, national respect for international trade and investment rules is more a matter of self-discipline than litigation.

For both reasons, a "legalistic" answer to the spreading use of LCRs is not wholly satisfactory.

Alternatives to LCRs

This Policy Analysis explores six alternatives to LCRs that could deliver more job creation, impose fewer costs on the economy, and generate more economic growth.

- *Promoting a business-friendly environment.* A proven way to create jobs and stimulate investment over the long term is to upgrade conditions for doing business. Low corporate tax rates and honest officials are key ingredients.

- *Encouraging corporate social responsibility.* Governments can encourage multinational corporations to search out local firms for their supply base without crossing the line into "forced localization." Many multinational corporations have adopted corporate social responsibility guidelines with this feature.

- *Providing training.* Quality training programs are critical: For every 1 percent increase in the number of workers participating in training for new positions, the employment rate and labor force participation rate in countries in the Organization for Economic Cooperation and Development rose by more than 1 percent (OECD 2004).

- *Improving logistics.* World trade today is characterized by global value chains: Trade transaction costs are incurred not just once in the trip from producer to consumer but many times, making good logistics critical. By reducing their own trade transaction costs burden, countries can become more competitive in world markets and create jobs at home.

- *Investing in infrastructure.* Infrastructure is critical for economic performance, and creating infrastructure jobs is a particularly good response to unemployment. Infrastructure projects in the United States create 18,000 jobs for every $1 billion in new outlays. In the average developing country, every $1 billion in infrastructure investment creates about 70,000 jobs (Heintz, Pollin, and Garrett-Peltier 2009).

- *Using tariffs or subsidies.* If a government has a political choice between a new LCR and a higher tariff or greater subsidy, the tariff or subsidy is the less bad economic choice. These instruments' cost is more visible, and properly done, their administration can be simple and transparent, unlike LCRs, which are more likely to "play favorites."

Survey Snapshot

We identified 117 LCR measures proposed or implemented since 2008. The list is undoubtedly incomplete, but it provides a rough approximation of the scope of LCR activity in the past few years.

Although some countries were more active and some industries more targeted, new LCR measures were found in all types of economies as well as in a broad range of industries. Many measures have effects beyond trade flows, directly and indirectly affecting investment, services, and employment. However, "affecting" does not translate into a one-for-one reduction in trade or investment.

We reviewed each LCR based on online information. Of the 117 cases, about 47 were systemically quantifiable: These cases explicitly target a subset of products that are traded internationally. Taken together, the quantifiable LCRs affected more than $373 billion in goods and services trade flows, about 2 percent of total global trade in 2010 (the year in which most measures were implemented).

We identified 70 cases that are not quantifiable because of their opaque nature, vague wording, or nontransparent application. Many of these cases directly targeted trade flows. Making various assumptions, our analysis suggests that the nonquantifiable cases adversely affected another $555 billion of trade, about 3 percent of global trade in goods and services.

In total, LCRs affected about $928 billion in trade in 2010, 5 percent of total global trade. The reduction in trade caused by LCRs—in contrast with the impact on trade—is a matter of greater speculation. We do not have estimates on the tariff-equivalent effect. As a conservative and speculative guess, we estimate that the tariff equivalent is 10 percent ad valorem. Assuming that the elasticity of import demand for foreign goods is about –1.0, we speculate that the reduction of trade as a result of LCRs in 2010 may have been about $93 billion. Nothing has happened since 2010 to reduce this guess.

Case Studies

This Policy Analysis presents six in-depth country-specific case studies to illustrate the impact of LCRs. The cases cover a range of industries, both advanced and developing countries, and measures that range from implicit and opaque to explicit and transparent. The purpose is to illustrate how LCRs are deployed by countries of different levels of development and in various geographic regions. The six countries account for nearly half of the LCR measures identified. They are not statistically representative of the survey findings, and in some cases the episode predates the survey period (roughly 2008–12). The cases do not present hard econometric findings; rather they provide context and present descriptive statistics. The case chapters (4 to 9) proceed alphabetically, starting with Brazil and ending with the United States.

■ *Healthcare industry in Brazil.* The Brazil case is messy—illustrative of what happens in many countries—because local content elements are offshoots of policies adopted for safety and infant industry reasons. Brazil is the largest market for healthcare goods and services in Latin America. However, cross-country analysis indicates that its healthcare market is underserved and that both the "device lag" and the "drug lag" are relatively long. If Brazil disentangled its LCRs from other policies, both its healthcare market and its exports and imports of medical devices and pharmaceuticals would grow.

- *Wind turbines in Canada.* Canada's LCR policies are clear cut and have been ruled inconsistent with its WTO obligations. Based on the "overnight cost" of onshore wind plants, we estimate that Canadian wind turbines cost about $386 more to install per kilowatt (kW) of electric capacity than US wind turbines. Since 2009, Ontario has installed about 800,000 kW of wind power, and Quebec has installed 500,000 kW. By our rough but conservative estimate, Ontario paid an extra $300 million and Quebec paid an extra $200 million as a result of their LCRs.

- *Automobile industry in China.* Chinese trade and investment barriers are often informal in nature and reflect opaque regulation, inconsistent law enforcement, weak protection for intellectual property rights, and corruption. The large share of state-owned enterprises in China may lead to a home bias for auto parts procurement. LCRs are often expressed as informal "requests" rather than mandates, which probably insulates them from a WTO challenge. However, cross-country analysis shows that, of the major automobile-producing countries, China has a very low level of imported auto parts content per automobile and the smallest share of imported autos as a portion of total sales. Indirect evidence suggests that Chinese auto prices are higher than they might be with reformed policies.

- *Solar cells and modules in India.* Most G-20 countries subsidize renewable energy in support of policies related to climate change, the environment, and energy security. To increase solar capacity, the Jawaharlal Nehru National Solar Mission auctions power purchase agreements to solar developers at a premium over the cost of coal-fired electricity. Developers must use cells and modules manufactured in India, with some exceptions. This LCR seems to have substantially distorted the Indian module market. The United States has challenged Indian policies; consultations are underway in the WTO.

- *Oil and gas in Nigeria.* The Nigerian Oil and Gas Content Development Act of 2010 was broadly worded to cover "all matters pertaining to Nigerian content in respect of all operations or transactions carried out in or connected with the Nigerian oil and gas industry." Assessing the efficacy and costs of the act's LCRs is difficult given the reported high levels of corruption and vandalism in the industry and the dearth of statistics. The act toggles between codifying current business practices (i.e., the 95 percent Nigerian employment requirement) and creating impossible standards for foreign companies. Based on rough arithmetic, we calculate that it imposes a heavy penalty on Nigeria in terms of lost tax revenue. Because Nigeria is a developing country and the act affects an industry generally not covered by WTO obligations, a legal challenge seems remote.

- *Buy America in the United States.* In February 2009, President Barack Obama signed the American Recovery and Reinvestment Act (ARRA), usually referred to as the stimulus bill. The act included a $787 billion mix of tax cuts and expenditures. It also mandated that all iron and steel procured using these funds be made in the United States; failure to meet this provision makes the entire project ineligible for ARRA funds. This requirement raised the costs and delayed the implementation of numerous projects. It also failed to provide a significant jobs dividend, as steel manufacturing is highly capital intensive and the labor force employed in the industry is deceptively small. The terms of ARRA were carefully crafted to fit within the strictures of the WTO and the North American Free Trade Agreement (NAFTA).

Plan of the Study

Chapter 1 describes the nature and motivation of LCRs. Chapter 2 summarizes six alternatives to LCRs that offer better outcomes in the long run, although they may not have comparable political appeal in the short run. Chapter 3 summarizes our survey of worldwide LCR measures enacted or proposed in recent years, roughly since January 2008 (appendix A provides the results of the survey itself). Chapters 4 to 9 present six case studies that illustrate the use and costs of LCR measures and their impact on domestic and international markets. Chapter 10 offers conclusions and recommendations.

1

Introduction:
The LCR Phenomenon

In the wake of the Great Recession of 2008–09, economists feared that protectionist policies might sweep the globe, echoing the wave of tariff escalation launched by the Smoot-Hawley tariff in the Great Depression of the 1930s. This time around, however, officials were far more restrained, largely avoiding traditional forms of protection (tariffs and quotas), and instead favoring opaque behind-the-border nontariff barriers (NTBs). These barriers to trade take many different forms, including difficult customs procedures, unreasonable standards (such as arbitrary packaging and labeling requirements), and direct government subsidies.

This Policy Analysis seeks to illuminate the use of local content requirements (LCRs), a form of NTB that has enjoyed growing popularity in the aftermath of the Great Recession. The line dividing LCRs from other forms of protection is not clear cut. All forms of protection discriminate against foreign goods, services, or investment and thereby favor their domestic counterparts. But LCRs have distinctive characteristics. The domestic preference is not expressed in terms of tariff lines but rather in terms of projects or firms.

To illustrate, ad valorem tariffs are expressed as a percentage duty on import value for each 8-digit Harmonized System (HS) line; sanitary and phytosanitary standards and technical barriers to trade are enumerated for very specific products. By contrast, LCRs are often expressed as a percentage of a project that must be supplied by local firms (akin to a quota) or as a subsidy available only to local firms. The closest LCRs to ad valorem tariffs are those that confer a price preference on domestic suppliers (e.g., 25 percent by comparison with the best foreign bid). LCRs are also expressed in terms of the domestic nationality of firms that are allowed to import certain items or invest in certain firms or sectors of the economy, which might be called a local ownership requirement. Unlike tariffs and quotas, LCRs are seldom announced in the national tariff schedule. Instead they are the object of separate legislation, for example, as part of a public expenditure program (such as road and port construction) or a financing program (such as official export loans). In this dimension, LCRs are similar to sanitary and phytosanitary standards and technical barriers to trade.

Regional parallels to national LCRs are present in nearly all free trade agreements (FTAs)—namely, rules of origin for trade in goods (and sometimes services). Rules of origin are also a prominent feature of the Generalized System of Preferences (GSP), under which advanced countries permit duty-free entry of limited quantities of goods from developing countries. Rules of origin are designed to ensure that a large percentage of the duty-free (or quota-free) value in goods or services circulated between regional partners (or arriving from developing countries) originates within the preferential trade area. The global costs of restrictive rules of origin very likely exceed the costs of LCRs, especially as the number of FTAs notified to the World Trade Organization (WTO) now exceeds 350, and 9 countries in the Organization for Economic Cooperation and Development (OECD)—counting the European Union as one country—have implemented GSP schemes. A rich body of literature exists on rules of origin; we leave their analysis to other scholars.

Historically, LCRs have been used in different contexts. Since 2008, the dominant motivation has been the simple but powerful appeal to create jobs at home rather than abroad. In an earlier era, the same appeal proved irresistible: The United States enacted its first Buy American statute in 1933, shortly after Congress passed the infamous Smoot-Hawley tariff of 1930. When the subprime financial crisis struck the US economy in 2008, sending shock waves across the world, many countries imposed LCRs. Congress tacked a Buy America provision on the American Recovery and Reinvestment Act (ARRA) of 2009 (the giant $787 billion fiscal stimulus bill), and other countries did likewise.

In these cases, government procurement and government-financed projects served as LCR transmission mechanisms. But high unemployment and stimulus spending are not the only LCR drivers. Infant industry arguments are often deployed to favor local firms, especially by developing countries entering high-tech sectors such as information technology and renewable energy.

A related motivation is the desire to ensure that local firms get a slice of the purchases arising from major investments and new business created by large foreign or domestic firms. In good times and bad, public procurement serves as a natural target for LCRs—in fact, LCRs are the norm rather than the exception in public procurement. The original Buy American Act of 1933 and its offspring were amended from time to time but never repealed. Regulated industries, such as airlines, broadcast networks, utilities, and telecommunications companies, as well as elastically defined "important" firms or "strategic" industries, are often subject to domestic ownership requirements. When state-owned enterprises are privatized, only domestic firms and citizens are eligible to buy them; when an "important" firm, such as Unocal or the Potash Company of Saskatchewan, becomes a takeover target, foreign multinational corporations may be blocked from bidding on them—the fate of China National Offshore Oil Corporation (CNOOC) and BHP Billiton.

Characteristics of LCRs

In one respect, classic LCRs bear a strong resemblance to import quotas: They use quantity rather than price signals to influence market outcomes. One big difference is that import quotas limit the quantity that can be purchased from foreign suppliers, whereas classic LCRs mandate the share that must be purchased from domestic suppliers. Another big difference is that when LCRs are tied to government-supported spending in a crisis, the political appeal of instantaneous job creation is powerful. Like quotas, LCRs are "off-budget," and although they impose an economic cost on society at large, they do not entail a fiscal cost—another attractive feature from a political vantage point.

In contrast to price preferences for domestic firms (a less frequent but also classic LCR), as well as tariffs and subsidies, quantity signals have marketing advantages, beloved by LCR advocates. The cost imposed on purchasers (whether households or firms) is opaque at best, often totally hidden. International obligations, agreed to in the WTO and regional trade agreements, may not be clear cut with respect to quantitative LCRs. Quantitative requirements tied to government-supported spending do not violate the WTO Government Procurement Agreement (or a regional counterpart) unless the country has specifically committed to liberalize the activity in question. LCRs tied to services seldom conflict with obligations scheduled in the General Agreement on Trade in Services (GATS), because for the most part those commitments are narrowly limited to preexisting market access enjoyed by foreign service providers.

In the wake of the Great Recession, countries considered or implemented more than 100 new LCRs. Several of them depart from the classic format of mandated purchases or price preferences for domestic suppliers and instead mix price and quantity signals. The LCR forms observed since January 2008 include the following:

- classic mandatory LCR percentages for goods or services,
- tax, tariff, and price concessions conditioned on local procurement,
- import licensing procedures tailored to encourage domestic purchases of certain products,
- certain lines of business that can be conducted only by domestic firms, and
- data that must be stored and analyzed locally or products that must be tested locally.

Table 1.1 identifies advanced and developing countries that have imposed LCRs since January 2008 and compares them with the average for all advanced or developing countries. The number of LCR cases since 2008 is an important indicator of how often policymakers invoke LCRs to address economic problems (unemployment, strategic sector development, etc.). However, the number of cases in any given country does not necessarily indicate their significance. For example, although Mongolia has only one recorded LCR since 2008, it could restrict foreign investment in mining and therefore has the potential to affect projects that far exceed the annual GDP of the entire country.

Table 1.1 shows that LCR-using countries have larger than average GDPs (not surprisingly) and consequently are less reliant on foreign trade and investment as a share of GDP. Because these countries are somewhat less engaged in the global economy than their peers, and have a wider array of local suppliers, they may be less mindful of the costs associated with LCR policies, and the costs are probably much lower than they would be in a smaller country.

Reflective of the spread and magnitude of LCRs is the Latin American Local Content Forum 2012, held July 23–25, 2012, in Rio de Janeiro. The advertisement for the forum read as follows:

> With 12.86 billion barrels of oil to extract off the coast of Rio de Janeiro, what is the best way forward to get this done on time and budget, while building a competitive workforce and supply chain?
>
> Discover all you need to know to meet your certification requirements, develop foolproof systems and processes to measure and manage local content across your supply chain and discover how the regulatory updates to investment reporting and certification will impact you.
>
> The Latin American Local Content Forum in November 2011 brought together over 100 [of] Latin America's regulators, NOCs [national oil companies], IOCs [international oil companies] and domestic and international suppliers to take part in key discussions on the future of Local Content in Latin America—where it is and where it is heading.
>
> Getting to the heart of the regulatory, certification, and systems and processes challenges when trying to comply with Local Content will be central to the program in 2012.

Why LCRs Are Bad Policy

LCRs enacted in the aftermath of the Great Recession have two great attractions: They provide instant jobs to unemployed workers, and they give immediate gratification to the sponsoring politician. Other policies can provide more jobs at lower cost, and with less damage to the system, but they require discipline and deliver results only over the long term.

Of course, LCRs are not enacted solely as palliatives for unemployment. Their supporters find numerous justifications, running from the infant industry argument to national ownership sentiments.

Table 1.1 Comparative statistics for countries that impose LCRs, 2008 to present

Country	Number of LCR cases since 2008	GDP, 2010 (billions of US dollars)	Total two-way goods and services trade, 2010		Inward FDI stock, 2010 (billions of US dollars at current exchange rates)	Inward FDI stock, 2010 (percent of GDP)
			Billions of US dollars at current prices	Percent of GDP		
Advanced economies[a]						
Australia	7	1,132	511	45	508	45
Canada	5	1,577	948	60	561	36
France	2	2,560	1,409	55	1,008	39
Greece	1	301	143	48	34	11
Korea	2	1,014	1,073	106	127	13
Switzerland	2	528	493	93	539	102
United States	14	14,587	4,137	28	3,451	24
Average of advanced economies with LCR cases	5	3,100	1,245	62	890	38
Average of all other advanced economies	0	905	650	72	321	84
Developing and other economies						
Argentina	8	369	151	41	87	24
Azerbaijan	1	52	39	75	10	19
Botswana	1	15	12	78	1	9
Brazil	15	2,088	483	23	473	23
China	10	5,927	3,335	56	579	10
Egypt	1	219	116	53	73	34
India	9	1,727	809	47	198	11

(table continues next page)

Table 1.1 Comparative statistics for countries that impose LCRs, 2008 to present (continued)

Country	Number of LCR cases since 2008	GDP, 2010 (billions of US dollars)	Total two-way goods and services trade, 2010 Billions of US dollars at current prices	Total two-way goods and services trade, 2010 Percent of GDP	Inward FDI stock, 2010 (billions of US dollars at current exchange rates)	Inward FDI stock, 2010 (percent of GDP)
Indonesia	12	707	335	47	122	17
Kazakhstan	5	149	105	70	81	55
Kenya	2	32	22	68	2	7
Mexico	1	1,036	645	62	327	32
Mongolia	1	6	7	117	4	67
Nigeria	2	203	151	75	60	30
Paraguay	1	18	17	91	3	17
Russia	5	1,480	766	52	423	29
Saudi Arabia	1	435	419	96	170	39
South Africa	3	364	207	57	132	36
Tanzania	1	23	16	70	8	35
Turkey	2	734	82	11	182	25
Uganda	1	17	9	53	6	34
Ukraine	2	138	141	102	58	42
Average of developing economies with LCR cases	4	749	375	64	143	28
Average of all other developing economies	0	44	47	105	18	40

a. IMF designations for "advanced economies," available at www.imf.org/external/pubs/ft/weo/2008/02/weodata/groups.htm#ae.

Sources: Number of LCR measures drawn from table A.1 in appendix A; GDP and trade data from World Bank, World Development Indicators database, http://data.worldbank.org/indicator/NY.GDP.MKTP.CD; and World Trade Organization statistics database, http://stat.wto.org/Home/WSDBHome.aspx; foreign direct investment data (FDI) data from UNCTADStat database, http://unctadstat.unctad.org/.

In an early paper, Gene M. Grossman (1981) identifies some of the weaknesses of LCRs. Other problems have become apparent as LCRs have become more widespread:

- The extent of assistance to the local activity is highly variable. Some LCRs are mere window dressing, with no protective effect, because local firms are already the low-cost supplier. Others have a tariff equivalent impact of 100 percent or more, because few local suppliers can supply the requisite good or service. Government officials often have no clue as to the effectiveness of the LCR.

- LCRs are particularly nontransparent. In nearly all instances, no cost entry shows up in budget accounts. The price impact on downstream producers may be all but impossible to calculate, especially for people not intimately familiar with the industry. Consequently, it is difficult or impossible for responsible legislators and officials to assess the cost and benefits of LCRs.

- In some circumstances, LCRs create unnecessary delays and raise costs. This is particularly true of LCRs applied to major infrastructure projects, such as renewable energy, waterworks, roads, ports, and telecommunications.

- LCRs are susceptible to corruption and playing favorites, especially when local producers and investors are few in number. All government policies are vulnerable to corruption and favoritism, but in the realm of trade and investment policy, LCRs seem particularly susceptible.

- LCRs seldom contain a "sunset" provision, and, with the exception of the WTO Government Procurement Agreement and parallel provisions in some regional trade agreements, many of them are never subject to removal through international negotiations.

Motives behind and Effects of LCRs

An extensive literature analyzes the impact of LCRs on domestic production, trade, and investment, with an eye toward price and welfare effects. As a nontariff barrier, LCRs distort the input decisions of producers and increase the costs for importers (Deardorff and Stern 1997). But measuring their net effects is seldom straightforward. Research suggests that the impacts depend on market conditions. Moreover, LCRs can not only lead to inefficient outcomes but also fail to achieve policy objectives—whether to increase industrywide domestic value added, promote competitive indigenous industries, or shield domestic suppliers through procurement favoritism. As a result, the impact of LCRs, like many other performance requirements, is "at best uncertain, and at worst negative" (Balasubramanyam 2001).

The seminal analysis by Grossman (1981) assesses the effects of LCRs on resource reallocation using a partial equilibrium model and assuming perfect competition.[1] It shows that, unlike tariffs, LCRs offer a degree of protection that is "variable and difficult to predict." Grossman (1981) shows that specific price effects of LCRs depend largely on factor use, input substitution, and market structure. He concludes that LCRs may not succeed in achieving the objectives of policymakers. Indeed, he writes, LCRs implemented to increase domestic value added in an industry can easily have the opposite effect. Although LCRs increase the demand for domestic intermediate goods, this boost to domestic value added can be partially or fully offset by a concomitant decrease in final goods production, because the price of final goods will rise. In turn, this effect leads purchasing firms to substitute other inputs, such as labor, for higher-cost intermediates. On balance, whether domestic value added rises or falls following the imposition of LCRs depends on input substitution and the price elasticity of final demand. Furthermore, in the case of monopolistic firms, LCRs allow domestic producers of intermediates to exercise monopoly power (reduce output and raise prices). Thus, LCRs may even fail to induce domestic production of intermediates—a necessary prerequisite for "dynamic gains from learning." This possibility undercuts the common infant industry justification for LCRs.

Michael Mussa (1984) analyzes the impact of LCRs when inputs are imperfect substitutes and the industry has monopolistic characteristics. His analysis confirms that LCRs distort production and diminish incentives for technical efficiency. But, he argues, as an alternative to tariffs, LCRs could serve as a second-best policy instrument, because they avoid the consumption distortion created by a tariff.[2]

Kala Krishna and Motoshige Itoh (1988) consider LCRs in an oligopolistic industry. They conclude that they decrease the profits of suppliers of domestic intermediate goods when inputs are complements in demand but increase them when inputs are substitutes.

A common finding from the academic literature is that the impact of LCRs depends critically on assumptions about industry structure: Although LCRs unambiguously distort production and reduce welfare in perfectly competitive markets, other outcomes are more likely in imperfectly competitive markets.[3] In the case of oligopolistic industries, LCRs shift rents and producer surplus to the host country of foreign direct investment (FDI). In the most

---

1. The analysis considers local content schemes in both physical terms (i.e., the proportion of domestic intermediate goods required in final goods production) and value-added terms (i.e., the minimum value of domestic intermediate goods required in the final good), as well as content preference programs (e.g., preferential rules of origin for developing countries).

2. However, Mussa (1984, 13) concludes that "diminished incentives for improvements in technical efficiency that save on domestic inputs provides a serious argument against the use of content protection to provide temporary protection for infant industries or mature industries that need to regain international competitiveness."

3. These differences stem from the contest between the neoclassical framework of perfect competition and the strategic trade framework of oligopoly and imperfect competition. For an overview of both theoretical and empirical studies on LCR outcomes (and other performance requirements) that build on these two schools of thought, see UNCTC (1991).

effective cases, LCRs shift rents and surplus to firms that can take advantage of "increasing returns to scale" and "dynamic gains from learning" (UNCTC 1991).[4] In particular, the potential benefit from spillover effects has been central to the debate over the merits of LCRs, and other trade-related investment measures (TRIMs), as tools for development.

LCRs fit into the broad category of performance requirements within TRIMs, namely, "trade policy measures that affect the volume, sectoral composition and geographical distribution of foreign direct investment" (WTO and UNCTAD 2002).[5] Imposing LCRs on foreign investors is often framed as a means of building competitive indigenous industries by enhancing "industrial deepening" and "supplier creation" as well as creating "backward linkages" (Moran 1998, 41). However, LCRs are seldom the first-best tools for such objectives, for three reasons:

- LCRs are often redundant, in that they require firms to undertake operations they would have undertaken in the absence of LCRs (e.g., seeking local suppliers).

- LCRs should enable domestic producers to capture economies of scale and thereby penetrate global markets, but in most cases they merely insulate high-cost operations from competition and generate lags in the introduction of new technology.

- LCRs can raise production costs and deter inflows of "market-seeking and efficiency-seeking" FDI (UNCTC 1999, WTO and UNCTAD 2002). Indeed, empirical studies from the 1970s and 1980s that focus on industries in both developed and developing countries in which LCRs were concentrated (e.g., electrical, automobiles, chemicals, mining and petroleum) often find such outcomes.[6]

Following a general review of the evidence, Theodore H. Moran (1998, 43) concludes:

> Attempts to "improve" the functioning of markets by imposing domestic content requirements on foreign firms generate technical, economic, managerial, and political-economic problems for the investors and for the host country. These problems interact in a perverse manner and tend to reinforce each other toward inefficiency and stasis rather than lead to some new level of dynamic learning, enhanced efficiency, or accelerated growth.

---

4. Martin Richardson (1993), for example, uses general equilibrium modeling to show that effective LCRs can induce foreign firms to increase their domestic production of inputs and increase capital inflows to the host country. Sajal Lahiri and Yoshiyasu Ono (1998) use partial equilibrium modeling to assess the optimal policy combination of imposing a profit tax and LCR to compete for inward FDI. They argue that LCRs can have positive effects on employment and the price level depending on both the number and relative efficiency of domestic firms.

5. The United Nations Conference on Trade and Development (UNCTAD) uses this definition of TRIMs; there is no commonly accepted definition in the literature.

6. For a summary of empirical studies, see Moran (1998) and WTO and UNCTAD (2002).

In the case of LCRs in renewable sectors, creating green jobs and building a competitive industry are not the only objectives. In addition, countries seek social and environmental objectives relating to the twin challenges of energy security and climate change (IEA and World Bank 2013). Indeed, both energy security and the promise of green jobs have inspired the use of LCRs to support renewable energy generating capacity, particularly since 2008 (table 1.2).[7] Underlying the use of LCRs is the "political reality that high financial support for renewable programmes might not be publicly supported if there were no local benefits attached" (Kuntze and Moerenhout 2013, 34).

Recent research explores the effectiveness of LCRs in achieving economic and environmental objectives. Nic Rivers and Randy Wigle (2011) used partial equilibrium analysis to assess the economic impact of tying support for renewably generated electricity to LCRs in the case of wind power. They find that LCRs can reduce the production of renewable electricity, as well as the overall level of employment in the renewable energy industry in the short run. Joanna I. Lewis and Ryan H. Wiser (2007, 1846) evaluate the conditions for achieving successful localization in wind power and conclude that "policy incentives may need to be designed and targeted differently depending on the specific goals for localization." The research consensus holds that LCRs must be "linked with other policies that support and catalyze learning" (Johnson 2013, 12). LCRs that are used as "indefinite protection subsidies" that preclude exposure to domestic and international competition will often result in insufficient incentives to invest in research and development (R&D) and innovation (Kuntze and Moerenhout 2013, 19). These authors offer a framework for determining the economic effectiveness of LCRs in renewable energy. The determinants include the size of the local market; the restrictiveness of LCRs; accompanying support measures, such as financial incentives; and innovation potential and technology knowledge. From their review of the evidence, they conclude that LCRs have increased domestic output under certain conditions, but they cannot say that LCRs added to innovative capacity. They conclude that countries "often fail to combine proper incentives and policies" (p. 31).[8]

LCRs are perhaps most commonly embedded in government procurement policies. Like TRIMs, these policies are based on industrial objectives, but they may also reflect national security concerns or socioeconomic objectives (e.g., protection of minority-owned or small and medium enterprises)

---

7. The increasing incidence of LCRs in renewables spurred both a rise in allegations of WTO violations and the use of trade defense instruments (TDIs) against imported renewable components. Jonas Kasteng (2013, 3) reports that the European Union's use of TDIs directed toward renewable energy sources such as solar and biofuels affected nearly €14 billion of imports, almost 75 percent of all TDI measures currently in place.

8. The build-up of China's domestic wind industry has generally been seen as a success story for the infant industry argument and the transfer of technology through the use of LCRs combined with other policy measures. Its success has been attributed to the fact that many of the "effectiveness conditions" outlined here were met (see Kuntze and Moerenhout 2013).

Table 1.2 Incidence of LCRs in renewable energy

Country/province and technology	LCR percent (start year), LCR percent (2012)[a]	Vertical cooperation and financial support
China (wind)	20 (1996), 70 (2009)	Joint venture, Clean Development Mechanism, state tariffs, national tender requirement
Ontario (wind)	25 (2009), 50 (2012)	Feed-in tariff conditionality
Quebec (wind)	40 (2003), 60 (2012)	Tender requirement
Spain (wind)	70 (2012)	Market entry requirement (provincial), noncoupled feed-in tariff (national)
Turkey (wind)	Variable (2011)	Additional feed-in tariff / local content used
Brazil (wind)	60 (2002), 60 (2012)	Condition for subsidized Brazilian Development Bank loans
South Africa (wind)	35 (2011), >35 (2012)	Tender requirement
Ontario (solar)	50 (2009), 60 (2012)	Feed-in tariff conditionality
Italy (solar)	Variable (2011)	5 to 10 percent bonus / local content used
France (solar)	60 (2012)	10 percent bonus on Électricité de France repurchasing price
Turkey (solar)	Variable (2011)	Additional feed-in tariff / local content used
India (solar)	30 (2011), 30 (2011)	Feed-in tariff conditionality

a. LCR percent provided in 2012 or the latest year applicable.

Source: Kuntze and Moerenhout (2013, table 5).

(Evenett and Hoekman 2002).[9] LCRs and other discriminatory policies against foreign competitors introduced in the context of post-2008 stimulus packages were drivers of an overall decrease in the openness of government procurement markets. Patrick Messerlin (2013) calculates the "import penetration" ratios, the share of public imports to total demand for public goods and services. He shows that between 2008 and 2009, most countries saw their ratios decrease by more than 10 percent (table 1.3).

Robert Baldwin and J. David Richardson (1972) use a partial equilibrium model to analyze the impact of LCRs and discriminatory procurement policies on welfare and market access. They argue that government demand relative to domestic supply crucially affects outcomes: Only when government demand is greater than domestic supply will a procurement ban on foreign suppliers raise prices paid by the government and thus domestic output, causing a reduction in imports and welfare.

Simon J. Evenett and Bernard M. Hoekman (2002) extend this analysis and confirm that government demand is often too weak to affect market outcomes,

---

9. Studies that analyze these objectives show that procurement discrimination results in inefficient outcomes. Other studies find there may be an efficiency rationale in imperfectly competitive markets (McAfee and McMillan 1989, Branco 1994). For a concise overview of the literature, see Evenett and Hoekman (2002, 3–5).

Table 1.3 Import penetration ratios for public procurement in selected countries, 1995–2009

Country	1995	1996	1997	1998	1999	2000	2001	2002	2003	2004	2005	2006	2007	2008	2009
Australia	5.1	5.0	5.4	5.4	5.9	5.9	5.8	6.1	5.9	5.9	6.0	5.9	6.2	5.7	5.3
Brazil	2.1	2.0	2.1	2.1	2.7	3.1	3.5	3.5	3.3	3.3	3.1	2.9	3.0	3.3	2.8
Canada	4.2	4.3	4.6	4.9	5.1	5.1	5.0	4.9	4.7	4.7	4.9	4.6	4.6	4.8	4.8
China	3.8	3.1	3.3	2.8	3.0	3.4	3.3	3.6	5.5	5.5	5.6	5.7	5.2	7.9	6.1
EU-27[a]	2.6	2.7	2.8	2.7	2.8	3.6	3.7	3.5	3.7	3.7	4.2	4.6	4.5	5.3	4.5
EU-2[b]	2.2	2.2	2.4	2.3	2.3	2.8	3.1	2.9	2.8	3.0	3.4	3.8	3.9	4.3	3.5
India	4.2	4.4	4.0	4.4	4.5	4.4	4.0	3.5	4.6	4.6	5.8	6.3	6.3	6.2	5.7
Indonesia	7.9	7.8	7.9	13.9	9.3	11.4	11.6	9.5	9.9	9.9	10.6	8.9	8.8	8.8	6.1
Japan	1.9	2.2	2.3	2.1	2.0	2.3	2.3	2.4	2.8	2.8	3.2	3.8	4.2	5.3	3.5
Korea	7.5	7.5	8.4	8.1	7.7	9.6	9.3	8.9	9.7	9.7	9.9	9.9	10.2	13.9	11.2
Mexico	4.8	4.9	5.2	5.1	4.9	5.2	4.9	4.5	5.6	5.6	5.8	5.9	6.3	6.4	5.7
Russia	3.3	3.5	3.6	4.6	6.2	5.3	4.7	4.2	3.7	3.7	3.8	3.3	3.1	3.1	2.5
Taiwan	9.9	10.1	10.8	11.9	10.7	10.5	10.2	11.3	12.4	12.4	11.9	12.9	13.5	12.9	11.9
Turkey	5.4	7.3	6.5	5.2	4.4	5.8	7.2	8.3	8.8	8.8	9.5	11.3	10.9	13.0	9.5
United States	2.7	2.8	2.9	2.8	3.0	3.6	3.5	3.3	4.0	4.0	4.4	4.3	4.4	4.8	3.7
Rest of world	6.4	6.8	6.9	6.9	6.7	7.1	7.2	7.9	8.8	8.8	9.4	9.1	9.1	10.1	8.3
World	4.2	4.5	4.6	4.6	4.6	5.1	5.2	5.2	6.0	6.0	6.4	6.7	6.8	7.6	6.3

a. EU-27 ratios take into account only extra-EU public imports.
b. EU-2 ratios designate the sum of France and Germany and take into account only extra-EU public imports.

Note: Import penetration ratios measure the share of public imports to total expenditure on public goods and services.

Source: Messerlin (2013, table 2).

making discriminatory procurement policies ineffective in the short run. Moreover, they contend, given free entry by new firms, such policies are also ineffective in the long run. However, in such cases, "much of the adverse impact on market access may well not be reversed upon [subsequent] liberalization . . . the damage to market access will already have been done" (p. 20).

Pushback against LCRs

The eruption of LCRs has not gone unnoticed by affected trading partners. The US Trade Representative (USTR) established the Trade Policy Staff Committee Task Force on Localization Barriers to Trade to develop a coordinated approach to LCR practices. The goal of the task force, established in mid-2012, is to raise the profile of the forced localization issue within the US government and to forge a common position so that US negotiators can engage trading partners on the problem. With this goal in mind, the USTR flagged LCRs as a growing problem at the Asia-Pacific Economic Cooperation (APEC) Senior Officials Meeting held in Surabaya, Indonesia, in April 2013. APEC officials were sufficiently concerned that they put LCRs on their agenda as a topic of discussion in subsequent meetings.

Meanwhile, three LCR cases are working their way through the WTO Dispute Settlement Body:

- In November 2012, China requested consultations with the European Union, Greece, and Italy regarding domestic content restrictions that affect renewable energy generation as a byproduct of the feed-in tariff programs of EU member states.

- In February 2013, the United States requested consultations with India concerning India's LCRs and subsidies in the solar energy sector, specifically addressing the Jawaharlal Nehru National Solar Mission (JNNSM).

- In May 2013, the WTO Appellate Body sided with the European Union and Japan in ruling that LCRs within Canada's renewable energy and feed-in tariff program violated WTO obligations.

Several WTO provisions seemingly limit or forbid LCR practices. In practice, they have important gaps. Four are worth flagging.

Article III of the General Agreement on Trade and Tariffs (GATT)

The first paragraph of Article III on National Treatment on Internal Taxation and Regulation states:

> The contracting parties recognize that internal taxes and other internal charges, and laws, regulations and requirements affecting the internal sale, offering for sale, purchase, transportation, distribution or use of products, and internal quantitative regulations requiring the mixture, processing or use of products in specified amounts or proportions, should not be applied to imported or domestic products so as to afford

protection to domestic production.* [The footnote allows for reasonable exceptions for subfederal governments in a free trade area or customs union.]

The language is strong, and in past WTO cases, the national treatment obligation has been strictly interpreted. A key weakness, however, is that government procurement by federal and subfederal agencies is subject to Article III and other GATT provisions only to the extent scheduled in the WTO Government Procurement Agreement (GPA). Only 41 countries have signed on to the GPA (another 10 are currently negotiating accession). Their schedules often leave out more government procurement than they include, and the benefits run only to other GPA members.

WTO Agreement on Subsidies and Countervailing Measures

The Agreement on Subsidies and Countervailing Measures (ASCM) enables any WTO member to bring a case when it suffers "adverse effects" from the subsidy practices of another WTO member. However, the ASCM definition of subsidies does not include all practices that economists might regard as subsidies, and the complaining country must provide evidence of an "adverse effect" on its own commercial interests. In the Canada wind turbine case (chapter 5), a majority of the three-member panel determined that the LCR, which was coupled with a preferential feed-in tariff for electricity, did not constitute a subsidy covered by the ASCM.

WTO Agreement on Trade-Related Investment Measures

The TRIMs agreement contains strong language that seems to preclude the imposition of LCRs in connection with authorizing or incentivizing investment. The text is reinforced by an illustrative list that includes these examples (among others):

1. TRIMs that are inconsistent with the obligation of national treatment provided for in paragraph 4 of Article III of GATT 1994[10] include those which are mandatory or enforceable under domestic law or under administrative rulings, or compliance with which is necessary to obtain an advantage, and which require:
    (a) the purchase or use by an enterprise of products of domestic origin or from any domestic source, whether specified in terms of particular products, in terms of volume or value of products, or in terms of a proportion of volume or value of its local production; or
    (b) that an enterprise's purchases or use of imported products be limited to an amount related to the volume or value of local products that it exports.

2. TRIMs that are inconsistent with the obligation of general elimination of quantitative restrictions provided for in paragraph 1 of Article XI of GATT 1994[11] include those which are mandatory or enforceable under domestic law or under adminis-

---

10. Article III of GATT 1994, www.wto.org/english/res_e/booksp_e/analytic_index_e/gatt1994_02_e.htm#article3A4.

11. Article XI of GATT 1994, www.wto.org/english/res_e/booksp_e/analytic_index_e/gatt1994_05_e.htm#article11A1.

trative rulings, or compliance with which is necessary to obtain an advantage, and which restrict:

(a) the importation by an enterprise of products used in or related to its local production, generally or to an amount related to the volume or value of local production that it exports;

(b) the importation by an enterprise of products used in or related to its local production by restricting its access to foreign exchange to an amount related to the foreign exchange inflows attributable to the enterprise; or

(c) the exportation or sale for export by an enterprise of products, whether specified in terms of particular products, in terms of volume or value of products, or in terms of a proportion of volume or value of its local production.

The TRIMs text, along with other GATT provisions, was strictly enforced by the Dispute Settlement Body against Indonesia in the automobile case brought by the United States, the European Union, and Japan in 1996.[12] However, in the vast majority of cases, when a country couples investment incentives with LCRs, no one complains. The multinational firm receiving incentives quietly and happily complies, and its home government feels absolutely no pressure to raise an objection. Moreover, although TRIMs provide a theoretical answer to a large class of LCRs, the agreement applies only to goods, not to services.

WTO Government Procurement Agreement

Buried in the National Treatment article of the 1947 GATT was an important exception: Article III(8)(a) excluded government procurement from coverage.[13] In 1994, government procurement was likewise carved out from the main commitments in the GATS.

As government procurement typically represents 10 to 15 percent of GDP, and LCRs go hand in glove with government procurement, these exclusions wall off a considerable amount of commerce—a fact that has prompted several editions of the GPA. The first GPA was signed in 1979, as part of the Tokyo Round. It was amended in 1987, and an enlarged GPA was signed in 1994 as part of the Uruguay Round. Further enlargements are under discussion in the current Doha Round.

All editions of the GPA are plurilateral agreements (included in Annex 4 to the Marrakesh Agreement), meaning that only parties to the GPA are

---

12. Specifically, the Dispute Settlement Body ruled that Indonesia's LCRs and additional taxes and charges against imported vehicles violated most-favored nation treatment (GATT Article I) and national treatment (GATT Article III: 2); qualified as LCRs prohibited by Article 2 of the TRIMs agreement; and qualified as specific subsidies that caused "serious prejudice," thus violating Article 5(c) of the ASCM. For a summary of these key findings, see www.wto.org/english/ tratop_e/dispu_e/cases_e/1pagesum_e/ds54sum_e.pdf.

13. John Jackson, the leading scholar of GATT jurisprudence, contends that government procurement was likewise excluded from the obligation of general most-favored nation treatment set forth in Article I (Jackson 1969, 291). This view is widely accepted. For details on the GPA, see www.wto.org/english/tratop_e/gproc_e/gp_gpa_e.htm.

bound by its rules and entitled to its benefits. This feature distinguishes the GPA from other WTO provisions that, to some extent, discipline the use of LCRs by all WTO members.

Through negotiations, parties to the GPA schedule their federal and subfederal agencies, meaning that other parties are eligible to bid for the procurement conducted by these agencies. To that extent, the GPA eliminates LCRs as between the parties. However, because the GPA has only 41 signatories out of 159 members (mainly advanced countries, including 27 members of the European Union) and the schedules are parsimonious with respect to covered agencies and even then have numerous exceptions, by far the lion's share of government procurement remains outside the multilateral trading system and thus remains subject to discretionary LCRs.

Difficulties Enforcing WTO Provisions

Beyond the technical difficulties of enforcing WTO provisions lie three central weaknesses of WTO disciplines against the eruption of LCRs. First, only WTO member governments have the legal standing to bring a case. Private firms that lose business because of LCRs must first convince their government that bringing a case is a worthwhile endeavor. Doing so is not easy. Second, bringing a WTO case is an arduous process for the complaining government in terms of time, money, and diplomatic relations. Third, WTO cases take two years or more to resolve, and WTO remedies offer no retroactive relief for the aggrieved firm. If a foreign firm loses a contract because of an LCR, no compensation will ever be paid, even if its own government wins in the WTO.

With the exception of the European Union, customs unions and FTAs currently offer few safeguards against LCRs. Although their legal provisions may well inscribe stronger limitations than the WTO, their dispute settlement provisions are generally weak. When Buy American restrictions were tacked on to ARRA in 2009, Canada discovered that provisions of the North American Free Trade Agreement (NAFTA) did not shield it from discrimination. It resorted to a somewhat unsatisfactory diplomatic settlement with the United States (see chapter 9).

Plan of the Book

Chapter 2 describes six alternatives to LCRs that offer better economic results in the long run, although they may not have comparable political appeal in the short run. Chapter 3 summarizes our survey of worldwide LCR measures enacted or proposed since roughly January 2008. The survey itself, a lengthy spreadsheet, is presented in appendix A. Chapters 4 to 9 present six cases studies, which illustrate the use and costs of LCR measures and their impact on domestic and international markets. Chapter 10 offers conclusions and recommendations.

2

Alternatives to Local Content Requirements

Almost by definition, once a local content requirement (LCR) is enacted, it satisfies two primary objectives: It creates identifiable jobs and gives local firms a better shot at targeted markets. The jury is still out as to whether LCRs enacted since the Great Recession have launched any infant industries to world-class performance. Whether or not an LCR does so, the jobs created often come at high costs—in terms of jobs destroyed elsewhere in the economy, distorted investment, delays in implementation, and wasteful expenditure of public funds. Moreover, although LCRs offer instant political gratification—the economic equivalent of cotton candy—they rank very low among paths to development. In fact, most LCRs probably retard development.

Six alternatives to LCRs could deliver more job creation, impose fewer costs on the economy, and generate more economic growth:

- creating a business-friendly environment,
- encouraging corporate social responsibility,
- expanding training,
- improving logistics,
- increasing investment in infrastructure, and
- imposing tariffs and subsidies.

Creating a Business-Friendly Environment

LCRs usually target specific projects or sectors. A better way to create jobs and stimulate investment is to upgrade the national environment for doing business. Multinational corporations are concerned about corruption, bureaucratic delays, investor protection, contract enforcement, and other aspects of normal business operations. International firms accept a certain amount of risk and delay in starting a new venture in a foreign country, but anything a host government can do to reduce the costs and delays will improve business prospects and encourage investment.

Quantifying these obvious points, table 2.1 summarizes rankings from the World Bank's *Doing Business 2012* report for the LCR-using countries identified in table 1.1 (World Bank and IFC 2011). The indicators show each country's rank for ease of doing business across 10 dimensions: starting a business, dealing with construction permits, accessing electricity, registering property, obtaining credit, protecting investors, paying taxes, trading across borders, enforcing contracts, and resolving insolvency. Most of the dimensions reflect characteristics of governance.

Without diving into all the details, it is evident that many LCR-using countries have ample room to improve their performance in the business beauty contest—often by simple reforms. Other countries have done just that. Morocco led the pack in improving its *Doing Business* ranking, advancing 21 places between the 2010 and 2012 surveys, primarily by streamlining construction permits, improving its electronic tax administration, and strengthening investor protections (World Bank and IFC 2011, 72). Armenia also ranks among the most improved countries in the 2012 rankings. It rose by merging the administrative processes that govern business and tax registrations; lowering the corporate income, property, and land tax rates (and improving tax compliance); and eliminating the requirement to obtain an environmental impact assessment for small projects (World Bank and IFC 2011, 66).

Corporate taxation and corruption deserve special attention. Low tax rates and simple tax systems demonstrably attract business firms and spark economic growth. Corruption is a proven killer of trade and investment. Table 2.2 shows the latest profit tax rates for the LCR-using countries and the number of hours required by the average firm to complete its corporate tax return, as reported in *Paying Taxes 2012* (PwC, World Bank, and IFC 2011). Large firms, especially multinational corporations, spend multiples of the hours listed in table 2.2, but as an indicator of relative tax system complexity, the average number of hours is a good measure. As table 2.2 shows, LCR countries have higher tax rates on profits and more burdensome tax systems than their peers. The scope for improvement is obvious.

The summary statistics in table 2.2 suggest that LCR countries score near the average level for all countries in terms of corruption. This leaves ample room for improvement, especially among developing countries that have embraced LCRs. Reducing corruption a few notches would be far more effective at promoting local business than imposing LCRs on selected projects. If anything, LCRs are an invitation to favoritism that abets corruption and worsens the business climate.

Table 2.1 Doing Business rankings, LCR countries, 2012

Country	Overall ease of doing business rank	Starting a business	Dealing with construction permits	Accessing electricity	Registering property	Obtaining credit[a]	Protecting investors	Paying taxes	Trading across borders	Enforcing contracts	Resolving insolvency
				Advanced economies[a]							
Australia	15	2	42	37	38	8	65	53	30	17	17
Canada	13	3	25	156	41	24	5	8	42	59	3
France	29	25	30	62	149	48	79	58	24	6	46
Greece	100	135	41	77	150	78	155	83	84	90	57
Korea	8	24	26	11	71	8	79	38	4	2	13
Switzerland	26	85	46	6	14	24	166	12	41	23	43
United States	4	13	17	17	16	4	5	72	20	7	15
Average of advanced economies with LCR cases	28	41	32	52	68	28	79	46	35	29	28
Average of all other advanced economies	23	45	52	40	60	46	44	51	23	38	18
				Developing and other economies							
Argentina	113	146	169	58	139	67	111	144	102	45	85
Azerbaijan	66	18	172	173	9	48	24	81	170	25	95
Botswana	54	90	132	91	50	48	46	22	150	65	28
Brazil	126	120	127	51	114	98	79	150	121	118	136
China	91	151	179	115	40	67	97	122	60	16	75

(table continues next page)

19

Table 2.1 Doing Business rankings, LCR countries, 2012 (continued)

Country	Overall ease of doing business rank	Starting a business	Dealing with construction permits	Accessing electricity	Registering property	Obtaining credit	Protecting investors	Paying taxes	Trading across borders	Enforcing contracts	Resolving insolvency
Egypt	110	21	154	101	93	78	79	145	64	147	137
India	132	166	181	98	97	40	46	147	109	182	128
Indonesia	129	155	71	161	99	126	46	131	39	156	146
Kazakhstan	47	57	147	86	29	78	10	13	176	27	54
Kenya	109	132	37	115	133	8	97	166	141	127	92
Mexico	53	75	43	142	140	40	46	109	59	81	24
Mongolia	86	97	119	171	26	67	29	57	159	33	124
Nigeria	133	116	84	176	180	78	65	138	149	97	99
Paraguay	102	106	66	23	64	78	65	132	154	106	140
Russia	120	111	178	183	45	98	111	105	160	13	60
Saudi Arabia	12	10	4	18	1	48	17	10	18	138	73
South Africa	35	44	31	124	76	1	10	44	144	81	77
Tanzania	127	123	176	78	158	98	97	129	92	36	122
Turkey	71	61	155	72	44	78	65	79	80	51	120
Uganda	123	143	109	129	127	48	133	93	158	116	63
Ukraine	152	112	180	169	166	24	111	181	140	44	156
Average of developing economies with LCR cases	95	98	120	111	87	63	66	105	116	81	97
Average of all other developing economies	107	100	99	101	100	96	97	101	105	106	109

a. IMF designations for "advanced economies," available at www.imf.org/external/pubs/ft/weo/2008/02/weodata/groups.htm#ae.

Source: World Bank and IFC (2011).

Table 2.2 Corporate tax and corruption indicators, LCR countries

Country	Profit tax rate (percent)	Number of hours, on average, to complete a corporate tax return	2011 Transparency International Corruption Perceptions Index
Advanced economies[a]			
Australia	26.0	37	8.8
Canada	9.4	45	8.7
France	8.2	26	7.0
Greece	13.4	88	3.4
Korea	15.2	100	5.4
Switzerland	8.9	15	8.8
United States	27.6	99	7.1
Average of advanced economies with LCR cases	15.5	59	7.0
Average of all other advanced economies	9.7	48	7.6
Developing and other economies			
Argentina	2.8	105	3.0
Azerbaijan	12.9	64	2.4
Botswana	15.9	40	6.1
Brazil	22.4	736	3.8
China	6.0	74	3.6
Egypt	13.0	69	2.9
India	24.6	45	3.1
Indonesia	23.6	88	3.0
Kazakhstan	15.9	75	2.7
Kenya	33.1	60	2.2
Mexico	24.5	157	3.0
Mongolia	10.2	57	2.7
Nigeria	22.3	398	2.4
Paraguay	9.6	387	2.2
Russia	9.0	130	2.4
Saudi Arabia	2.1	32	4.4
South Africa	24.4	100	4.1
Tanzania	20.2	60	3.0
Turkey	17.9	46	4.2
Uganda	23.3	45	2.4
Ukraine	12.2	112	2.3
Average of developing economies with LCR cases	16.5	137	3.1
Average of all other developing economies	15.3	71	3.3

a. IMF designations for "advanced economies," available at www.imf.org/external/pubs/ft/weo/2008/02/weodata/groups.htm#ae.

Sources: Data on profit tax rate and corporate tax returns from PwC, World Bank, and IFC (2012); Corruption Perceptions Index from Transparency International, http://cpi.transparency.org/cpi2011/results.

Encouraging Corporate Social Responsibility

A study by the Organization for Economic Cooperation and Development (OECD) published a decade ago (Gordon 2001) found that many multinational corporations had issued corporate social responsibility (CSR) guidelines for their own use. Because there is wide variation in the quality and content of private guidelines, several international institutions have issued their own CSR guidelines. Among these are the Caux Principles for Business, the Global Reporting Initiative, the Global Sullivan Principles, and the OECD Guidelines for Multinational Enterprises.

CSR norms have many elements. They cover human rights; workplace conditions, in both multinational corporation operations and their suppliers; environmental safeguards; and relations with government officials. CSR obligations aimed at strengthening the base of local suppliers are an alternative to LCRs.

The Global Reporting Initiative[1] recommends that manufacturing multinationals report on how much they buy locally. The OECD guidelines[2] offer 2 relevant points (out of 15 general policies):

> Encourage local capacity building through close co-operation with the local community, including business interests, as well as developing the enterprise's activities in domestic and foreign markets, consistent with the need for sound commercial practice.

> Encourage human capital formation, in particular by creating employment opportunities and facilitating training opportunities for employees.

Similar guidance is found in the second of the Caux Principles, which states that "businesses should contribute to economic and social development not only in the countries in which they operate, but also in the world community at large, through effective and prudent use of resources, free and fair competition and emphasis upon innovation in technology, production methods, marketing and communications."[3] Seventh on the list of the Sullivan Principles is the principle that multinational corporations will work "with governments and communities in which [they] do business to improve the quality of life in those communities—their educational, cultural, economic and social well-being—and seek to provide training and opportunities for workers from disadvantaged backgrounds."[4]

---

1. Global Reporting Initiative, 2006, *Sustainability Reporting Guidelines: Version 3.0,* Amsterdam, www.globalreporting.org.

2. *OECD Guidelines for Multinational Enterprises*, 2011 edition, May 25, 2011, Paris, www.oecd.org/daf/inv/mne/48004323.pdf.

3. Caux Round Table, *Principles for Business*, 2010, www.cauxroundtable.org/index.cfm?menuid=8.

4. Leon H. Sullivan Foundation, *Global Sullivan Principles*, http://thesullivanfoundation.org/about/global-sullivan-principles (accessed on May 31, 2012).

CSR pressures can inspire targeted actions on the part of multinational corporations. Socially responsible multinational corporations can ask themselves several questions. Has the firm designated a manager to be a "talent scout" to search out potential indigenous suppliers? Does the firm provide production assistance, managerial advice, and advance purchase orders to potential indigenous suppliers? Does the firm have procedures to "qualify" and "certify" potential indigenous suppliers (e.g., ISO 9000 certification)? Does the firm have a program to introduce qualified indigenous suppliers to sister affiliates in the region, thereby promoting exports? (Moran 2011, 137).

Governments can help implement the CSR prescriptions. Singapore and Malaysia, for example, have set up industrial parks for local suppliers adjacent to their export processing zones that house multinational corporations. They have also established programs to link foreign multinationals with lists of indigenous firms in each sector; they finance equipment recommended by the foreign firms and offer certification instruction (Moran 2011).

Expanding Training

LCRs are one example of preventive measures designed to avoid dislocation by protecting an industry and its workers from foreign competition.[5] Preventive measures should be contrasted with direct measures aimed at the immediate needs of workers, such as unemployment insurance, job search assistance, and training programs.

Training programs fall into two broad categories: those that provide basic language and math skills to people with low educational attainment and those that provide specific job-related skills. Workers in developing countries often have less than high school education. The lack of basic skills makes it difficult for them to enter the labor force. Basic skills, however, are largely the responsibility of public education systems.

Job-related skills, by contrast, are the mixed responsibility of government and firms. Recent years have seen more private sector efforts at offering specific job-related skill training, often prompted by government. The best known examples are in advanced countries. In Germany, tax credits encourage firms to hire and train new workers. In the United States, the government finances training delivered by private institutions. Workers are given vouchers, which they use to purchase training from the institution of their choice.

Systematic evaluation of training programs is severely limited by the lack of data concerning who gets trained, for what, and at what cost and how useful the training is in helping the worker find a new job. The absence of data is particularly acute in developing countries. However, analysis by the OECD finds a relatively strong relationship between the training participation rate, on the one hand, and employment and labor force participation rates on the other. Data

---

5. This section is based on work by Howard Rosen (2005).

from the second half of the 1990s indicate that for every 1 percent increase in the number of workers participating in training, the employment rate and labor force participation rate rose by more than 1 percent (OECD 2004).[6]

The effectiveness of various training schemes tends to correlate with their links to specific employment opportunities. At a minimum, these links can take the form of training for broad vocational skills for which demand has been documented (e.g., plumbing or machine-tool skills). Training received through a closer link to potential employers—for example, through apprenticeship programs or technical or vocational courses—tends to be even more effective. Other tools, such as tax incentives and skill certifications, can also link worker training to private sector employers. Corporate tax systems typically treat training as a business expense, although this incentive is limited for firms that have few taxable profits. In these cases, the government could consider a refundable tax credit to cover all or some of the costs associated with training.

Given the important linkage between training and job opportunities, the ultimate effectiveness of any training program depends on the availability of accurate, detailed, and timely information about labor market conditions. Governments and private employers need to work together in collecting and publishing information on demand for workers by industry, occupation, skill requirements, and location.

Governments have many tools at their disposal to alleviate economic adjustment pains, ranging from outright industry protection to the use of tariffs and nontariff barriers (including LCRs) to government support of labor market flexibility through job transition assistance, including worker training.

Table 2.3 presents average imports as a percent of GDP between 2003 and 2007 and average public spending on active labor market programs (ALMPs) as a percent of GDP between 2003 and 2007 for 10 OECD member countries (the 5 economies with the highest and lowest ALMP/GDP ratios) as well as the average for all 31 OECD members. The correlation between the two indices for 31 OECD member economies (0.43) is strong but not statistically significant.

Economists generally argue that labor market adjustment programs can substitute for trade protection, but only a few examples can be cited. Denmark, the Netherlands, and Sweden have extensive labor market adjustment programs and are extremely open to imports. The ALMP/GDP ratio for the top five economies is more than twice the average for all OECD members. In other words, to the extent that there is a relationship between spending on ALMPs and openness to imports, it seems to be stronger in economies that spend a significant amount on ALMPs. Although comparable data for developing countries are not readily available, it seems clear that these countries would have to devote considerable resources, as well as significantly reform existing labor laws, to enhance workers' skills and promote labor market flexibility.

---

6. This relationship was statistically significant at the 1 percent level. The relationship between participation in training and a country's unemployment rate was not statistically significant.

Table 2.3 Imports and labor market spending of 10 OECD countries, 2003–07 (percent of GDP)

Country	Average imports	Average public spending on active labor market programs
Denmark	42.12	1.57
Netherlands	51.51	1.29
Sweden	37.49	1.23
Belgium	93.69	1.09
Germany	31.29	0.95
Israel	26.85	0.18
United States	13.55	0.14
Korea	24.00	0.12
Estonia	51.54	0.07
Mexico	17.20	0.02
OECD average	21.35	0.56

OECD = Organization for Economic Cooperation and Development

Source: OECD, Labor Market Programs data from OECD.Stat Extracts database, http://stats.oecd.org/Index.aspx?DatasetCode=LMPEXP.

Improving Logistics

No longer is the bulk of global commerce confined to raw materials and finished manufactures. In between are vast webs of trade in intermediate goods and services, linked in global value chains with ingredients from multiple countries and coordinated by numerous business trips and data exchanges. This change increases the importance of trade transaction costs (TTCs), which are incurred not just once in the trip from producer to consumer but many times.

It turns out that TTCs decisively separate countries that participate fully in world commerce and those that are somewhat isolated. TTCs are not simply a matter of geography and fate. Targeted policies—grouped under the label of "trade facilitation"—can sharply reduce the TTC burden even for landlocked countries. Singapore, for example, ranks first in trade facilitation, not only because of its excellent natural port but also because of its superb governance. Landlocked Austria ranks 11th, owing entirely to government emphasis on quality infrastructure and efficient border management.

Table 2.4 presents estimates drawn from the work of John S. Wilson, Catherine L. Mann, and Tsuneihiro Otsuki (2004). They used a gravity model to tease out the consequences of inefficient ports, inadequate services, poor customs administration, and excessive regulation. Port characteristics are largely a matter of hard infrastructure, inadequate services are a mixture of hard infrastructure (telecom systems) and soft infrastructure (internet access), and customs administration and regulation are purely soft infrastructure. In making their calculations, the authors did not assume that every country

Table 2.4 Estimated gains from trade facilitation improvements to merchandise exports

Region	Export gains	
	Billions of US dollars	Percent
East Asia	180.7	24.0
Eastern Europe and Central Asia	41.7	30.0
Latin America and Caribbean	35.8	20.0
Middle East and North Africa	0.9	3.3
Organization for Economic Cooperation and Development	103.9	3.8
South Asia	14.5	40.3
Sub-Saharan Africa	1.2	10.9
Total	376.3	9.7

APEC = Asia Pacific Economic Cooperation forum

Note: World Bank model assumes all below average countries improve port efficiency, customs environment, regulatory environment, and e-business usage to average APEC levels. See Hufbauer, Schott, and Wong (2010, appendix F) for a review of the methodology.

Source: Wilson, Mann, and Otsuki (2004).

attains Singapore's level of performance; instead, they assumed that countries below the average lifted themselves halfway to the average. Even so, the potential trade gains are spectacular. According to these estimates, a sharp improvement in trade facilitation could boost the merchandise exports of non-OECD countries by $272 billion and OECD countries by $103 billion.[7] Table 2.5 reports the potential gains to per capita GDP for several countries.

A subsequent study published by the World Economic Forum (2013), based on research conducted in collaboration with the World Bank and Bain & Company, confirms the huge potential payoff from slashing TTCs. Ambitious improvement in border administration and transport and communications infrastructure—beyond the upgrades contemplated by Wilson, Mann, and Otsuki (2004)—could raise world GDP by 4.7 percent ($2.6 trillion) and boost world exports by 14.5 percent ($1.6 trillion). These figures are substantially greater than the potential payoff from complete worldwide tariff elimination.

Both in the aggregate and on a per capita basis, potential TTC gains are huge. Are they believable? The World Bank first published its Logistics Performance Index (LPI) for 2007; the latest is for 2012. The index covers 150 countries and 5,000 individual components (roughly 30 per country). For

---

7. The OECD (2003) reports several earlier studies of the trade and GDP benefits from improved trade facilitation and offers its own estimates. In our view, most of the early studies are too conservative, a judgment supported by the enthusiasm of the business community for advancing the trade facilitation agreement in the Doha Round of WTO negotiations. However, the Wilson, Mann, and Otsuki (2004) estimates are on the high side and substantially larger than the estimates reported in Hufbauer, Schott, and Wong (2010).

Table 2.5   Estimated GDP gains from substantial improvements in trade facilitation

Country	GDP per capita change	
	US dollars	Percent
Australia	946	4
Canada	766	3
Chile	270	5
China	56	7
Hong Kong	483	2
Indonesia	73	7
Japan	1,921	5
Korea	614	5
Malaysia	105	3
Mexico	336	7
New Zealand	653	4
Peru	303	13
Philippines	121	10
Russia	336	14
Singapore	1,173	4
Taiwan	112	4
Thailand	836	5
United States	1,331	4
Vietnam	16	5

Source: Wilson, Mann, and Otsuki (2003).

convenience, the components are grouped into seven categories: customs, infrastructure, international shipments, logistics competence, tracking and tracing, domestic logistics costs, and timeliness. In 2007, the best performer was Singapore, with an overall score of 4.19 (out of 5); the worst was Afghanistan, at 1.21.

As might be expected, scores improve with per capita GDP. More interesting, however, is the fact that after normalizing for per capita income, LPI outperformers enjoy faster trade expansion, more rapid economic growth, and more diversified exports. Illustrative is the export growth comparison between LPI outperformers and underperformers over the 2005–10 period. The 2010 LPI report identifies 10 outperformers and 10 underperformers (after adjusting for income levels) among non-high-income, non-oil-producing countries. Table 2.6 compares their export growth. On average, LPI outperformers increased their exports about twice as rapidly as LPI underperformers. However, an examination of the LPI components turns up no magic bullets. All seven components are important. India, for example, which increased its exports by 56 percent between 2005 and 2010, scored relatively high on logistics quality and competence in 2012 and relatively low on infrastructure. Vietnam, where exports rose 54 percent over the same time period, scored relatively high on international shipments and relatively low on logistics quality and competence.

Table 2.6 Export growth, LPI ranks, and trade facilitation components of overperforming and underperforming countries

Country	Total export growth, 2005–10 (percent)	Overall LPI rank, 2010	Best component rank, 2012	Worst component rank, 2012
Overperformers in 2010				
Democratic Republic of the Congo	124	143	Customs (133)	Timeliness (149)
Madagascar	26	88	Timeliness (11)	Customs and tracking and tracing (120)
Uganda	206	66	Customs (44)[a]	Tracking and tracing (114)[a]
Bangladesh	96	79	Infrastructure (65)	Customs (121)
Vietnam	121	53	International shipments (57)	Logistics, quality, and competence (82)
India	121	47	Logistics, quality, and competence (38)	Infrastructure (56)
Philippines	29	44	Tracking and tracing and logistics, quality, and competence (39)	Customs (62)
Thailand	77	35	International shipments (35)	Timeliness (99)
China	107	27	International shipments (23)	Timeliness (54)
South Africa	58	28	Infrastructure (19)	Timeliness (93)
Average	93	52		

Underperformers in 2010

Eritrea	n.a.	154	Shipment (135)	Customs (151)
Fiji	15	144	Timeliness (85)	Customs (137)
Namibia	100	152	Customs (54)	Timeliness (14)
Montenegro	n.a.	121	Timeliness (11)	Customs and logistics, quality, and competence (120)
Botswana	5	134	Customs (48)	International shipments (111)
Gabon	66	122	Timeliness (23)	Infrastructure (140)
Russia	64	94	Timeliness (29)	Customs (138)
Croatia	35	74	Infrastructure (32)	Timeliness (65)
Slovenia	35	57	International shipments (31)	Timeliness (46)
Greece	35	54	Tracking and tracing (63)	Timeliness (125)
Average	44	106		

n.a. = not available
LPI = World Bank's Logistics Performance Index

a. Data not available for 2012; taken from World Bank, *Connecting to Compete*, 2010.

Sources: Export growth data are from World Bank, *World Development Indicators* database, June 2012, http://data.worldbank.org/indicator, World Bank, World Integrated Trade Solution (WITS), June 2012, http://wits.worldbank.org/wits, and IMF, *Direction of Trade Statistics*, June 2012; trade facilitation components are from World Bank, *Connecting to Compete*, 2007 and 2012, http://web.worldbank.org/WBSITE/EXTERNAL/TOPICS/TRADE/0,,contentMDK:23188613~pagePK:2100 58~piPK:210062~theSitePK:239071,00.html.

Another piece of evidence comes from an Inter-American Development Bank study entitled *Unclogging the Arteries* (Blyde, Moreira, and Volpe 2011), which shows that TTCs are much greater impediments to commerce for most Latin American countries than tariffs. The authors estimate that a 10 percentage point decrease in the unusually high TTC figures in Latin America would boost intraregional exports by more than 60 percent. The biggest source of trade costs is port inefficiency, directly attributable to poor infrastructure and weak administration.

Twenty case studies presented in the World Economic Forum report (2013) convincingly show that the statistical results summarized above are not artifacts. The economic payoff, in jobs and income, from reducing supply chain barriers is large—and can be realized by any country with a do-it-yourself attitude.

Increasing Investment in Infrastructure

LCRs often create a guaranteed market for goods or services supplied by local firms to public infrastructure projects. Jill Wells and John Hawkins (2008), of the UK Institution of Civil Engineers, argue that they can help "level the playing field" in procurement markets that are fraught with advantages for foreign state-owned enterprises and disadvantages for local suppliers and small and medium-size enterprises. Other advocates give a positive assessment of LCRs based on the notion that they increase the market share of local producers (see, for example, Levett and Chandler 2012).

But these justifications leave no space for the fact that LCRs usually raise costs, impair quality, and create delays (for an example from Indonesia, see World Bank 2007). In a study of nearly 2,000 projects financed by the World Bank over nearly 30 years, Nicola Limodio (2011) reaches an obvious conclusion: The higher the quality of implementation, the more likely the project outcome will be favorable. Although there may be capable local firms that can undertake infrastructure projects, many policymakers tout LCRs as a means to develop strategic or infant industries. That argument speaks to the weakness of local firms, not their strength.

As a means of creating jobs and boosting local firms, an alternative to LCRs on existing infrastructure projects is to enlarge the infrastructure portfolio by opening infrastructure opportunities to the private sector.[8] A report by the World Bank's Public-Private Infrastructure Advisory Facility (Schur et al. 2008) finds that policy uncertainty in local markets limits both the size and scope of infrastructure projects that private investors are willing to undertake. If the obstacles of policy uncertainty cannot be surmounted, and tax revenues are scarce, new public projects can instead be financed with user fees of various kinds.

---

8. Privately owned infrastructure, whether domestic or foreign owned, often performs better than public sector projects (see Moran 2011).

Table 2.7 Global infrastructure needed to modernize obsolescent systems and meet growing demand, 2005–30

Projected investment	Water	Power	Road and rail	Air/seaports
Total projected cumulative investment (trillions of US dollars at 2005 prices)	22.6	9.0	7.8	1.6
By region (percent)				
Asia/Oceania	40	47	27	32
Europe	20	12	40	27
Latin America/South America	22	16	13	4
United States and Canada	16	17	12	27
Africa	1	6	4	1
Middle East	1	2	4	9

Sources: Doshi, Schulman, and Gabaldon (2007, Exhibit 1).

User fees, whether publicly or privately administered, stand out among financing tools in their ability to efficiently allocate investment. The logic behind user fees is simple: The people who use the good or service provided by the infrastructure should pay the costs of construction and maintenance. User fees are typically collected at the initial point of consumption, thereby providing the consumer with a clear cost for each use of the infrastructure. User fees certainly have their limitations, explored by Edward Gramlich (1990, 1994) among others, but the question must always be asked: What is the alternative? If no better financing alternative exists, policymakers should impose user fees rather than leave a promising project on the drawing board.

Infrastructure will be big business across the globe over the coming decades. In 2010, the World Economic Forum projected that the world is facing a global infrastructure deficit of about $2 trillion a year over the next 20 years. There is thus latent demand for modernization and expansion. Viren Doshi, Gary Schulman, and Daniel Gabaldon (2007) of Booz & Company, a US-based management and consulting firm, break down this roughly $40 trillion global demand by project type and region. More than half the demand represents future investments in water infrastructure, and a quarter reflects energy infrastructure (table 2.7). Asia and Oceania lead demand for infrastructure development, with a projected need of $16 trillion in investment, primarily for water and power projects.

All these figures represent needs, not available financing. But the message is clear: If countries around the world can turn to public-private partnerships and user fees to fund needed infrastructure, global productivity will enjoy a significant boost and millions of good jobs will be created. The potential vastly exceeds any job creation associated with new LCR mandates.

Infrastructure jobs are particularly relevant to unemployment in construction and other cyclical sectors that were hit hard by the Great Recession (see Lin and Doemeland 2012). Moreover, infrastructure projects indirectly create jobs in various manufacturing and service sectors. In the United States, researchers estimate that infrastructure projects for energy, public schools, transportation, and water systems create 18,000 jobs for every $1 billion in new outlays; about 40 percent of these jobs are in the construction sector, with the other 60 percent spread across the economy (Heintz, Pollin, and Garrett-Peltier 2009). In a developing country with one-quarter of the United States' per capita GDP, the job creation effect of infrastructure projects is about four times as great—more than 70,000 jobs per billion dollars. This mechanism, not LCRs, is where policy should be pointed.

Imposing Tariffs and Subsidies

Most developing countries have retained substantial policy space between their maximum tariff rates bound in World Trade Organization (WTO) schedules and their currently applied tariff rates. Table 2.8 illustrates this phenomenon: In extreme cases, such as Tanzania, the difference between the bound rate and the applied rate is more than 100 percentage points. Substantial empirical work shows that progressive liberalization, not higher protection, best promotes economic growth (see Krueger 1998, Stiglitz 1998, Frankel and Romer 1999, Wacziarg and Welch 2008). However, if a government that decides to protect a certain activity or sector has a political choice between a new LCR and a higher tariff, the tariff is the better economic choice. The cost impact of a tariff is visible; the cost impact of an LCR is hard to determine. LCR specifications are more likely than tariffs to "play favorites" between local firms, because, in principle, tariffs are uniform and provide equal protection to all local firms whereas LCRs often favor a few firms. Tariffs do not delay the larger project; LCRs more often than not ensure delay. So while higher tariffs are far from a first-best policy, as a means of targeted protection they are superior to LCRs.

Economists generally agree that subsidies are preferable to tariffs or other forms of trade protection, because they are more visible, they do not foreclose the market to competitive foreign firms, and they do not impose a deadweight loss, through higher prices, on household and business consumers. The WTO Agreement on Subsidies and Countervailing Measures (ASCM) has very strict rules against subsidies that are preferentially targeted on exports, but subsidies that target the domestic market are actionable only when (among other characteristics) they are specific to an industry and cause "adverse effects" to the interests of another WTO member. In reality, few WTO dispute cases have arisen when subsidies alter market conditions solely within the territory of a WTO member. Only when the subsidized firm exports to foreign markets does it become likely that another WTO member will bring a countervailing duty case. In practice, countries thus have a great deal of room within the WTO rulebook to subsidize domestic firms; probably the greater constraint is their own budget capacity. Almost as a footnote, it deserves mention that the history of public subsidies, whether to farmers or manufacturers, is a history of domestic preferences. Foreigners are off limits when it comes to most public subsidies.

Table 2.8 Bound and MFN applied tariff rates, 2010 (percent)

Country	Binding coverage (percent of tariff lines)	Average bound	Average MFN applied	Difference between bound and MFN applied
Tanzania	13	120	13	108
Nigeria	19	119	12	107
Kuwait[a]	100	100	5	95
Mauritius	18	94	1	93
Gambia	14	103	14	89
Ghana	14	93	13	80
Saint Kitts and Nevis	98	76	9	67
Jamaica	100	50	8	42
Costa Rica	100	43	5	38
India[a]	74	49	13	36
El Salvador	100	37	6	31
Indonesia	96	37	7	30
Colombia	100	43	13	30
Mexico	100	36	9	27
Peru	100	29	5	24
Egypt[a]	99	37	17	20
Philippines	67	26	6	19
Chile	100	25	6	19
Thailand	75	28	10	18
Brazil	100	31	14	18
Norway	100	20	7	13
South Africa	96	19	8	11
New Zealand[a]	100	10	2	8
Korea	95	17	12	5
Gabon[a]	100	21	18	4
Canada	100	7	4	3
Vietnam	100	11	10	2
China	100	10	10	0
United States	100	4	4	0
European Union	100	5	5	0

MFN = most favored nation

a. Data are from 2009.

Source: World Trade Organization, World Tariff Profiles, 2011, www.wto.org/english/res_e/booksp_e/tariff_profiles11_e.pdf.

Exchange rate policy occupies an opposite pole to targeted subsidies and tariffs: Whereas these policies zero in on specific industries and products, exchange rates broadly affect all of the entire commercial relations with the outside world. This sharp distinction might seem to make exchange rate policy a poor alternative to LCR measures. But LCRs are sometimes imposed because political leaders are concerned about a trade deficit or poor export growth or a seeming absence of international competitiveness. In these circumstances,

Table 2.9 Tariff dispersion, 2010 (percent)

Country	Simple average	Minimum rate	Maximum rate	Standard deviation	Trade balance (percent of GDP, average 2000–2010)	Growth of value in exports (average 2000–2010)
Hong Kong	0.0	0	0.0	0.0	8.5	8.1
Singapore	0.0	0	0.0	0.0	24.0	9.1
Switzerland	0.0	0	0.0	0.0	8.2	4.6
Chile	6.0	0	15.6	0.6	6.8	4.4
Australia	2.8	0	10.0	2.8	–1.2	3.5
New Zealand	2.1	0	10.0	3.0	0.3	3.0

Sources: World Trade Organization, World Tariff Profiles, 2011, www.wto.org/english/res_e/booksp_e/tariff_profiles11_e.pdf; World Bank, *World Development Indicators* database, http://data.worldbank.org/indicator.

addressing currency overvaluation can respond to these concerns more effectively than a series of LCRs.

When national leaders decide they want to spark the economy, attract investment, and integrate with world commerce, it would be far better in economic terms, albeit more challenging politically, to flatten the tariff schedule and eliminate sector-specific subsidies—thereby curbing distortions and taking away targeted protection—while removing the drag on growth of output and employment generated by currency overvaluation. Hong Kong and Singapore were early practitioners of this combination, to great success. Later practitioners included Chile, New Zealand, and Australia. Table 2.9 shows tariff dispersion for these countries, as measured by the standard deviation of the country's tariff lines as well as their average trade deficit and average annual export growth from 2000 to 2010. As the table shows, these countries are not incurring persistent trade deficits, and all of them have enjoyed solid export growth.

Conclusion

The appeal of LCRs springs from instant political gratification—a consequence of walling off economic activity from foreign competition. Other policies generally take longer to show their positive effects, but they are superior in terms of attracting investment, delivering jobs, and fostering growth—and, unlike LCRs, they do not undermine the international trading system or distort the domestic economy to the same extent.

In their own national interest, governments should resist imposing new LCRs and lay plans to phase out existing ones. Toward this end, it might be useful to convene a fact-finding meeting under WTO auspices and to consider a common definition and coordinated standstill of LCR practices.

3

Survey and Case Studies

Local content requirements (LCRs) are a protective device with three simple but powerful appeals: to create jobs at home rather than abroad; to nurture domestic firms so that they become world-class competitors; and to ensure that important industries, such as civil aviation, broadcasting, and electric power, are locally owned (these might be called local ownership requirements). Each appeal has variants that speak to particular conditions. For example, creating jobs at home seems like a natural corollary to public subsidies that support green energy. Nurturing domestic firms can have the added feature of helping disadvantaged groups (such as leatherworkers in Japan). Important industries have been elastically defined to include almost any state-owned enterprise on the verge of privatization (the Russian story) and iconic private firms subject to a foreign takeover bid (the Unocal story).

This book uses two approaches to size up and illustrate the LCR phenomenon. The first approach is a global survey of about 100 recent LCR episodes, basically instances identified since the onset of the US financial crisis in 2008, summarized in appendix A. Of course, LCRs predate the Great Recession. The norm for public procurement for at least 100 years has been preferential purchases from local firms. Both to make our task manageable and to keep a focus on contemporary trade and investment challenges, we surveyed only recent episodes.

The second approach is the compilation of six case studies. Case studies are, in a sense, anecdotes; their value is to illustrate larger phenomena. Ideally, case studies should be statistically representative of the phenomenon under consideration. We make no claim that our six cases are statistically representative.[1] The cases were selected to illustrate the LCR phenomenon in both advanced and emerging economies, to cover several different industries, and to show the range of LCR policies, from highly explicit and transparent to highly implicit and opaque. LCRs in some cases are mixed with other policy goals, such as making select pharmaceuticals widely available at low cost (the Brazilian healthcare case). The six case studies are presented in chapters 4 to 9 in alphabetical order of the countries imposing the LCR.

Most of the LCRs described in the case studies were launched well before the Great Recession of 2008–09. Unlike the new LCRs covered in the survey (discussed in the next section), the earlier LCRs were not inspired primarily by the severe unemployment of a collapsing world economy. Instead, targeted job creation was mixed with other motives, often variants of the infant industry argument (present to some degree in the Brazilian healthcare, Canadian wind turbine, Chinese automobile, Indian solar power, and Nigerian oil and gas cases).

To size up the dimensions of this problem, we undertook a global screening of LCR mandates. The goal of this screen was to identify and list all LCRs enacted since the onset of the Great Recession. The analysis began with the Global Trade Alerts database (www.globaltradealert.org), coordinated by the Centre for Economic Policy Research in London and supported by the World Bank. The analysis built off that backbone by monitoring various sources around the globe. This research demonstrated that the proliferation of LCR policies is substantial and widespread.

Appendix A lists all LCR measures proposed or implemented since 2008 that we were able to identify, some 117 cases. Although some countries were more active and some industries more targeted, new LCR measures were found in all types of economies as well as virtually all industries. By case count, Brazil was the worst perpetrator, with 15 episodes, but LCRs are not limited to developing countries. Many measures have effects beyond trade flows, directly and indirectly affecting investment, services, and employment. The affected industries cover a wide range, including agriculture, healthcare, information technology, automobiles, and many others.

We analyzed each case based on the online information we could find. Of the 117 cases, about 47 were systemically quantifiable. These cases explicitly target a subset of products or services that are traded internationally. In these cases, the analysis identified all 4-digit Harmonized System (HS) codes affected by the measure. For example, Argentina implemented an "import balance" measure that requires automobile companies to maintain a neutral trade balance. This measure affected several sections of Chapter 85 of the HS (specifically, 8703, 8704, 8706, 8707, and 8708). We used common trade data sources, such the World Bank's World Integrated Trade Solutions (WITS), to quantify the affected trade flows.

---

1. Indeed, as work on our global survey was completed in parallel with work on the case studies, it would have been impossible to select in advance cases that represented the survey outcome.

Table 3.1   Estimated goods and services trade affected by LCR measures since 2008

LCR measure	Estimated affected goods and services trade (billions of dollars)[a]	Speculated estimate of trade reduced (billions of dollars)[b]
47 quantifiable measures	373	37
70 nonquantifiable measures[c]	555	56
117 total LCR measures	928	93

a. Cumulative trade figure calculated from table A.1 in appendix A.
b. The reduction in trade on account of LCRs—by contrast with the impact on trade—is a matter of greater speculation. As a conservative but speculative guess, we calculate reduced trade using an estimated tariff-equivalent of 10 percent ad valorem and assuming the elasticity of import demand for foreign goods as approximately –1.0.
c. For nonquantifiable LCR measures, the estimated affected trade was calculated by multiplying the 70 measures by the average of $7.9 billion affected trade per quantifiable LCR measure.

Note: Quantifiable LCR measures explicitly target a subset of products or services that are traded internationally and could be identified by 4-digit Harmonized System (HS) codes. By contrast, although most nonquantifiable LCR measures directly target trade flows, they could not be easily quantified, due to their opaque nature, vague wording, or nontransparent application.

Source: Authors' calculations.

Although by design, all of the LCRs negatively affect trade, the term "affecting" does not translate into a one-for-one reduction in trade. Future research might establish the tariff equivalents of these measures; doing so was beyond the scope of our work. Some researchers have begun to estimate the tariff equivalent of other nontariff barriers, but their work has focused primarily on the trade cost of deficient soft and hard infrastructure. Our analysis suggests that, taken together, the quantifiable LCRs affected more than $373 billion in goods and services trade flows (table 3.1), about 2 percent of total world trade in 2010 (the year when most measures were implemented).

In addition to the 47 cases that our analysis tried to quantify, we identified 70 cases that are not quantifiable, because of their opaque nature, vague wording, or nontransparent application. Many of these cases directly targeted trade flows: 10 limited or prohibited foreign investment; 23 limited services (the majority required firms to store all data in local data centers and prohibited firms from moving these centers abroad); and 4 limited foreign employment. These measures likely had spillover effects on trade flows. We assumed that the 70 cases had the same average impact as the more clearly targeted, or systemically quantifiable, cases. We believe this is a conservative assumption. Making this assumption, the analysis suggests that the 70 nonquantifiable cases adversely affected another $555 billion of trade (see table 3.1), about 3 percent of world trade in 2010.

Based on these assumptions, LCRs affected almost $928 billion in trade in 2010, about 5 percent of total global trade in goods and services ($18.5 trillion). The reduction in trade as a result of LCRs—by contrast with the impact on trade—is a matter of greater speculation. We do not have estimates on their tariff-equivalent effect. As a conservative and speculative guess, we would say that the tariff equivalent is 10 percent ad valorem. Assuming that the elasticity of import demand for foreign goods is about –1.0, we speculate that the reduction in trade as a result of LCRs in 2010 may have been about $93 billion a year. This figure could be too high or too low. Whatever the correct estimate, there is no reason to think that the volume of trade lost in the years after 2010 is smaller, as very few LCRs have been withdrawn. In fact, according to the latest issue of the Global Trade Alert, the "body count" of new instances of protection (every category, including LCRs) in the fourth quarter of 2012 showed no decline from previous quarters (Evenett 2012).

Greater speculation is required to estimate the number of targeted jobs supported by cumulative LCRs since the beginning of 2008. Our estimates suggest that advanced economies imposed LCRs that negatively affected about $39 billion of trade (4 percent of the total), while the rest of the world (mainly developing countries) imposed LCRs that affected $889 billion of trade (96 percent) (see table 3.2). If our speculation as to the global reduction in trade is correct—roughly $93 billion—advanced economies may have cut targeted imports by $4 billion and the rest of the world may have cut targeted imports by $89 billion. In the Organization for Economic Cooperation and Development, the average number of jobs per billion dollars of GDP is 5,500; in the rest of the world the figure is 42,500. Based on these averages, LCRs may have supported 22,000 targeted jobs in advanced economies and 3.7 million targeted jobs in the rest of the world. Of course, policy support for targeted jobs does not translate into net employment gains, because foreign countries lose exports from "beggar-my-neighbor" LCRs and because domestic buyers (households and business firms) of more expensive products from LCR sectors experience a reduction in their own purchasing power.

Table 3.2 Estimated jobs affected by LCR measures since 2008

Country group	Estimated trade affected by 117 LCR measures (billions of dollars)[a]	Speculated estimate of trade reduced (billions of dollars)	Estimated jobs affected by LCR measures		
			Employees per billion US dollars value added in industry[b]	Estimated employees per billion US dollars in import-competing firms (halved)[c]	Speculated estimate of jobs affected by LCRs (thousands)[d]
Advanced economies	39	4	11,000[e]	5,500	22
Rest of world	889	89	85,000[f]	42,500	3,763
Total	928	93	—	—	3,784

a. Calculations of the estimated trade affected by 117 LCR measures by country group were based on the following: Advanced economies accounted for about 4 percent or $15.7 billion of the total trade affected by the 47 quantifiable LCR measures, namely $373 billion (see table 3.1). The rest of the world accounted for about 96 percent or $357.1 billion of the total trade affected by the 47 quantifiable LCR measures. These percentage shares were applied to the total estimated trade affected by all 117 LCR measures, namely $928 billion.

b. Value added in industry was used as the best estimate of GDP from tradables. Industry corresponds to International Standard Industrial Classification (ISIC) divisions 10 to 45 and includes manufacturing.

c. Values are halved to better estimate the higher labor productivity of import-competing firms.

d. Figures calculated by multiplying estimated trade reduced by the ratio of employees per billion US dollars in import-competing firms. Figures rounded to nearest thousand.

e. The ratio of employees per billion US dollars in import-competing firms for advanced economies is calculated as the average for countries in the Organization for Economic Cooperation and Development (OECD).

f. The ratio of employees per billion US dollars in import-competing firms for the rest of the world is calculated as the regional average for developing countries.

Note: Advanced economies comprise seven developed countries—Australia, Canada, France, Greece, Korea, Switzerland, and the United States—and account for a total of 33 LCR measures. The rest of the world comprises 21 developing and other countries and accounts for a total of 84 LCR measures.

Sources: Trade affected and trade reduced are from table 3.1; industry value added data from World Bank, World Development Indicators database, http://data.worldbank.org/indicator; employment data from International Labor Organization, Global Employment Trends, 2012, www.ilo.org/wcmsp5/groups/public/@dgreports/@dcomm/@publ/documents/ publication/ wcms_171571.pdf; estimated jobs affected from authors' calculations.

4

Healthcare Industry in Brazil

The Brazilian healthcare sector illustrates the combination of policy goals that has, both intentionally and unintentionally, forced the localization of medical equipment suppliers and pharmaceutical firms. One goal is to keep hospitals and health insurance either publicly owned or owned by Brazilian firms. Another appears to be infant industry support for domestic medical equipment firms. A third is to ensure public safety, especially with respect to new pharmaceuticals. A fourth is to ensure public access to affordable drugs, especially for serious diseases (notably HIV/AIDS). Lurking behind these goals is Brazil's trade deficit in healthcare products, an economic feature that probably troubles some economic officials.

Brazil is the largest market for healthcare goods and services in Latin America, spending about $142 billion, or 8.8 percent of GDP, on healthcare in 2009. The sector can be divided into three broad categories: hospitals and other health services, medical devices, and pharmaceutical products. Expenditures on hospital care and medical services accounted for 5.6 percent, medical devices outside the hospital 1.3 percent, and pharmaceuticals purchased outside the hospital 1.9 percent of GDP in 2009 (JETRO 2010).

As of 2012, no Brazilian hospitals or other healthcare service providers were owned by foreign firms, and foreign firms were not allowed to participate directly or indirectly in Brazil's health insurance industry. In contrast, foreign firms play a prominent role in the Brazilian market for medical devices and pharmaceutical products. These segments are the focus of this case study.

Imported medical devices accounted for about 60 percent of the Brazilian market in 2011 (figure 4.1). Imported pharmaceuticals accounted for 24 percent of the Brazilian market; about 70 percent of Brazilian pharmaceuticals

**Figure 4.1 Brazilian trade in medical devices, market size and
import share, 2008–11**

exports, imports, market size, and
trade balance (millions of US dollars)   import share (percent)

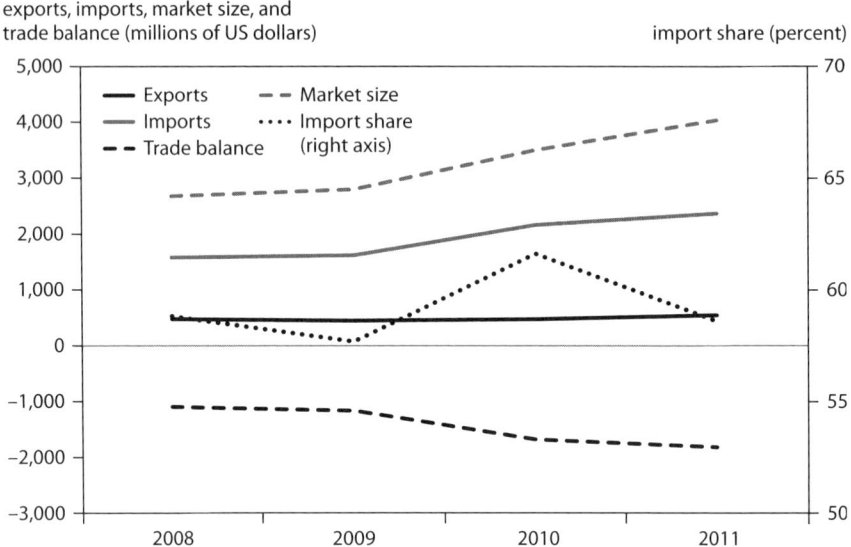

Source: Trade figures are from UN Comtrade database, http://comtrade.un.org/db, and authors' calculations;
market size from Espicom Business Intelligence, *Medistat Worldwide Market Forecasts* to 2016, June 2011.

are manufactured by foreign companies operating in Brazil as a result of local
content requirements (LCRs) and other factors (figure 4.2).[1]

Brazilian imports of healthcare products have generated a growing trade
deficit in this sector, rising from about $700 million in the late 1980s to $7.5
billion in 2011 (Oliveira 2011, UN Comtrade data). About 75 percent of the
trade deficit in healthcare products was generated in pharmaceutical products, a reflection of the much larger market for these products. The sectoral
trade deficit is one (but certainly not the most important) reason behind
Brazil's implicit pursuit of medical sector localization, using various policies
and practices.

Healthcare Industry Trade

LCRs come in different flavors. Perhaps the most direct and explicit is a
requirement that all materials in a contract be supplied locally by domestic
firms. Next are bid preferences for local suppliers (e.g., a 25 percent price preference for Buy America suppliers in the United States). More subtle are licensing requirements that give a preference to local firms or local products. Most

---

1. "A Latin Swing," *World Pharmaceuticals Frontiers*, March 2010, www.worldpharmaceuticals.net/
editorials/017-march10/WPF017_latin-swing.pdf (accessed on June 28, 2012).

Figure 4.2 Brazilian pharmaceuticals trade, 2001–11

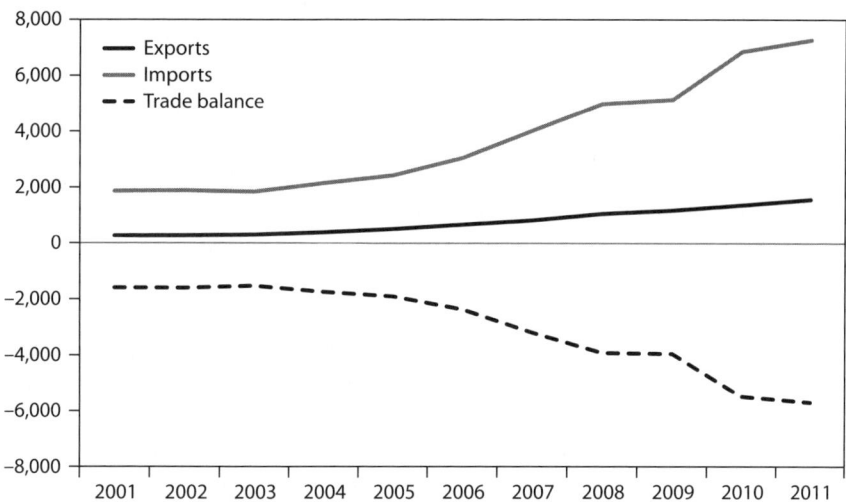

millions of US dollars

Source: UN Comtrade database, http://comtrade.un.org/db, and authors' calculations.

subtle and implicit are ostensibly nondiscriminatory regulations or licensing tests that, in practice, disadvantage foreign firms or products by lengthy delays or more rigorous testing. A few LCRs in the Brazilian healthcare sector are explicit, but most are implicit.

In 2011, Brazil imported $226 billion worth of goods, of which almost $10 billion (about 4.4 percent) were healthcare products. Brazil exported $256 billion worth of goods, of which about $2 billion (about 0.8 percent) were healthcare products.[2] Thus, the Brazilian trade deficit in healthcare totaled $7.5 billion, and the overall Brazilian trade balance showed a surplus of about $30 billion.

The most important reason behind the adoption of LCR policies and practices in this sector is probably the Brazilian government's desire to create a world-class healthcare industry. Box 4.1 sketches the history of policies introduced in the 1980s to create a world-class information technology (IT) sector. Elements of the healthcare sector may be traveling a similar policy path.

Despite the continuing controversy over its computer policy in the 1980s, Brazil still uses LCRs to foster the growth of selected industries. Interventionist industrial policies, including LCRs, gained prominence in 2003, after Brazil abandoned exchange rate management as its preferred policy tool (CEBRI 2012). Unlike previous industrial policies, which stressed the creation of production capacity, the new industrial approach focused on the promotion

---

2. UN Comtrade data and authors' calculations.

Box 4.1   Protecting the computer sector in Brazil

Import protection has often been used to promote particular industries. In the 1980s, Brazil imposed severe import restrictions in an effort to grow its local computer industry. By the end of the 1980s, Brazil had a diversified set of information technology (IT) corporations with a significant presence in the local market. The output of local computer hardware producers grew from less than $200 million in 1979 to more than $4 billion in 1990 (Botelho et al. 1999). This policy spurred high levels of smuggling and gray market activity, because Brazilian IT products were both more expensive and less advanced than hardware produced in Europe, Japan, and the United States.

Fear of being left behind drove a change in Brazilian policy in the early 1990s. Under the new, more liberal approach, the local computer industry progressively lost its "greenhouse" protection and was exposed to international competition. Many Brazilian firms disappeared, sold out to foreign technology partners, or moved into specialized niches. The content of locally manufactured components and technology declined sharply. But the removal of import restrictions slashed prices for computers and stimulated dramatic growth in Brazilian computer usage.

Was the Brazilian computer policy of the 1980s a failure? Some argue that it was, as most local firms could not survive in an unprotected market and Brazil did not become an international player in global IT production. But supporters argue that the policy prompted the Brazilian IT sector to invest significantly in the accumulation of technological capabilities and that important backward linkages were developed. These capabilities, combined with the country's market size, attracted foreign direct investment by firms such as Compaq, Dell, and Gateway to serve the Brazilian and South American markets.

of particular sectors associated with new technology. A study by the Centro Brasileiro de Relações Internacionais (CEBRI 2012, 14) suggests that in most cases, LCRs do not help achieve "diversification of the economy into new sectors as a way of assuring an increase in productivity of the economy." Instead, by shielding the domestic industry from international competition, they discourage innovation and productivity. CEBRI recommends good-quality education, investment in infrastructure, strong protection of property rights, and streamlined bureaucracy as public policies that would better promote competitive local industries.

Healthcare sector trade can be divided into two broad categories: medical devices and pharmaceuticals. The Brazilian pharmaceutical market (drugs for human or veterinary use) was about $30 billion in 2011; the market for medical devices was about $4 billion. Pharmaceuticals account for about 75 percent of the sector trade deficit; medical devices account for about 25 percent (see figures 4.1 and 4.2). Pharmaceuticals represent a much larger market than medical devices, a category that includes everything from simple bandages to complex pacemakers and imaging systems. Table 4.1 lists the pharmaceutical products and medical device products examined in this chapter.

Brazil controls the sale of foreign and domestic healthcare products through a licensing system. The Ministry of Health's regulatory branch, the National Health Surveillance Agency (Agência Nacional de Vigilância Sanitária [ANVISA]), was established in 1999 "to foster protection of the health of the population by exercising sanitary control over production and marketing of products and services subject to sanitary surveillance."[3] This licensing system creates costly and time-consuming hurdles for foreign firms with respect to the registration of medical devices—hurdles that translate into implicit LCRs.

Recently, the Brazilian government announced a new procurement program for government hospitals. Starting in the second half of 2012, the procurement plan will establish preferences of up to 25 percent for Brazilian medical technologies and medications in government contracts—a highly explicit LCR policy. This program has two main components: centralized government procurement through the Unified Health System (SUS), launched in early 2012, and fiscal support that was to be launched during the second half of 2012.

The main purpose of the government procurement policy is to create demand for domestic products, thereby increasing employment. A long-term objective is to foster technology-intensive sectors. But according to CEBRI (2012, 28), use of LCRs to help established sectors to be more competitive "is not only unnecessary, but can make achieving additional gains in competitiveness difficult by protecting domestic producers from international competition." The report also suggests that in the medical care case, "the benefits in terms of employment and income hardly justify the cost in terms of price increases. This unfavorable trade-off tends to be especially serious in the case of health products" (p. 28).

In Brazil, 74 percent of the population depends on public health insurance and public hospitals. However, about half of hospitals are private; they supply 65 percent of the nation's hospital beds. They are better equipped and generally offer superior services. For example, private hospitals carry out 44.3 CT scans and 19.8 MRIs per million patients, pushing Brazil into third place in the world, after Japan and Australia. By contrast, public hospitals carry out only 6.0 CT scans and 2.9 MRIs per million patients, about the same as Mexico and Eastern Europe (JETRO 2012a, 31).

As per capita income rises, more Brazilians will buy private health insurance, expanding demand for private hospital services. The number of private insurance contracts grew from 31.7 million in 2003 to 46.6 million in 2011, an increase of 47 percent, in a period when population grew by 9 percent (JETRO

---

3. See ANVISA's website at http://portal.anvisa.gov.br/wps/portal/anvisa-ingles (accessed on June 26, 2012).

Table 4.1   Pharmaceutical and medical device products by Harmonized System (HS) code

HS code	Pharmaceutical products
H3-2936	Provitamins and vitamins, natural or reproduced by synthesis (including natural concentrates), derivatives thereof used primarily as vitamins, and intermixtures of the foregoing, whether or not in any solvent
H3-2937	Hormones, prostaglandins, thromboxanes and leukotrienes, natural or reproduced by synthesis; derivatives and structural analogues thereof, including chain modified polypeptides, used primarily as hormones
H3-2939	Vegetable alkaloids, natural or reproduced by synthesis, and their salts, ethers, esters, and other derivatives.
H3-2941	Antibiotics
H3-30	Pharmaceutical products
	Medical devices
	Consumables
H3-300510	Adhesive dressings and other articles having an adhesive layer
H3-300590	Wadding, gauze, bandages and similar articles (e.g., dressings, adhesive plasters, poultices), impregnated/coated with pharmaceutical substances/put up in forms/packings for retail sale for medical, surgical, dental or veterinary purposes (excluding 3005.10)
H3-300610	Sterile surgical catgut, similar sterile suture materials (including sterile absorbable surgical/dental yarns) and sterile tissue adhesives for surgical wound closure; sterile laminaria and sterile laminaria tents; sterile absorbable surgical/dental/veterinary purposes
H3-300620	Blood-grouping reagents
H3-300650	First-aid boxes and kits
H3-300691	Appliances identifiable for ostomy use
H3-401511	Surgical gloves of vulcanized rubber
H3-901831	Syringes, with or without needles
H3-901832	Tubular metal needles and needles for sutures
H3-901839	Catheters, cannulae, and the like
H3-300510	Adhesive dressings and other articles having an adhesive layer
H3-300590	Wadding, gauze, bandages, and similar articles (e.g., dressings, adhesive plasters, poultices), impregnated/coated with pharmaceutical substances/put up in forms/packings for retail sale for medical, surgical, dental/veterinary purposes(excluding 3005.10)
	Dental devices
H3-300640	Dental cements and other dental fillings; bone reconstruction cements
H3-901841	Dental drill engines, whether or not combined on a single base with other dental equipment
H3-901849	Instruments and appliances used in dental sciences (excluding drills)

(continued on next page)

Table 4.1   Pharmaceutical and medical device products by Harmonized System (HS) code *(continued)*

H3-902121	Artificial teeth
H3-902129	Dental fittings (excluding artificial teeth)
H3-902213	Apparatus based on the use of X-rays (excluding 9022.12) for dental uses
H3-940210	Dentists' chairs; barbers' similar chairs with rotating as well as reclining and elevating movements, and parts thereof

Diagnostic imaging

H3-300630	Opacifying preparations for X-ray examinations; diagnostic reagents designed to be administered to the patient
H3-370110	Photographic plates and film in the flat, sensitized, unexposed, of any material other than paper/paperboard/textiles, for X-ray
H3-370210	Photographic film in rolls, sensitized, unexposed, of any material other than paper/paperboard/textiles, for X-ray
H3-901811	Electro-cardiographs
H3-901812	Ultrasonic scanning apparatus
H3-901813	Magnetic resonance imaging apparatus
H3-901814	Scintigraphic apparatus
H3-902214	Apparatus based on the use of X-rays (excluding 9022.12), for medical/surgical/veterinary uses
H3-902221	Apparatus based on the use of alpha/beta/gamma radiations, for medical, surgical, dental, veterinary uses, including radiography/radiotherapy apparatus
H3-902230	X-ray tubes
H3-902290	X-ray generators (excluding tubes), high tension generators, control panels and desks, screens, examination/treatment tables, chairs, etc.

Orthopedic and prosthetic devices

H3-902110	Orthopaedic and fracture appliances
H3-902131	Artificial joints
H3-902139	Artificial parts of the body other than teeth, dental fittings, and joints

Patient aid

H3-901820	Ultraviolet, infrared ray apparatus used in medical, surgical, dental, or veterinary sciences
H3-901910	Mechano-therapy appliances; massage apparatus; psychological aptitude-testing apparatus
H3-901920	Ozone therapy, oxygen therapy, aerosol therapy, artificial respiration, other therapeutic respiration apparatus
H3-902140	Hearing aids (excluding parts and accessories)
H3-902150	Pacemakers for stimulating heart muscles (excluding parts and accessories)
H3-902190	Appliances which are worn, carried, or implanted in the body, to compensate for a defect or disability (excluding 9021.10-9021.50)

(continued on next page)

Table 4.1   Pharmaceutical and medical device products by Harmonized System (HS) code *(continued)*

	Other
H3-841920	Medical/surgical/laboratory sterilizers, whether or not electrically heated
H3-871310	Carriages for disabled persons, not mechanically propelled
H3-871390	Carriages for disabled persons, motorized/otherwise mechanically propelled
H3-901850	Ophthalmic instruments and appliances, n.e.s. in 90.18
H3-901890	Instruments and appliances used in medical, surgical, or veterinary sciences, incl. other electro-medical apparatus and sight-testing instruments, n.e.s. in 90.18
H3-940290	Medical, surgical, veterinary furniture (e.g., operating tables, examination tables, hospital beds with mechanical fittings; parts of the foregoing articles)

n.e.s. = not elsewhere specified

Sources: Pharmaceuticals data are from US International Trade Commission, *Pharmaceutical Products and Chemical Intermediates, Fourth Review,* 2010, www.usitc.gov/publications/332/pub4181. pdf; medical device data from Espicom Business Intelligence, *Medistat Worldwide Medical Market Forecast to 2016,* June 2011; UN Comtrade database, http://comtrade.un.org/db/mr/rfCommoditiesList.aspx?.

2012a).[4] According to the Instituto Brasileiro de Geografia e Estatistica, the Brazilian population will grow from its current level of 180 million to 220 million by 2040, an average annual increase of 0.5 percent. Meanwhile, average life expectancy, now about 73 years, is slowly rising (JETRO 2012a, 29). Combined, these factors ensure growing demand in an already large market for healthcare.

Medical Devices

In 2011 imports accounted for about 60 percent of the $4 billion Brazilian market for medical devices (see figure 4.1). Brazil depends heavily on imported products for certain medical devices, including patient aids (89 percent), appliances such as wheelchairs and medical furniture (81 percent), and diagnostic imaging (63 percent). The import share for orthopedic and prosthetic devices (48 percent), consumables (41 percent), and dental devices (30 percent) is much lower (figures 4.3 and 4.4).[5] In 2010 the United States was Brazil's dominant supplier, accounting for 32 percent of total medical device imports, followed by Germany (15 percent) and China (7 percent) (table 4.2).

---

4. Population data are from Históricas and Estatisticas, Instituto Brasileiro de Geografia e Estatística, http://seriesestatisticas.ibge.gov.br/series.aspx?vcodigo=POP300&sv=35&t=revisao-2008-projecao-da-populacao-do-brasil (accessed on June 29, 2012).

5. Authors' calculations based on data from UN Comtrade database.

Figure 4.3   Brazilian market for medical devices, 2008–11

millions of US dollars

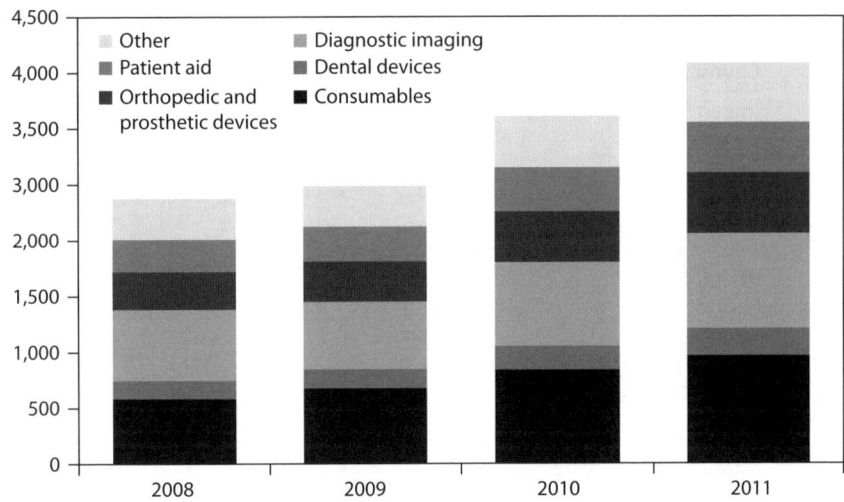

Source: Espicom Business Intelligence, *Medistat Worldwide Medical Market Forecasts to 2016*, June 2011.

Figure 4.4   Brazil's import share of medical devices, 2011

percent

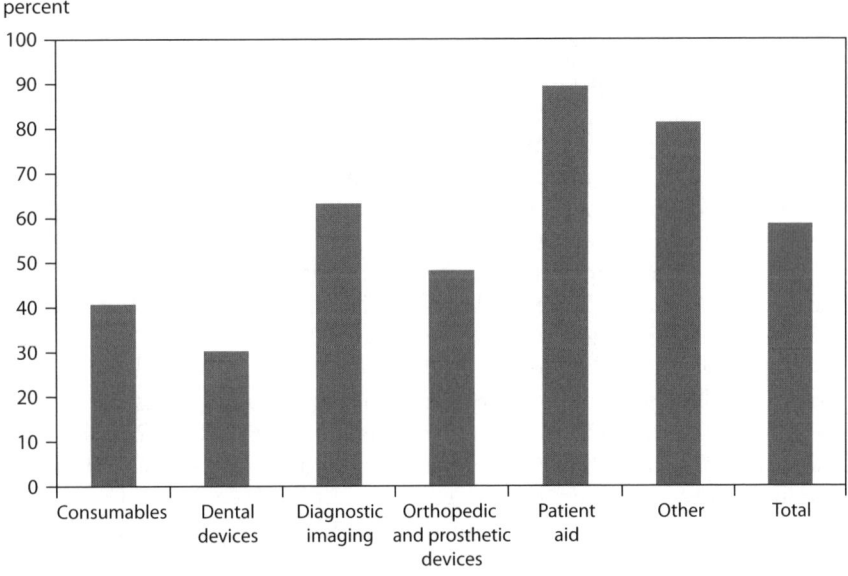

Source: Espicom Business Intelligence, *Medistat Worldwide Medical Market Forecasts to 2016*; UN Comtrade database, http://comtrade.un.org/db; authors' calculations.

Table 4.2   Import value of medical devices, by major countries, 2010

Country	Imports (millions of US dollars)	Percent share of total imports
United States	1,179	32
Germany	550	15
China	241	7
Japan	224	6
Malaysia	152	4
Switzerland	129	4
Ireland	123	3
Poland	109	3
Sweden	106	3
United Kingdom	97	3
Other countries	752	21
Total	3,667	100

Source: JETRO (2012a).

Regardless of where healthcare products are manufactured—locally or abroad—in order to sell pharmaceuticals, medical devices, health and fitness equipment, and cosmetics in Brazil, a manufacturer must obtain a license and receive product registration approval from ANVISA. This process is not unique to Brazil; it was adapted from other industrial countries, especially in Europe.

Brazil has two registration processes: *cadastro* for low-risk products and *registro* for high-risk products. The applicable process depends on whether a Good Manufacturing and Control Practices (GMP) certificate is required, the norm for high-risk products. All healthcare products are regarded as high risk, so the GMP is required across the board. When healthcare products are manufactured abroad, ANVISA staff must travel to the factory to carry out the GMP inspection. Because ANVISA does not have enough budget or staff to carry out certification abroad in a timely manner, the waiting time for GMP certification for a healthcare product manufactured overseas is 18 months or longer—an implicit LCR.

To accelerate the approval process, some foreign firms have started to localize their operations, by either acquiring Brazilian firms or erecting greenfield factories. The Brazilian government often offers foreign firms inducements, such as low interest rate loans and tax concessions. However, manufacturing firms must have an environmental license to build a new factory and meet other local regulations. The conditions for acquiring a license and following other regulations vary across municipal governments. It usually takes about two months to get licensing and regulatory approval, but in metropolitan areas, it may take about a year. If a plant uses any type of nuclear material, the firm must get approval from the Comissãno Nacional de Energia Nuclear (CNEN), except when nuclear emissions are below the threshold level specified by CNEN Resolution No. 112/2011. These regulations confer an advantage on established firms.

Registration requirements do not overtly discriminate between foreign and domestic firms, but registration procedures grossly disadvantage exports to Brazil and thus promote domestic production to avoid lengthy delays in foreign inspections and approvals. The Brazilian government then reinforces the incentive to produce locally by offering tax and financial concessions.

Pharmaceutical Products

Although 75 percent of the trade deficit in the healthcare sector in Brazil is from pharmaceutical products, Brazil imports a relatively small share (about 25 percent) of its pharmaceutical products from abroad (see figure 4.2). Instead, foreign direct investment has been much more active in the pharmaceutical sector. Table 4.3 lists the major foreign companies that have operations in Brazil.

Pharmaceutical firms face the same time-consuming registration process as medical device firms. In addition, they face serious patent protection issues. Brazil signed the World Trade Organization (WTO) Agreement on Trade-Related Aspects of Intellectual Property Rights (TRIPS) in 1996; however, Brazilian patent regulations require that a patented drug be manufactured in Brazil within three years of its introduction on the local market (JETRO 2010). If domestic production does not start within this time frame, the Brazilian government can license a domestic firm to produce a generic version of the patented drug. This provision severely limits exports by multinational pharmaceutical firms to Brazil. Instead, these firms often launch manufacturing operations in Brazil for new products—another implicit LCR.

The Brazilian government puts strong pressure on pharmaceutical firms to lower their prices, using informal contacts, cheaper generic medicines, and public subsidies as tools of persuasion. For example, the national AIDS program, established in 1996, provides free medication to more than 180,000 people with HIV. The cost of drugs for severe illness often features in public campaigns that seek lower prices from foreign-based multinational corporations that sell in the Brazilian market. These practices are not LCRs, but they illustrate the Brazilian government's strong preference for cheap generic drugs, especially for serious illnesses.

Issuing a compulsory license is one way the government sometimes obtains cheaper generic drugs. In May 2007, for example, it issued a compulsory license to produce a generic version of Efavirenz for the national HIV/AIDS program. By switching from Efavirenz to its generic version, the government expects to save more than $400 per patient per year.

Table 4.3 Major foreign pharmaceutical firms operating in Brazil

Company	Number of years in Brazil	Number of employees	Number of offices	Number of factories	Core business
Abbott Laboratórios do Brazil	70	1,000	2	1	Drugs and medicine, supplements, diabetes
Becton Dickinson Indústrias Cirúrgicas	56		2		Diabetes, medical, surgery systems, ophthalmology systems, pharmaceuticals
Eli Lilly of Brazil	80	600	3	1	Mental illness, oncology, diabetes, women's health
Johnson & Johnson S.A. Indústria e Comércio	77	4,500		2	
Merck Sharp & Dohme Brazil	60	700	1+	1	Pain killers, eye disease, HIV, vaccines
Pfizer of Brazil	60	1,800	9	1	Human and veterinary drugs, cardiac disease, central nervous system, pain killers, anti-inflammatory, oncology, endocrine secretion, erectile dysfuntion; for pets and animals, anti-inflammatory, antiphrastic drugs, auxiliary reproductive medicine, vaccines

Note: Data are for US firms.

Source: JETRO (2010).

Farmanguinhos/Fiocruz, which is managed by the Brazilian Ministry of Health, manufactures 2 billion units of generic Efavirenz annually and expects to reap annual savings of $900 million. In effect, these policies switched purchases from the patented product made by a foreign firm, Merck Sharp & Dohme, to a generic product manufactured locally.

A related Brazilian bargaining tool is to deny patent applications. In 2008, California-based Gilead Sciences was denied its patent application for Tenofovir on the grounds that the drug lacked uniqueness. Denying the patent application allows Brazil to import a generic of Tenofovir. The government currently imports a generic version of Tenofovir from India that costs about one-ninth what Gilead charges (about $158 per patient per year instead of $1,387). Because the generic is not manufactured in Brazil, the patent denial cannot be counted as an LCR, but the situation illustrates the broad thrust of government policy toward cheap generic pharmaceuticals.

As the examples illustrate, Brazilian policies erect substantial obstacles for foreign producers of healthcare products. However, the healthcare sector is growing rapidly—Brazil's population exceeds 180 million and per capita incomes are rising—meaning that multinational pharmaceutical firms find it difficult to ignore Brazil. Moreover, Brazil is an attractive country for clinical trials, because it has a diverse population with varied cultures, dietary habits, and genetic backgrounds. Recent deregulation has made Brazil an even more attractive location for clinical testing (JETRO 2010).

Global Harmonization Movement

Most countries regulate healthcare products for safety reasons. Some countries regulate excessively, imposing high costs as a result. The cost of regulation is not always reflected in the cost of a product. Instead, some firms may choose to avoid a country that imposes complex, time-consuming, or opaque regulation. In this case, the country will experience a long "drug lag" or "device lag."

Japan has been criticized for taking too long to approve the sale of new drugs and medical devices. A stent for large bowel obstruction that was introduced in 1990 in the United States was not approved in Japan until 2012—a device lag of more than 20 years. The Japanese government acknowledges the problem, and the Japanese Ministry of Health and Welfare has tried to shorten the lag by facilitating cooperation in joint clinical trials in the United States, Japan, and Europe.[6]

Efforts to speed up approval processes are global. In 1992, the European Union, the United States, Canada, Australia, and Japan conceived the Global Harmonization Task Force (GHTF). Its purpose is to encourage convergence in regulatory practices related to ensuring the safety, effectiveness, perfor-

---

6. In one successful case, in January 2012, the Japanese government approved the use of health insurance to pay for a stent that dilates a clogged artery of the thigh; US authorities are still reviewing the data.

mance, and quality of medical devices, promoting technological innovation and facilitating international trade.[7] Developing countries such as Brazil, Chile, China, India, Indonesia, Malaysia, Mexico, South Africa, Thailand, and Vietnam participate in the GHTF through their regional organizations, the Asian Harmonization Working Party (AHWP) and the Latin America Harmonization Working Party (LAHWP). A new group, the International Medical Device Regulators Forum (IMDRF), will focus on implementing the GHTF regulatory model.

Harmonizing the regulation of healthcare products is one way to reduce the industry's burden and ensure maximum accessibility of safe, effective healthcare products by patients. International regulatory harmonization would eliminate or reduce redundant regulatory procedures, device lag, and drug lag, and could point the way to some liberalization of Brazil's implicit LCR policies.

Cost of LCRs and Related Barriers

Countries with implicit or explicit LCRs in healthcare products likely experience longer device lags and drug lags. These lags are one cost of LCRs and related trade barriers. Other possible costs include higher prices and lower quality.

Device Lag

One way to assess device lags is to examine medical device density, a measure of the availability of medical devices. If regulations are too tight, the prices of medical devices may be high, reflecting LCRs and related trade barriers. As a result, people are underserved, and medical device density is low.

Statistics on device density often relate to diagnostic imaging, such as MRI and CT. However, the universe of medical devices is much broader, ranging from wound care products to sophisticated imaging equipment. We used per capita spending on medical devices to calculate the medical device density of 20 major countries in 2011 (figure 4.5).

Per capita medical device spending in Brazil is low. It would be useful to determine whether the device lag reflects tough regulation, LCRs, or both. Device lag can result from many factors, including the size of the economy, the level of income, the culture, other features of the healthcare and insurance systems, and various regulations. We did not build a mathematical model that would single out the impact of regulation and LCRs. We can nevertheless say that, given its income level, Brazil seems to spend less than other countries on medical devices. It is probably experiencing at least a modest device lag, possibly caused by regulation coupled with LCRs.

What about trade activity? One reason for the Brazilian regulation system, in which ANVISA must approve the sale of medical device products, is to

---

7. See the website of the Global Harmonization Task Force at www.ghtf.org/about (accessed on June 29, 2012).

Figure 4.5 Medical device density in selected countries, 2011

US dollars

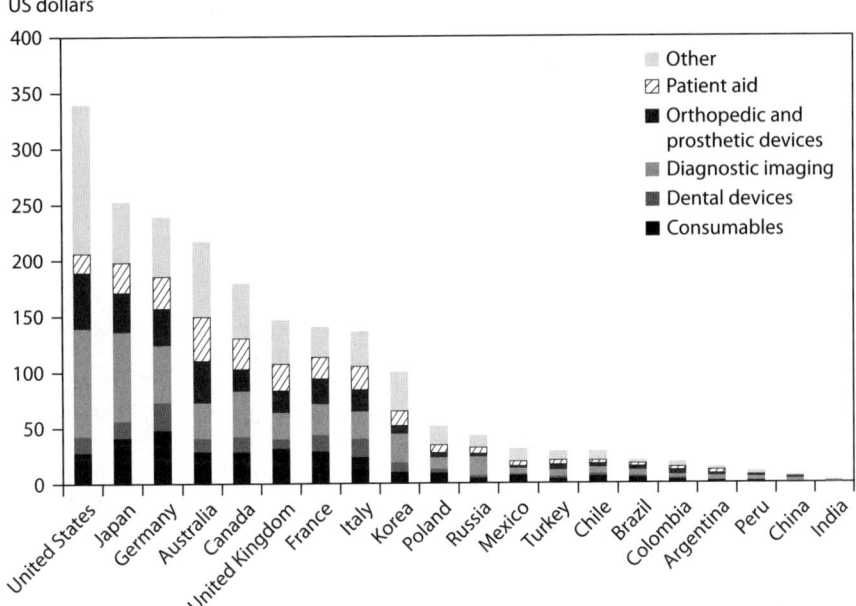

Note: Medical device density is approximated by per capita market size and expressed in US dollars.

Sources: Espicom Business Intelligence, *Medistat Worldwide Medical Market Forecasts to 2016,* June 2011; IMF, *World Economic Outlook* database, www.imf.org/external/pubs/ft/weo/2013/01/weodata/index.aspx (accessed on September 20, 2012).

promote the medical device industry in Brazil. If the system really nurtured an infant industry, Brazil should be a net exporter of medical devices. Table 4.4 shows medical device market sizes and trade balances for 21 countries in 2011. Figures 4.6 and 4.7 show exports and imports of medical device products by major countries in 2011. Brazilian trade activity seems low and its trade deficit rather large (figure 4.8). Japan, another country with tight regulation and long device lags, also has a trade deficit in medical devices. This deficit may reflect the fact that firms choose production sites where they do not have to spend extra money and time to get approvals. Japan recently announced its decision to speed up the approval process for medical device and pharmaceutical products in order to help grow the healthcare industry.

The impact of liberalizing trade barriers (including LCRs) might differ sharply across medical device categories, because products are regulated based on their risk features. In general, high-tech medical devices are more tightly regulated than low-tech medical devices. Hence, if Brazil removed LCRs and accelerated the approval process, high-tech medical devices would benefit more than low-tech devices. As a result, two-way trade in high-tech medical devices would likely grow faster than trade in low-tech products.

Table 4.4　Medical device market size and trade balance, selected countries, 2011 (millions of US dollars)

Country	Market size	Exports	Imports	Trade balance
United States	105,761	36,040	31,893	4,147
Japan	32,257	5,330	11,031	−5,701
Germany	19,547	25,364	16,329	9,035
United Kingdom	9,164	5,579	6,896	−1,316
China	8,940	9,483	7,602	1,881
France	8,839	9,242	10,937	−1,695
Italy	8,222	3,721	6,041	−2,321
Canada	6,153	1,539	4,761	−3,222
Russia	6,006	93	4,169	−4,076
Australia	4,926	1,472	4,151	−2,678
Korea	4,879	1,603	2,598	−995
Switzerland	4,663	10,547	3,889	6,658
Brazil	4,034	547	2,364	−1,817
Mexico	3,489	5,938	2,844	3,094
India	2,643	774	1,963	−1,189
Turkey	2,116	246	1,906	−1,660
Poland	1,944	888	1,666	−778
Colombia	864	76	753	−677
Argentina	579	111	603	−492
Chile	495	18	550	−532
Peru	318	8	242	−233

Notes: Medical device density is approximated by the market size of medical device products divided by the country's population. See table 4.1 for the list of products in each category.

Sources: Espicom Business Intelligence, *Medistat Worldwide Medical Market Forecasts to 2016,* June 2011; IMF, *World Economic Outlook* database, www.imf.org/external/pubs/ft/weo/2013/01/weo data/index.aspx (accessed on September 20, 2012); trade figures are from UN Comtrade database, http://comtrade.un.org/db; authors' calculations.

Drug Lag

We used per capita spending on pharmaceutical products as a proxy for drug lag. Per capita spending on pharmaceutical products is likely correlated with the variety of drugs available in the market; thus, higher spending means greater variety. Greater variety also means that people are more adequately served; less variety reflects a drug lag.

Table 4.5 presents market size, exports, imports, trade balances, and import shares for 12 sample countries. Brazil ranks sixth in the size of its pharmaceutical market. However, per capita spending on pharmaceutical products was just $153 in 2011, a little lower than Korea and a little higher than Russia (figure 4.9). It would be necessary to construct a full mathematical model to determine whether Brazil has a drug lag as a result of tight regulation or LCRs, an exercise that was beyond our resources. However, removing LCRs and other

Figure 4.6　Export of medical devices, selected countries, 2011

millions of US dollars

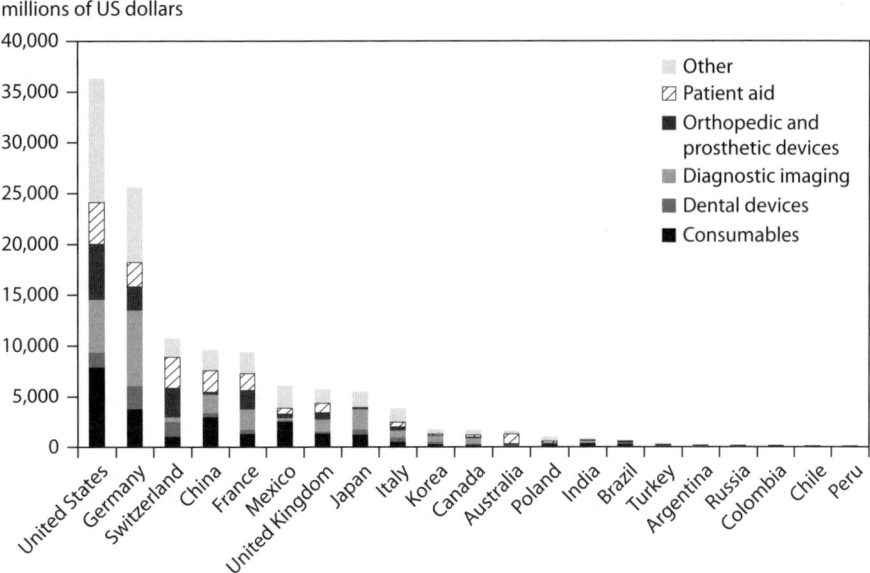

Sources: Trade figures are from UN Comtrade database, http://comtrade.un.org/db; authors' calculations.

Figure 4.7　Import of medical devices, selected countries, 2011

millions of US dollars

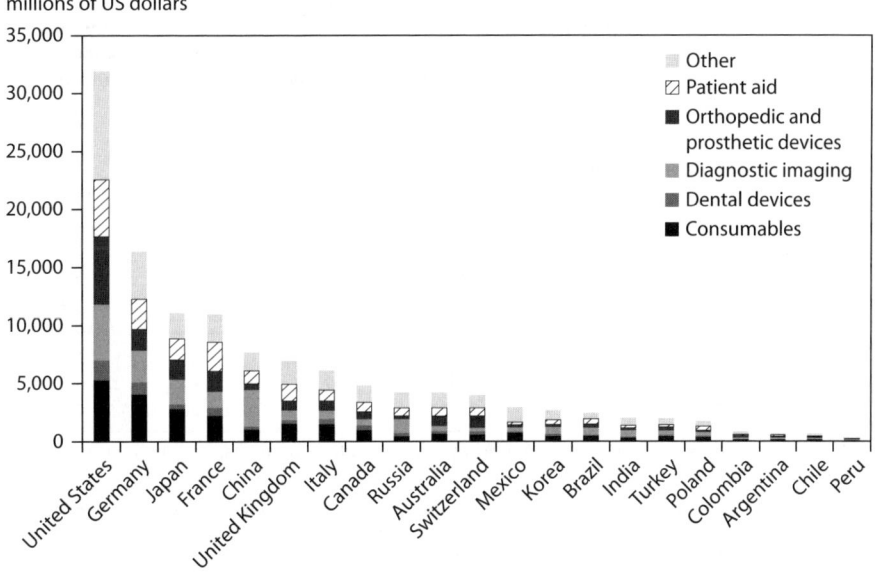

Sources: Trade figures are from UN Comtrade database, http://comtrade.un.org/db; authors' calculations.

Figure 4.8 Medical device exports, imports, and trade balance, selected countries, 2011

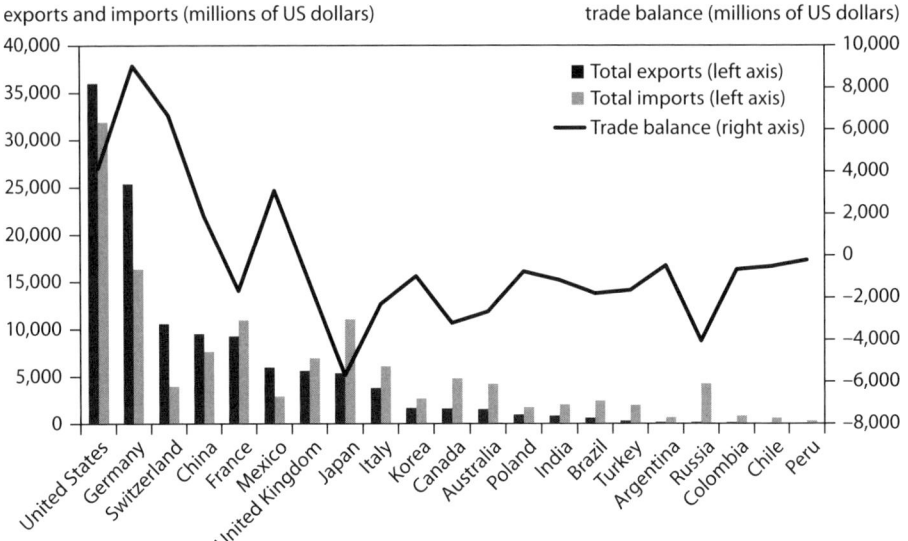

Sources: Trade figures are from UN Comtrade database, http://comtrade.un.org/db; authors' calculations.

Table 4.5 Pharmaceutical market, selected countries, 2011

Country	Market size (billions of US dollars)	Pharmaceutical trade (billions of US dollars)			Percent share of imports
		Exports	**Imports**	**Trade balance**	
United States	322	43.1	69.9	−26.8	22
Japan	111	4.5	21.6	−17.1	19
China	67	11.5	11.2	0.3	17
Germany	45	70.2	53.3	17.0	118
France	41	33.8	29.8	4.0	72
Brazil	30	1.6	7.3	−5.7	24
Italy	29	20.4	25.1	−4.7	88
Canada	22	5.6	13.1	−7.5	59
United Kingdom	22	35.9	26.4	9.5	123
Russia	16	0.3	13.5	−13.1	86
India	14	9.5	2.7	6.8	19
Korea	12	1.3	4.3	−3.0	35

Note: Due to differences in the definition of pharmaceutical products, import figures exceed domestic sales for some countries.

Sources: Market size data are from IMS Institute for Healthcare Informatics, *The Global Use of Medicines: Outlook through 2016,* July 2012, www.imshealth.com/ims/Global/Content/Insights/IMS%20 Institute%20for%20Healthcare%20Informatics/Global%20 Use%20of%20Meds%202011/Medicines_Outlook_Through_2016_Report.pdf (accessed on September 16, 2012); trade data are from UN Comtrade database (HS codes 2936, 2937, 2939, 2941, chapter 30), http://comtrade.un.org/db.

Figure 4.9 Per capita spending on pharmaceutical products, selected countries, 2011

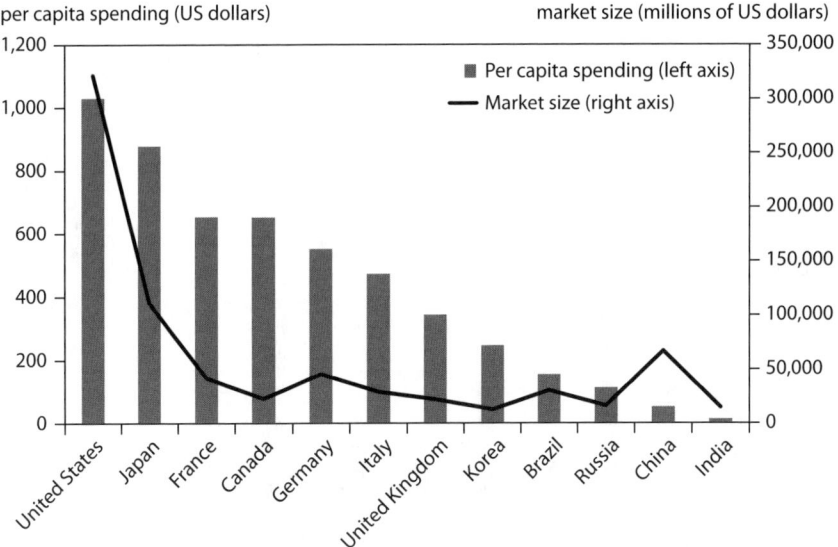

Sources: Market size data are from IMS Institute for Healthcare Informatics, *The Global Use of Medicines: Outlook through 2016,* July 2012, www.imshealth.com/ims/Global/Content/Insights/IMS%20Institute%20for%20Health care%20Informatics/Global%20Use%20of%20Meds%202011/Medicines_Outlook_Through_2016_Report.pdf (accessed on September 16, 2012).

trade barriers would likely boost both the export and import of pharmaceutical products (figure 4.10). Countries with tight regulations and long drug lags, such as Japan, seem to have larger trade deficits. Likewise, Brazil's pharmaceutical trade seems low and its trade deficit large.

Alternatives to LCRs

Brazil is the largest market for healthcare goods and services in Latin America, and its market will expand as income and population grow. Some LCRs in the sector are explicit—new procurement programs for public hospitals give a preference up to 25 percent for Brazilian medical technologies and medications, for example. Most LCRs are implicit, however—often in the form of sales controls on foreign and domestic healthcare products. These control and licensing systems—which are not unique to Brazil—create costly and time-consuming hurdles for foreign firms that translate into implicit LCRs.

Because Brazil is not a member of the WTO Government Procurement Agreement, price preferences do not breach WTO rules. Moreover, the implicit LCRs are sufficiently embedded in safety practices to escape WTO scrutiny.

Figure 4.10 Exports and imports of pharmaceutical products, selected countries, 2011

millions of US dollars

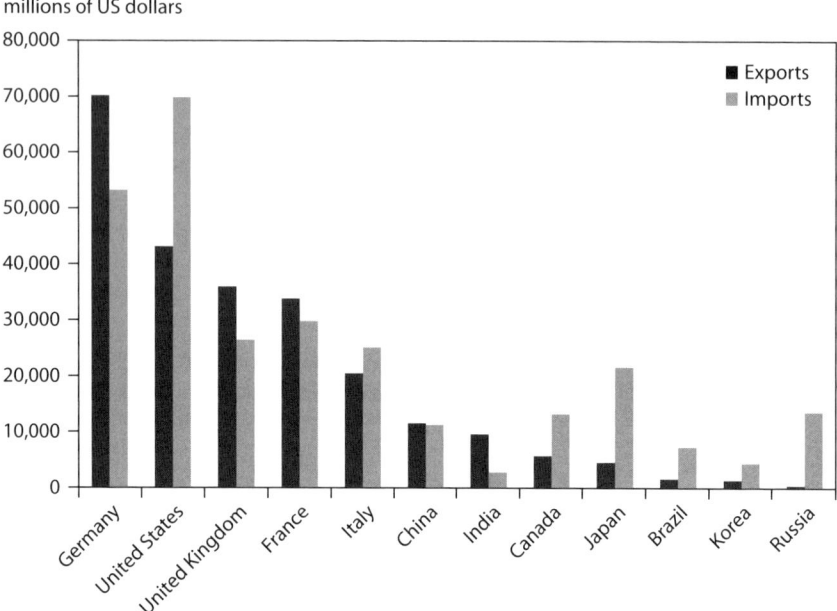

Sources: Market size data are from IMS Institute for Healthcare Informatics, *The Global Use of Medicines: Outlook through 2016*, July 2012, www.imshealth.com/ims/Global/Content/Insights/IMS%20Institute%20for%20Health care%20Informatics/Global%20Use%20of%20Meds%202011/Medicines_Outlook_Through_2016_Report.pdf (accessed on September 16, 2012).

That said, given the multiple goals of Brazilian healthcare policy, greater reliance should be placed on explicit price signals. The preference of up to 25 percent paid by public hospitals for Brazilian medical technologies and medications is a better policy than implicit LCRs. Similarly, foreign medical equipment and pharmaceutical firms should be permitted to speed up the vetting of their products by paying an explicit cost-of-service fee to the Brazilian authorities. To ensure access to affordable pharmaceuticals, Brazil can continue to license and import generics, provided international patent agreements are respected. To create a world-class healthcare sector, it should give serious thought to creating a friendlier environment for business. Creating well-situated industrial parks for healthcare firms and offering targeted tax relief could help it do so.

Major countries—the United States, Japan, European powers, and their Asian and Latin American counterparts—have joined to create healthcare forums. Forums such as the GHTF and the IMDRF aim to harmonize regulatory processes in order to eliminate redundant regulatory procedures, thereby reducing device and drug lags. Brazil participates in both forums through a regional organization (LAHWP). Assigning a higher profile to Brazilian participation could point the way to further liberalization of Brazil's implicit LCR policies.

Cross-country analysis indicates that Brazil's healthcare market is underserved and that device and drug lags are relatively long. Removing explicit and implicit LCRs would not only help Brazil's healthcare market grow but also increase the export and import of medical devices and pharmaceuticals. Brazil could even turn its deficit in medical device trade into a surplus by moving toward liberalization.

5

Wind Turbines in Canada

Along with the United States' Buy America policy, wind turbine policy in two Canadian provinces—Ontario and Quebec—exemplifies the explicit edge of local content requirement (LCR) measures. In the Canadian case, quantitative LCR percentages are the tool of choice. Promoting Canadian manufacturing firms, with the pitch to job creation and shades of infant industry argumentation, are the motivating themes.

According to the *World Wind Energy Report* (WWEA 2012), worldwide wind energy capacity has doubled every three years since the late 1990s (20 percent annual growth), reaching 237,000 megawatts (MW) in 2011. Ninety-six countries and regions now use wind power for electricity generation. At the end of 2011, wind turbines installed worldwide provided about 3 percent of global electricity consumption.

For many years, the wind energy industry has been driven by five markets: China, the United States, Germany, Spain, and India. Canada joined the top 10 major wind energy industry countries in 2010 (figure 5.1). On both Canadian coasts, across the Prairies, and in the Great Lakes region, new onshore and offshore wind development projects are underway.

Sources of Energy in Canada

Although Canada is a newcomer in wind energy, about 65 percent of Canadian energy comes from renewable sources, mostly hydro; 15 percent comes from nuclear plants, another 15 percent from coal, and 5 percent from natural gas facilities (figure 5.2). Rich natural resources enable Canadians to enjoy reliable

Figure 5.1 Top 10 countries by total wind energy capacity, 2011

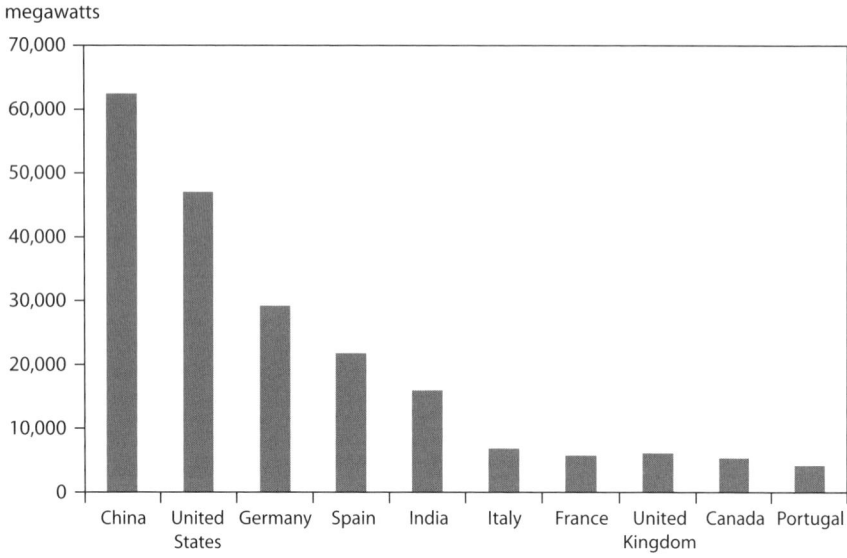

Source: WWEA (2012).

electricity at one of the world's lowest rates. Electricity prices in Canada were the fourth lowest among the countries of the Organization for Economic Co-operation and Development (OECD) (figure 5.3); the United States, Mexico, and Korea are the only countries where electricity prices are lower. However, Canadian users are facing steady price increases (figure 5.4) and will soon need new power sources to meet growing demand and to compensate for the shutdown of coal-fired plants.

A 2005 study by the International Energy Agency projected that Canada would need about $185 billion of new investment in electricity generation, transmission, and distribution infrastructure by 2030 (CANWEA 2008). Provincial power authorities have already announced $115 billion in new capital spending to produce and distribute power over the next two decades. The difficulty lies in striking the balance between higher demands for electricity and environmental concerns.

Efforts to Reduce Greenhouse Gas Emissions

Canada has worked to reduce greenhouse gas emissions since the 1980s. In 2010, as a signatory to the Copenhagen Accord, it adopted a new target: a 17 percent reduction from 2005 levels by 2020. To achieve this target, the Canadian government initiated a sector-by-sector approach. Stationary energy emissions from fuel combustion for electric power accounted for about 46

Figure 5.2 Canadian electric power generation, 2011 (percent)

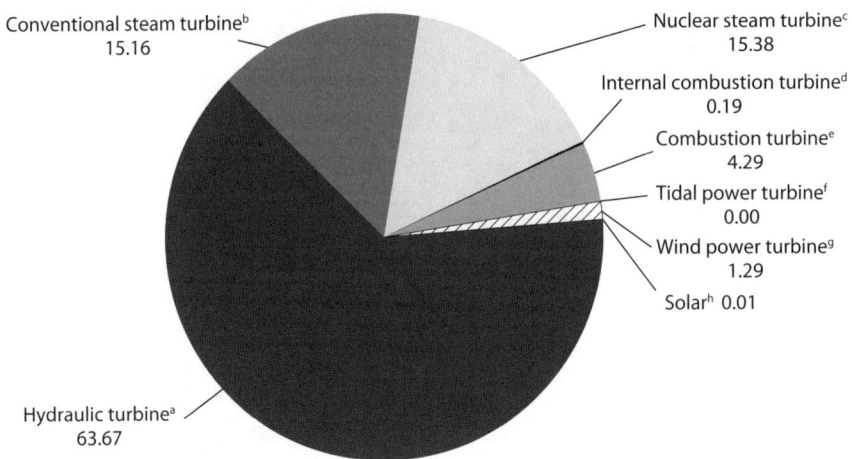

Conventional steam turbine[b]
15.16

Nuclear steam turbine[c]
15.38

Internal combustion turbine[d]
0.19

Combustion turbine[e]
4.29

Tidal power turbine[f]
0.00

Wind power turbine[g]
1.29

Solar[h] 0.01

Hydraulic turbine[a]
63.67

a. Electric power generated from a plant in which the turbine generators are driven by flowing water.
b. A power plant in which the prime mover is a steam turbine. The steam used to drive the turbine is produced in a boiler where fossil fuels or other combustible materials are burned.
c. Electricity generated at an electric power plant whose turbines are driven by steam generated in a reactor by heat from the fission of nuclear fuel.
d. A power plant in which the prime mover is an internal combustion turbine. Electric power is generated by the rapid burning of a fuel-air mixture into mechanical energy.
e. A power plant in which the prime mover is a combustion turbine. Electric power is generated by the burning of a fuel into mechanical energy.
f. Electric power generated from a plant in which the turbine generators are driven by rushing water. The share of tidal power turbine is negligible.
g. A power plant in which the prime mover is a wind turbine. Electric power is generated by the conversion of wind power into mechanical energy.
h. Electricity created by using photovoltaic (PV) technology by converting solar energy into solar electricity from sunlight.

Sources: Statistics Canada, www.statcan.gc.ca/start-debut-eng.html (accessed on October 23, 2012); authors' calculations.

percent of total Canadian greenhouse gas emissions in 2009. As the centerpiece of the sector-by-sector approach, the government imposed a set of emissions performance standards on the electric power sector. According to the National Round Table on the Environment and the Economy (NRTEE 2012), greenhouse gas emissions from the electric power sector are expected to decrease 25 percent from their 2005 level by 2020. Provinces across the country have committed to reduce their own greenhouse gas emissions by measures such as public education campaigns and energy efficiency and renewable electricity programs—all in accordance with the national climate policy plan.

Wind energy has become a major renewable energy sources after hydro. The Canadian Wind Energy Association (CANWEA 2008) envisions satisfying 20 percent of Canada's electricity demand through wind energy by 2025. Doing so would entail installing about 22,000 wind turbines spread over 450 locations across Canada.

Figure 5.3 Household electricity prices, 2011

US dollars per megawatt hour

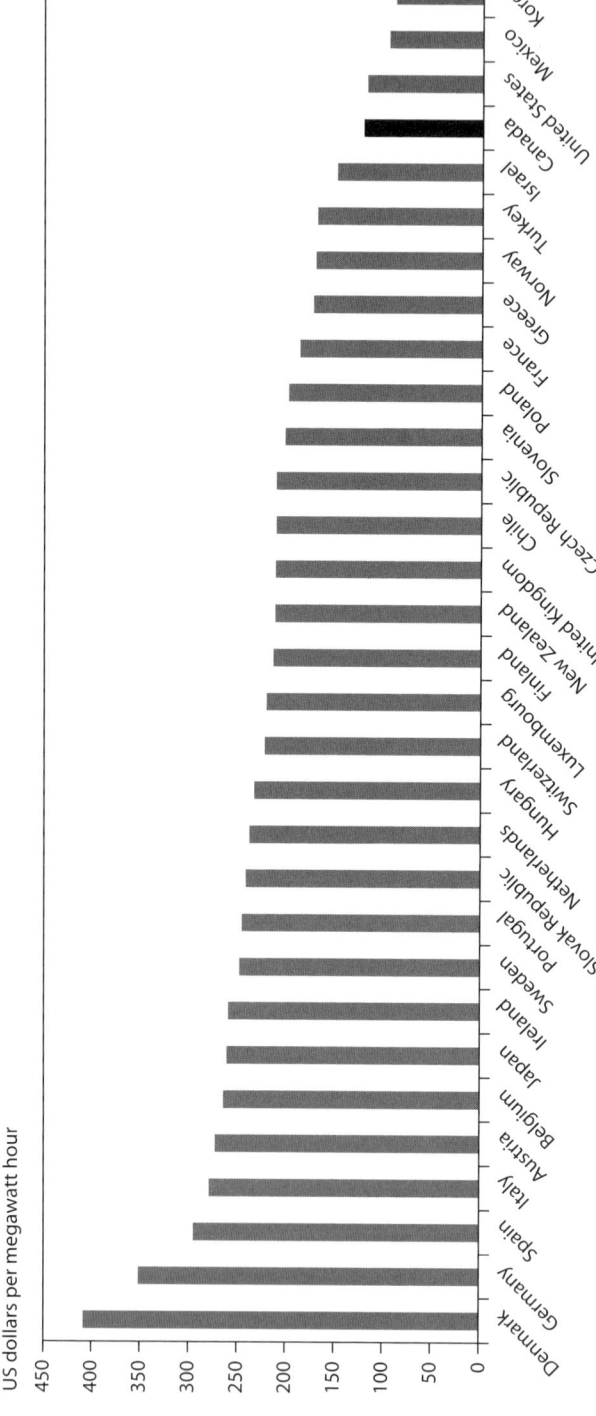

Source: International Energy Agency, *Energy Prices and Taxes, 3rd Quarter 2012,* www.iea.org/stats (accessed on October 23, 2012).

Figure 5.4   Average residential electricity prices in Canada, 1998–2011

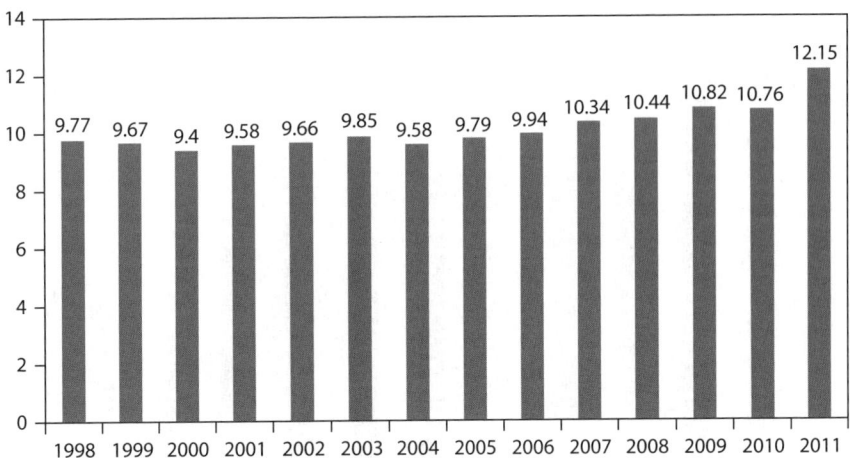

cents/kilowatt hour

Notes: Figures are in Canadian dollars and based on 1,000 kWh monthly consumption. Average electricity price is an average of 11 major Canadian cities for years 1998–2008 and an average of 12 major Canadian cities for years 2009–2011.

Source: Hydro Quebec, *Comparison of Electricity Prices in Major North American Cities, 1998–2011*, www.hydro quebec.com/en/index.html (accessed on December 12, 2012).

Wind Energy Regulations

Canada is a federal state comprising 10 provinces and 3 territories. Jurisdiction over electricity generation, transmission, and distribution rests primarily at the provincial and territorial levels of government. As a result, there are significant differences across Canadian electricity markets.

At the federal level, electricity industry regulation relates mainly to international and interprovincial power transmission and nuclear energy. Provincial regulatory bodies govern licensing and regulatory approvals. For wind power, almost all developments require municipal approvals, including site plan review and municipal building permits.

One of the significant differences by region is the price of electricity, which varies widely (figure 5.5). In 2011, Montreal had the lowest monthly residential bill, C$68 for 1,000 kilowatt hour (kWh); Ontario ranked in the middle, at about C$127. Calgary had the most expensive electricity (C$175), more than twice the cost in Montreal.

Wind Power in Ontario

Electricity generation, transmission, and distribution in Ontario are governed by five separate legal entities. Ontario Power Generation Inc., which is wholly

Figure 5.5 Monthly bills in major Canadian cities, 2011

Canadian dollars

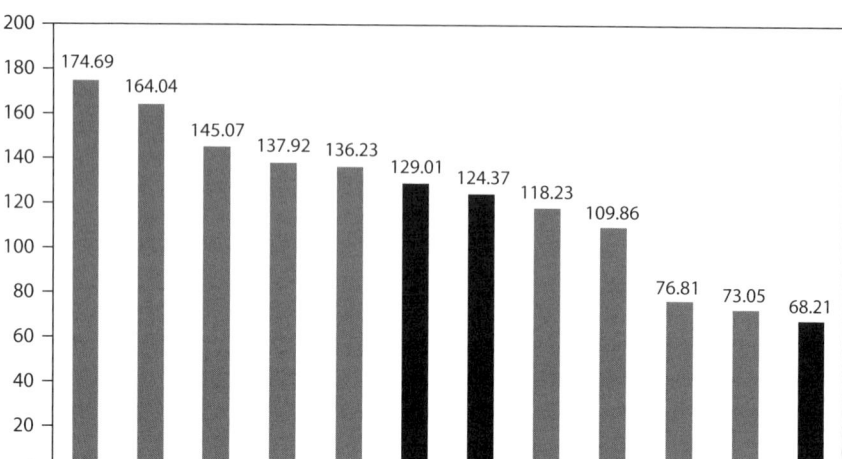

Notes: Figures represent monthly bills for residential service, for consumption of 1,000 kilowatt hours.

Source: Hydro Quebec, *Comparison of Electricity Prices in Major North American Cities,* April 2012, www.hydro
quebec.com/publications/en/comparison_prices/pdf/comp_2012_en.pdf (accessed on October 12, 2012).

owned by the Province of Ontario and operates the assets of the former Ontario Hydro Company, supplies more than 70 percent of provincial electricity.
Hydro One Networks, also wholly owned by the Province of Ontario, operates
97 percent of the transmission assets in the province, along with distribution
assets serving more than 1.2 million customers.

Ontario has deployed a feed-in tariff (FIT) program to promote green
energy, including wind. FIT programs are not unique to Canada; many other
countries, including the United States, use similar schemes (box 5.1). Under
this concept, electricity generated by renewable energy sources is supplied to
the grid at a price well above the cost of customary sources, such as coal. The
Ontario FIT program guarantees electricity purchase prices, grid access, and
long-term contracts to green energy producers, all of which make capital-
intensive investments worthwhile.

Ontario introduced its FIT program in 2009 to spur investment in renewable energy. At the same time, it sought to increase investment in manufacturing plants as a means of creating renewable energy jobs. Toward this
goal, Ontario's FIT program comes with an LCR. It mandates that renewable
energy supplies must meet a "minimum required domestic content level" to

Box 5.1 Feed-in tariff programs

Germany and Spain were the first countries to introduce feed-in tariff (FIT) programs to accelerate investment in renewable energy. Japan was a latecomer, starting its FIT program in July 2012. Within a few months, solar-powered electricity increased by 80 percent over the previous year. At the same time, the market share of imported solar panels, mostly from China and Korea, increased from 19 to 32 percent. Solar panels imported from those countries are 10 to 30 percent less expensive than Japanese panels.

In Germany, despite a big surge in demand, the top solar panel firm, Q-Cells, filed for bankruptcy. The bankruptcy prompted the European Union to launch an antidumping complaint against Chinese solar panel imports.

EU trade remedy complaints are emblematic of the conflict between the quest for renewable energy and existing "fair trade" rules embodied in antidumping and countervailing duty statutes, the national treatment obligation of the GATT, and the investment obligations of the WTO. The wide-ranging conflict affects international shipments of solar and wind power components, as well as biofuels, and challenges FIT programs.

China is the world's largest producer of solar panels, producing about 65 percent of all solar panels. The European Union is China's main export market, accounting for about 80 percent of all Chinese export sales.[1] The European Commission launched an antidumping and antisubsidy investigation in September 2012. After collecting and examining data, but within nine months of launching the investigation, the commission will issue its provisional findings (in this case, a deadline of June 2013).[2] The United States also claimed that imports of Chinese solar panels were subsidized. In October 2012, the US Commerce Department set antidumping duties ranging from 18 to 250 percent on solar energy cells imported from China.[3]

---

1. European Commission Trade Defence, "EU Initiates Anti-Dumping Investigation on Solar Panel Imports from China," September 6, 2012, http://trade.ec.europa.eu/doclib/press/index.cfm?id=829.

2. European Commission Trade Defence, "EU Initiates Anti-Subsidy Investigation on Solar Panel Imports from China," November 8, 2012, http://trade.ec.europa.eu/doclib/press/index.cfm?id=841.

3. Brian Wingfield, "U.S. Sets Anti-Dumping Duties on China Solar Imports," Bloomberg News, October 11, 2012, www.bloomberg.com/news/2012-10-10/u-s-sets-anti-dumping-duties-on-china-solar-imports.html.

---

be eligible for FIT benefits.[1] Those levels range from 25 percent for large wind projects to 60 percent for solar projects.

Japan and the European Union claimed that Canada's FIT scheme violates the Agreement on Subsidies and Countervailing Measures (ASCM), the

---

1. Ontario Power Authority, "Feed-in Tariff Program FIT Rules Version 2.0," August 10, 2012, http://fit.powerauthority.on.ca/august-10-2012-final-fit-20-program-documents-posted.

national treatment requirement of Article III of the General Agreement on Tariffs and Trade (GATT), and the Agreement on Trade-Related Investment Measures (TRIMs). Canada countered that because its FIT program is designed to ensure the affordable generation of clean energy, it is shielded by GATT Article XX (General Exceptions) from other provisions of the GATT and the TRIMS agreement. Canada also claims that Ontario's FIT program entails government procurement that is exempt from the ASCM.

On December 19, 2012, the final World Trade Organization (WTO) panel report agreed with Japan and the European Union that Ontario's LCR is not permissible. The report found that the LCR violates nondiscrimination rules in the GATT; however, it rejected (by a vote of 2 to 1) the claim that the LCR amounts to an illegal subsidy. After lodging its objections to the nondiscrimination finding on the interim report, the Ontario Energy Ministry said, "Should the panel disagree, we are ready to pursue all options with the federal government, including an appeal of the decision."[2] On February 6, 2013, the Canadian government announced that it had launched an appeal with the WTO Appellate Body. In a final ruling, in May 2013, the Appellate Body sided with the European Union and Japan and upheld the general findings of the December panel.[3]

Although the Ontario program was found to violate WTO rules, Ontario did succeed in attracting large-scale foreign direct investment to its renewable energy sector. Ontario's local newspaper, the *London Free Press*, reported that Ontario's LCR attracted $30 billion in new investment.[4] The largest deal under the province's green power plan is a complex of four wind and solar power clusters entailing an investment of US$6.7 billion by Korea's Samsung Group (Wilke 2011).

Wind Power in Quebec

The electricity industry in Quebec is dominated by Hydro-Quebec, a provincial monopoly. A number of specific authorizations are required for the development of wind energy facilities, including certificates from the Ministry of Sustainable Development, Environment and Parks, permits from local municipalities, authorizations from the Ministry of Natural Resources and Wildlife to locate facilities on public lands, and authorization from the Commission de protection du territoire agricole du Quebec (Agricultural Land Protection Commission) for the use of agricultural land (Gowlings 2010).

---

2. Richard Blackwell, "Ontario Loses WTO Ruling on Green Energy Policies: Reports," *Globe and Mail*, October 18, 2012, http://ictsd.org/i/press/ictsd-in-the-news/147621 (accessed on May 8, 2013).

3. For detail on the ruling, see "WTO Appellate Body Rules against Canada in Renewable Energy Case," *Inside US Trade*, May 8, 2013, www.insidetrade.com (accessed on May 9, 2013).

4. Debora Van Brenk, "Ontario to Defend Local Content Rules That Have Brought $30B in Investment," *London Free Press*, November 19, 2012.

Quebec's main energy source has been hydropower, which provided 97 percent of total provincial electricity in 2011. The most recent energy strategy document, *Quebec Energy Strategy 2006–2015*, views wind as a perfect complement to hydro and sets a goal of building 4,000 megawatts (MW) of wind power by 2015. Based on current technology, this capacity represents about 10 percent of peak electricity demand. New wind energy plants are built through requests for proposals (RFPs). Quebec has already issued three wind energy RFPs, totaling 3,500 MW of capacity. The most recent RFP, announced in July 2012, called for the procurement of an additional 700 MW of wind energy capacity.

The Quebec provincial government has announced its intention to maximize regional and provincial economic benefits through LCRs that require that 30 percent of the cost of the turbines be spent in the municipalities of Gaspesie and Matane and 60 percent of the overall costs be incurred in Quebec. The costs associated with several items were excluded from the determination of the 30 percent regional content figure. They include wind turbine warranties; transportation of the wind turbines to the project site; erection, testing, and commissioning of the turbines; and maintenance and operating costs (Government of Quebec 2006). These exclusions essentially say that Quebec is seeking hard capital investment in manufacturing plants and creation of associated jobs.

The LCR that 60 percent of overall costs be incurred in Quebec includes both "hard" and "soft" local content items, such as development costs, including the cost of resource, site, and environmental studies; the cost of the wind turbines; and total construction costs, including the costs associated with transporting wind turbines to project sites, testing, and commissioning. The costs associated with warranty coverage payments, operations and maintenance, and payments to local landowners are excluded.[5]

Impact of LCRs in Ontario and Quebec

Ontario and Quebec are using FIT and RFP programs to achieve their goal of increasing investment in the local renewable energy sector. Neither program is unique to Canada. What is unique is that both programs couple their incentives with LCRs.

As in the German and Japanese cases cited in box 5.1, the FIT program may or may not increase production of domestic renewable energy products, as less expensive products from China and Korea compete with domestic products. By mandating LCRs, the governments of Ontario and Quebec aim to increase both investment in renewable energy plant and the manufacture of renewable energy products. The problem is that, like any trade barrier, LCRs

5. Matthew Sherrad and Thomas J. Timmins, "Canada: Quebec Announces Procurement of 700 MW of Wind Energy," Gowlings Knowledge Centre, July 2012, www.gowlings.com/resources/article.asp?pubID=2577 (accessed on July 31, 2012).

Figure 5.6   Overnight cost of onshore wind energy plants, selected countries, 2009

US dollars per kilowatt of installed electric capacity

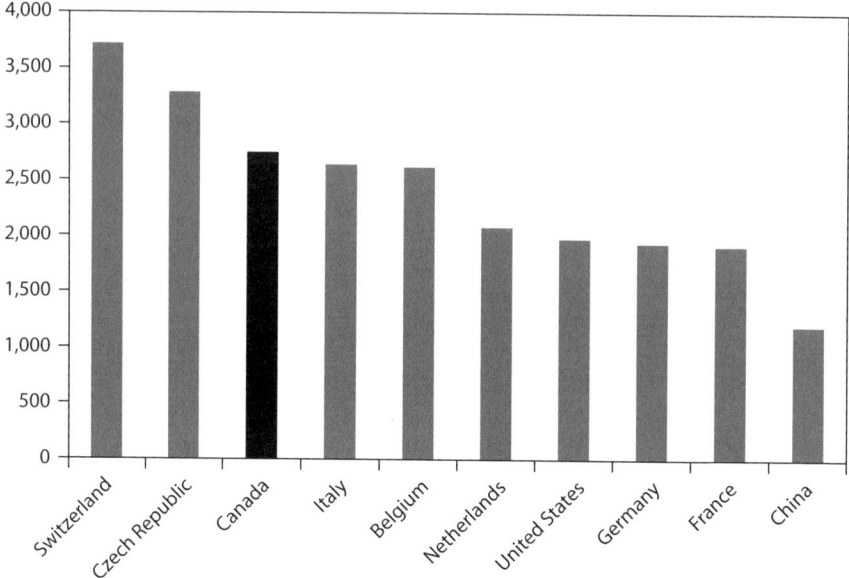

Notes: Overnight cost includes preconstruction (engineering, procurement, and construction) and contingency costs.

Source: International Energy Agency, *Projected Cost of Generating Electricity*, 2010 edition, www.iea.org/textbase/npsum/ElecCostSUM.pdf (accessed on October 22, 2012).

almost certainly increase the cost of installed capacity and, as a result, limit the expansion of renewable energy capabilities.

The impact of LCRs in Ontario and Quebec will eventually be reflected in the price of renewable energy—electricity generated from solar panels and wind turbines. In Japan, imported solar panels are generally 10 to 30 percent less expensive than domestic solar panels. However, most wind turbines are custom made, and differences in size, style, and quality make simple price comparisons impossible.

We used the "overnight cost" of onshore wind energy plant as a proxy for the price of wind turbines. Overnight cost includes preconstruction; construction (engineering, procurement, and construction); and contingency costs. Figure 5.6 presents the overnight cost of onshore wind plant in 10 countries, among which Canada ranked third highest. The United States ranked seventh, with costs about 28 percent less than Canada's. We assume that the United States represents the baseline cost in North America for onshore wind turbine plants. Although not all of the price differences between Canada and the

United States are the result of LCRs, we assume, conservatively, that half the differences can be attributed to policies.

The cost per kilowatt (kW) is about $1,980 in the United States and about $2,750 in Canada; half the difference is about $386 per kW of installed capacity. Since 2009, Ontario has installed more than 800,000 kW of wind power generation. At $386 extra per kW as a result of the LCRs, the capital cost would have increased by more than $300 million ($386 × 800,000 = $308.8 million). Quebec has installed more than 500,000 kW of wind power capacity since 2009. The extra capital costs as a result of the LCRs are estimated at almost $200 million.

Another way to measure the impact of LCRs is to compare the development of the renewable energy sector across countries. As shown in figure 5.1, Canada ranked 10th in terms of wind energy capacity. But Canada has fewer people and a smaller GDP than big wind energy countries. To use common metrics, we relate wind energy capacity to the population and the land area.

Figure 5.7 shows wind energy capacity relative to population. Canada ranks eighth, just above the average figure for the sample countries. This achievement reflects the large wind energy capacity on Prince Edward Island, where wind energy supplied more than half of total electricity generated in 2011. Ontario ranked 11th and Quebec 14th, just below the average.

Figure 5.8 shows wind energy capacity relative to country land area (measured by square kilometers). Canada ranked 27th among 31 countries, with a figure of 0.5 kW/square kilometer, much lower than sample average of 16.5 kW/square kilometer. Ontario (2.1 kW/square kilometer) and Quebec (0.8 kW/square kilometer) have slightly higher capacity than Canada as a whole. These comparisons indicate that Ontario and Quebec have enormous potential to build more wind energy fields.

Alternatives to LCRs

Like any other trade barrier, the LCRs used by the Canadian provinces are eventually reflected in higher prices, which we estimate at about $386 extra per kilowatt of electric capacity. Rather than using LCRs to spur the installation of wind turbines and assist Canadian firms, it would make more sense for Canada and its provinces to offer generous but temporary refundable tax credits for both hard costs (such as the costs of building turbines) and soft costs (such as the costs of training skilled machinists). The financial costs would be highly visible. After five years, the federal and provincial governments could assess whether the payoff in terms of creating a world-class domestic industry and accelerating the implementation of wind energy justified the public outlay.

Both Ontario and Quebec have huge potential to produce more wind energy. The LCRs mandated by Ontario's FIT program and Quebec's RFP program are probably discouraging this development.

74

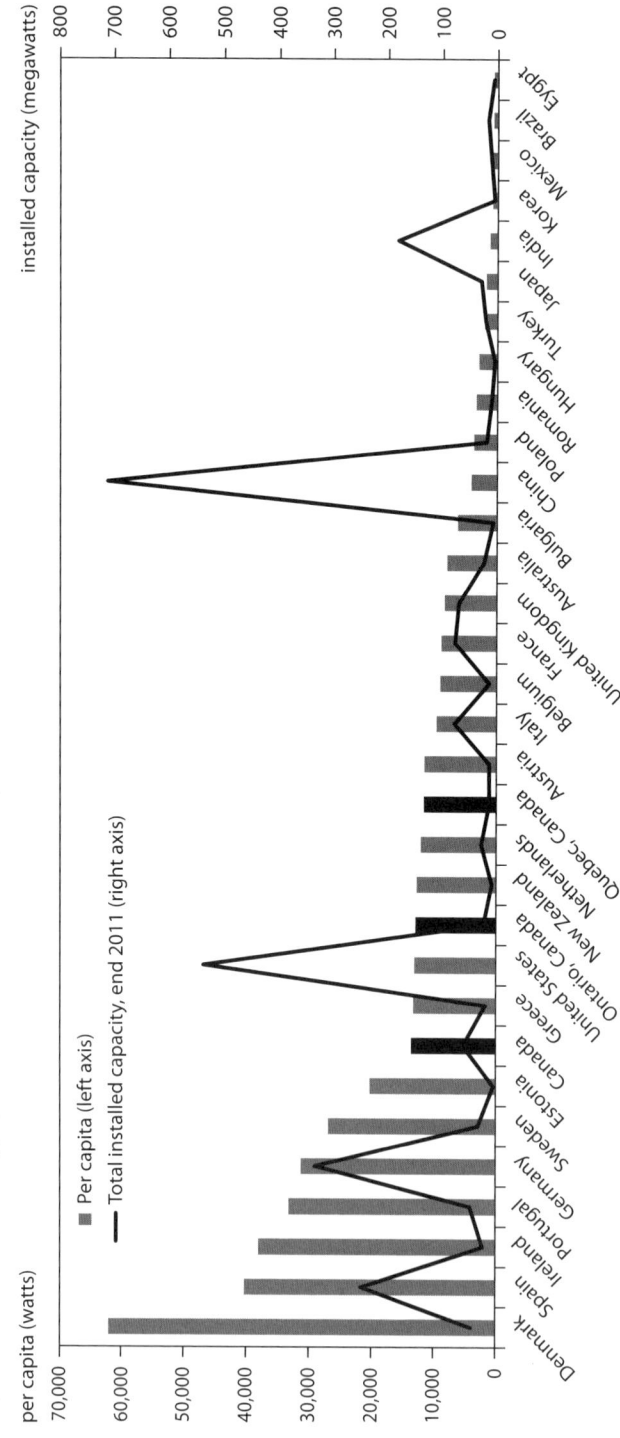

Figure 5.7 Wind energy, per capita and total capacity, 2011

per capita (watts)

installed capacity (megawatts)

- Per capita (left axis)
- Total installed capacity, end 2011 (right axis)

Denmark, Spain, Ireland, Portugal, Germany, Sweden, Estonia, Canada, Greece, United States, Ontario, Canada, New Zealand, Quebec, Canada, Netherlands, Austria, Italy, Belgium, France, United Kingdom, Australia, Bulgaria, China, Poland, Romania, Hungary, Turkey, Japan, India, Korea, Mexico, Brazil, Eygpt

Source: Authors' calculations are based on data from WWEA (2012); CIA World Fact Book, www.cia.gov/world-factbook/rankorder/rankorderguide.html (accessed on October 15, 2012).

Figure 5.8 Wind energy, per land area, 2011

per land area (kilowatt per square kilometer)

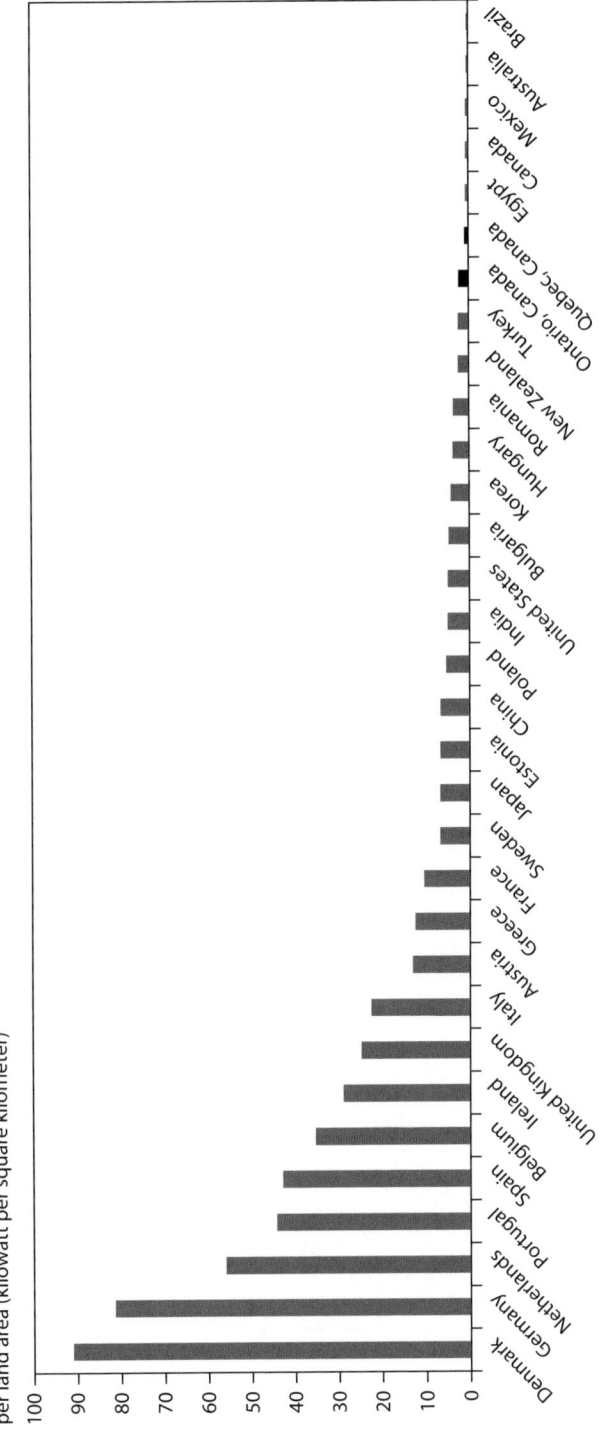

Source: Authors' calaculations are based on data from WWEA (2012); CIA World Fact Book, www.cia.gov/world-factbook/rankorder/rankorderguide.html (accessed on October 15, 2012).

6

Automobile Industry
in China

Local content requirements (LCRs) are embedded in China's approach to the automobile industry. LCRs have been in force in the sector for more than three decades, as a tool for consolidating and promoting the industry. Beginning in the 1980s, when China designated the auto industry as a pillar of economic growth, the government began subsidizing the industry and encouraging joint ventures with foreign investors, both to increase production and to acquire technology.

Upon its accession to the World Trade Organization (WTO) in 2001, China removed LCRs from its official laws and regulations. However, through foreign ownership requirements, financing arrangements, and government "suggestions," LCRs are alive and well. Their informal administration means that a WTO challenge—as a violation of Article III (National Treatment) of the Agreement on Subsidies and Countervailing Measures (ASCM) or trade-related investment measures (TRIMs)—would encounter very high evidentiary hurdles. Local ownership requirements that restrict foreign participation in joint ventures to less than 50 percent are not covered by WTO rules.

Automobile Production and Role of the State

In 2009, Chinese sales of automobiles surpassed those of the United States, making China the world's largest automobile market. In 2011, China sold 18.5 million cars, about 30 percent of global sales (figure 6.1) (JAMA 2012). China is also the number one producer of automobiles, turning out 18.4 million cars in 2011, about 24 percent of total world output (figure 6.2).

Figure 6.1 Domestic sales and imports of automobiles, selected countries, 2011

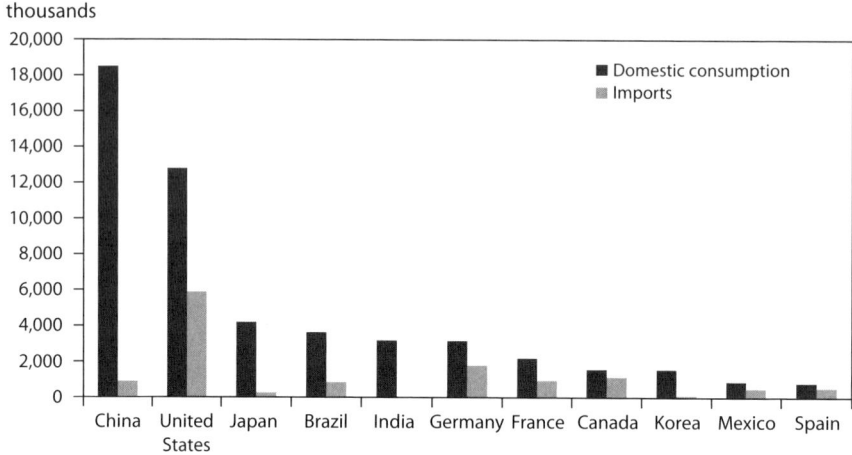

Notes: For Germany, Korea, and Spain, import figures are calculated as domestic sales minus (production minus exports). For Germany, the sales figures are the number of new cars registered. For India, figures are from Society of Indian Automobile Manufacturers for the years 2010-11. Based on these figures, India has a trade deficit of 13,000 autos, but the number of autos imported is unknown. For Spain, figures drawn from Japan Automobiles Manufacturers' Association and are for 2010.

Sources: International Organization of Motor Vehicle Manufacturers, Production Statistics, http://oica.net/category/production-statistics (accessed on May 12, 2012); JETRO (2012b); import figures are from UN Comtrade database, http://comtrade.un.org/db; for Mexico, import and sales figures are from export.gov, http://export.gov/mexico/leadingindustrysectors/eg_mx_042754.asp (accessed on May 31, 2012).

China's auto market and production will continue to grow rapidly in the years ahead. General Motors is planning to build four factories and increase production capacity by 70 percent to 5 million cars a year by 2015. Volkswagen plans to build new factories and increase production capacity by 40 percent to 3.4 million cars a year. Hyundai, which has the third-largest auto sales share in the world, is constructing four factories, increasing its annual production capacity to 2 million cars. Nissan and other Japanese automakers are also increasing production capacity in China; the combined capacity of Japanese auto firms is expected to reach 5.4 million cars a year by 2015.[1]

The expansion of auto production capacity is motivated by China's growing demand for cars, especially in the interior regions. According to the head of the Automotive Industrial Policy Research at the China Automotive Technology and Research Center, the Chinese auto market will expand to 30 million cars a year by 2020.[2] According to the deputy chief of the Development

---

1. "China Will Be the Largest Auto Producer in the World," *Nikkei Online*, May 21, 2013 (in Japanese) (accessed on May 21, 2013).

2. "30 Million Limit, Chinese Auto Industry and Next Generation Eco Car Is the Key," *Nikkei Online,* May 8, 2012 (in Japanese), www.nikkei.com/article/DGXNASDD070AJ_X00C12A5000000/ (accessed on May 23, 2012).

Figure 6.2   Automobile production and imported auto parts, selected countries, 2011

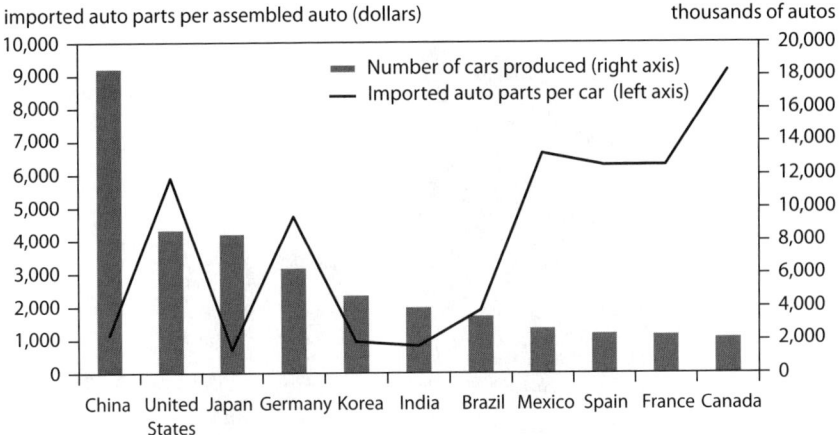

imported auto parts per assembled auto (dollars)   thousands of autos

Legend:
- Number of cars produced (right axis)
- Imported auto parts per car (left axis)

x-axis: China, United States, Japan, Germany, Korea, India, Brazil, Mexico, Spain, France, Canada

Notes: Auto production includes both commercial and passenger vehicles. All figures are based on 2011 data, except for Germany, India and Spain, where 2010 figures are used. Imported auto parts per car are calculated as total imported auto parts divided by the number of cars produced in a country.

Sources: International Organization of Motor Vehicle Manufacturers, Production Statistics. http://oica.net/category/production-statistics (accessed on May 12, 2012); UN Comtrade database, http://comtrade.un.org/db; authors' calculations.

Research Center of the State Council, "theoretically, Chinese auto production can reach 60 to 70 million per year." Whichever figure is correct, the Chinese auto market is booming.

Before foreign firms began their joint venture investments with Chinese automakers in the 1980s, China had more than 100 automakers, each producing a small number of cars and trucks. To promote the auto industry, the Chinese government gradually opened its door to foreign automakers. In 2011, Chinese brands, including Cherry and First Automobile Works, accounted for about 42 percent of the market; Japanese automakers accounted for 19 percent; European automakers for 19 percent; US automakers for 11 percent; and Korean automakers for 8 percent (figure 6.3). Table 6.1 lists the foreign automakers in China.

As in other Chinese industries, state-owned enterprises (SOEs) have majority stakes in big automobile firms. According to a recent trade policy paper by the Organization for Economic Cooperation and Development (OECD) (Kowalski, Büge, and Sztajerowska 2013), four Chinese auto companies (Dongfeng Motor Group, FAW Car, Guangzhou Automobile, and SAIC Motor) are included in the Forbes Global 2000 list of the world's largest public companies. Among the four, only one, Guangzhou Automobile, is a company in which the state owns less than half of the shares.[3] The other three companies are majority owned by the state.

---

3. Not all of the other auto manufacturing firms, which did not make the Forbes list, are SOEs.

Figure 6.3   Top 10 automakers in China by share of production, 2012
(percent)

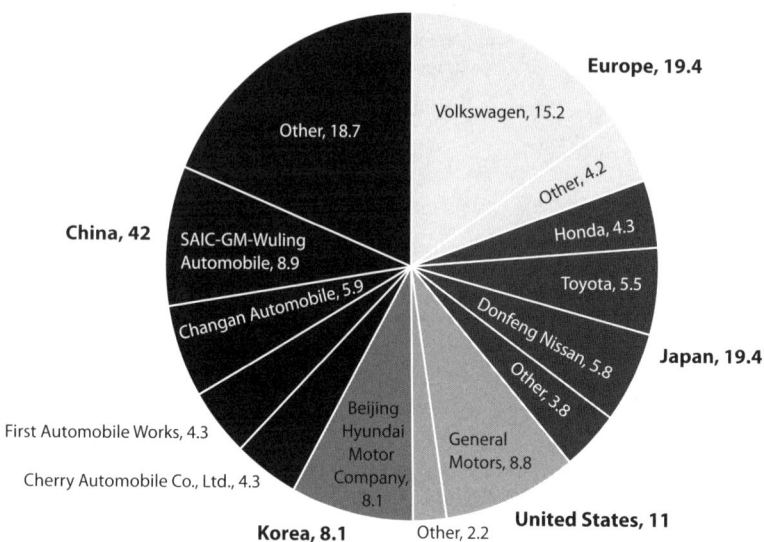

Source: Fourin, www.fourin.jp/report/CHINA_INDUSTRY_2012.html (in Japanese) (accessed on June 13, 2012).

Using comprehensive databases, P. Kowalski, Max Büge, and Monika Sztajerowska (2013) examine the importance of SOEs in the global marketplace and the practices that govern the international trade and investment activities of SOEs. Among the world's largest 2,000 companies, 204 are identified as SOEs (meaning the state owns more than half of the company's shares).

The number of SOEs varies by country and by industry. China has the largest number (about 70), followed by India (30), Russia (9), and the United Arab Emirates (9). SOEs in OECD countries are shrinking and concentrated mainly in network industries, such as energy, telecommunication, and transportation. In contrast, SOEs in emerging countries, such as China, Brazil, and India, remain significant.

Unlike in OECD countries, SOEs in China are fairly evenly spread across manufacturing, services, and finance (table 6.2). Within the manufacturing sector, auto SOEs account for 20 percent of sales and profits. These SOEs may enjoy government advantages, such as direct subsidies, exemptions from antitrust enforcement, and concessionary financing. Other manufacturing industries with a high SOE share include fabricated metal products, basic metals, electrical equipment, and other transport equipment. Usha C. V. Haley and George T. Haley (2013) claim that big Chinese SOEs received more than $300 billion in direct subsidies between 1985 and 2005.

Table 6.1 Foreign automakers in China

Model	Year of estimate	Capital (millions of US dollars)[a]	Production capacity	Shareholdings
FAW-Volkswagen Automobile Co. Ltd.	1991	582	n.a.	FAW 60 percent, Volkswagen AG 20 percent, Audi AG 10 percent, Volkswagen Automobile (China) Investment 10 percent
SAIC Motor Corporation (formerly Shanghai Volkswagen Automotive Company)	1984	28,175	n.a.	Shanghai Automotive Industry Corporation (SAIC) 50 percent, Volkswagen 50 percent
FAW Toyota-Tianjin	2002	1,266	n.a.	FAW group 20 percent, Tianjin FAW Xiali Corp Ltd. 30 percent, TMC 40 percent, Toyota Motoer (China) Investment Co. Ltd. 10 percent
FAW Toyota-Sichuan	2000	67	n.a.	FAW 50 percent, Toyota 45 percent, Toyota Tsusho Corporation 5 percent
SAIC-GM-Wuling Automobile Co., Ltd.	2002	n.a.	n.a.	SAIC 50.1 percent, GM 44 percent, Wuling (China) 5.9 percent
Shanghai GM (Shenyang) Norsom Motors	2004	227	n.a.	Shanghai GM 50 percent, GM China 25 percent, SAIC 25 percent
Shanghai General Motors (SGM)	1997	n.a.	n.a.	GM 50 percent, Shanghai Automotive Industry Corporation (Group) 50 percent
Shanghai GM Dong Yue Motors Co., Ltd.	2003	n.a.	n.a.	SAIC 25 percent, General Motors (China) 25 percent, Shanghai General Motors 50 percent
FAW-GM Light Duty Commercial Vehicle	2009	n.a.	n.a.	GM China 50 percent, China FAW Group 50 percent

(table continues next page)

Table 6.1 Foreign automakers in China (*continued*)

Model	Year of estimate	Capital (millions of US dollars)[a]	Production capacity	Shareholdings
Beijing Hyundai Motor Company	2002	n.a.	700,000 units	Hyundai 50 percent, Beijing Automotive Holdings 50 percent
Changan Suzuki Automobile Co., Ltd.	1993	190	100,000 units	Changan Automobile 51 percent, Japan Suzuki 25 percent, Japan Sojitz 14 percent, and Suzuki (China) Investment 10 percent
Changan Ford Mazda Automobile Co., Ltd.	2001	n.a.	410,000 units	Changan 50 percent, Ford 15 percent, Mazda 15 percent
Dongfeng Peugeot Citroen Automobile Company Ltd.	1992	n.a.	300,000 units	DFM China 31 percent, Chinese banks 39 percent, Citroen 26.9 percent, international banks 3.1 percent
Dongfeng Motor Co., Ltd.	2003	2,622	n.a.	Dongfeng Motor Corporation 50 percent, Nissan Motor Co. 50 percent
Guangqi Honda Automobile Co., Ltd.	1998	n.a.	360,000 units	Guangzhou Automobile Group 50 percent, Honda Motor Co., Ltd 50 percent
Dongfeng Honda Automobile	2003	200	n.a.	Dongfeng Motor Corporation 50 percent, Honda Motor Co. 50 percent

n.a. = not available

a. Original figures in renminbi (RMB) were converted to US dollars using the foreign exchange rate of 6.37 RMB/US dollar.

Sources: Company websites; "Company Overview of Beijing Hyundai Motors Co. Ltd.," *Bloomberg Businessweek*, http://investing.businessweek.com/research/stocks/private/snapshot.asp?privcapld=9171497; "Dongfeng Peugeot Citroen Automobile Company Ltd.," *Hubei*, January 26, 2005, www.cnhubei.com/200502/ca677337.htm; Changan, "JV Cooperation," www.globalchangan.com/About/cooper.shtml#; "Company Overview of Chongqing Changan Suzuki Automobile Co., Ltd.," *Bloomberg Businessweek*, http://investing.businessweek.com/research/stocks/private/snapshot.asp?privcapld=5533467; Guangqi Honda, "Company profile," www.ghac.cn/english/public/index_jsp_catid_1940_1947_1959_id_97398.shtml.

Table 6.2 Chinese state-owned enterprises, by industry, 2010–11

NACE code	Industry	Number of firms	Total sales (billions of US dollars)	Total profits (billions of US dollars)	Total market value (billions of US dollars)	Total assets (billions of US dollars)
11	Manufacture of beverages	3	3.4	1.4	54.5	7.0
21	Manufacture of basic pharmaceutical products and pharmaceutical preparations	1	6.9	0.1	8.3	4.1
23	Manufacture of other nonmetallic mineral products	1	4.7	0.3	7.8	11.2
24	Manufacture of basic metals	7	85.3	2.7	74.3	100.3
27	Manufacture of electrical equipment	2	13.1	0.6	24.8	23.8
28	Manufacture of machinery and equipment n.e.c.	4	18.8	1.7	41.0	22.9
29	Manufacture of motor vehicles, trailers and semi-trailers	3	39.2	2.1	45.1	35.0
30	Manufacture of other transport equipment	3	15.3	0.7	42.8	23.5
35	Electricity, gas, steam, and air conditioning supply	5	24.8	2.2	52.5	104.0
42	Civil engineering	4	177.0	4.3	57.9	175.7
46	Wholesale trade, except of motor vehicles and motorcycles	1	13.8	0.0	6.3	6.1
49	Land transport and transport via pipelines	1	3.3	1.0	19.4	9.9
50	Water transport	1	10.0	-1.1	14.7	19.9
51	Air transport	8	62.3	10.5	176.7	117.3
61	Telecommunications	4	349.1	42.6	599.9	502.7
64	Financial intermediation, except insurance and pension funding	11	237.5	64.4	872.9	6,636.1
65	Insurance, reinsurance and pension funding, except compulsory social security	2	62.5	5.1	110.2	203.8
66	Other financial activities	1	3.6	1.6	21.7	26.0
68	Real estate activities	2	14.5	1.8	18.8	47.8
91	Libraries, archives, museums, and other cultural activities	3	314.4	19.4	223.0	199.4
93	Sports activities and amusement and recreation activities	2	2.7	0.9	17.3	14.2
	Total	69	1,462.1	162.3	2,489.9	8,290.7

NACE = Nomenclature Generale des Activites Economiques (General Name for Economic Activities); n.e.c. = not elsewhere classified

Source: Based on data from Kowalski, Büge, and Sztajerowska (2013).

China's rapid growth has created many challenges, among them oil consumption and environmental damage. China's demand for oil—stemming largely from the rapid growth in its automobile and truck fleet—has been extraordinary. Dependence on foreign oil increased from less than 8 percent in 1995 to 54 percent in 2010.[4] Meanwhile, severe air pollution imposes serious health risks.

To address these challenges, the Chinese central government prioritized high-tech and high-value-added industries, as outlined in the 12th Five Year Plan and Foreign Investment Catalogue.[5] The Foreign Investment Catalogue divides industrial sectors into four categories: "encouraged," "restricted," "prohibited," and "permitted." Foreign investment in "encouraged" sectors is promoted by granting foreign firms benefits such as greater scope for foreign ownership, less governmental review, and lower taxes. The Catalogue reveals that the Chinese government is calling for further market opening and encouraging foreign investment in high-end manufacturing, new technologies, alternative energy, and other environmentally friendly industries. At the same time, the government discourages investment in industries that generate high levels of pollution and energy consumption, as well as those that export natural resources.

In the automobile industry, the government has shifted its focus toward energy-efficient cars, such as alternative fuel cars, hybrid cars, and electric cars, and it is supporting the development of better fuel-cell batteries. In April 2012, it announced production and sales targets for electric cars and plug-in hybrid vehicles of more than 500,000 in 2015 and more than 5 million in 2020.[6]

To achieve these goals, the government listed the New Energy Vehicle (NEV) as an "encouraged" industry in the most recent Foreign Investment Catalogue.[7] It moved traditional automobile assembly activity from the list of "encouraged" industries to the "permitted" category. In addition, it placed the manufacture of specified key components for NEVs—including certain types of batteries and battery components, battery and motor management systems, and certain types of electric vehicle drive motors—on the "encouraged" list.

---

4. "30 Million Limit, Chinese Auto Industry and Next Generation Eco Car Is the Key," *Nikkei Online*, May 8, 2012 (in Japanese), www.nikkei.com/article/DGXNASDD070AJ_X00C12A5000000 (accessed on May 23, 2012).

5. "2012 Foreign Investment Industrial Guidance Catalog Promulgated," *China Briefing*, December 30, 2012, www.china-briefing.com/news/2011/12/30/2011-foreign-investment-industrial-guidance-catalogue-promulgated.html (accessed on May 15, 2013).

6. "30 Million Limit, Chinese Auto Industry and Next Generation Eco Car Is the Key," *Nikkei Online*.

7. Foreign Investment Catalogues were first introduced in 1995. The most recent version was released in 2011 and implemented in January 2012.

Investment Barriers and Incentives

China is the world's second-largest destination for foreign direct investment (FDI) after the United States. In 2011, it received $124 billion in inward FDI (USTR 2012). However, investors continue to complain about lack of transparency, inconsistent law enforcement, weak intellectual property rights protection, and corruption.

US and other foreign automakers and automotive parts manufactures face significant challenges in China, which has implemented a series of policies that discriminate against foreign firms. Foreign automotive firms can operate only through joint ventures with Chinese firms, and foreign ownership is limited to less than 50 percent. Foreign auto parts makers can operate without a joint venture and are not subject to ownership limitation, although certain NEV parts, such as batteries, are subject to foreign ownership limitations.

The array of barriers and incentives, coupled with high tariffs on automobile parts, have encouraged foreign auto and parts makers to produce in China rather than export assembled autos or parts from their home countries. Table 6.3 shows automobile imports for major automobile-producing countries in 2011. Figure 6.2 displays the number of vehicles produced and the value of imported auto parts per vehicle in these countries. On average, each Chinese-made car contains $1,155 worth of imported auto parts, of which 40 percent is the transmission. This figure is considerably below the average for countries that have virtually free trade in auto parts. The United Kingdom has the highest imported auto parts content per vehicle ($10,853) followed by Canada ($9,156), Mexico ($6,638), France ($6,285), Spain ($6,279), the United States ($5,897), and Germany $4,737 (figure 6.4).[8] Countries not renowned for relatively free trade in auto parts have much lower imports per vehicle. Among these countries, Japan is the lowest, with just $705 per vehicle; the value of imported auto parts per vehicle is also low in India ($813) and Korea ($945). Although Ricardian comparative advantage may explain a good part of these differences, it seems likely that low levels of imported parts per assembled vehicle in Japan, India, Korea, and China reflect an array of overt and covert barriers to both trade and investment.[9]

Assembled auto imports present a similar pattern. The Chinese sold 18.5 million automobiles in 2011, 1.0 million (less than 6 percent) of which were imports (figure 6.5). The United Kingdom has the highest imported auto sales, at about 86 percent, followed by Australia (slightly less than 86 percent) and France (82 percent). In most countries, imported cars account for about

---

8. Under the North American Free Trade Agreement (NAFTA), auto parts may cross the same border several times during production to take advantage of plant specialization and production efficiencies. This phenomenon raises the calculated value of imported parts per vehicle, because the cited data make no adjustment for double counting the same part.

9. Our limited statistical efforts to explain the extent of parts trade by reference to elements of comparative advantage were not successful.

Table 6.3   Automobile imports by major automobile-producing countries, 2011

Country	Imported auto parts per vehicle (US dollars)	Imported assembled autos as a share of sales (percent)
Argentina	n.a.	62.5
Australia	n.a.	85.9
Brazil	1,893	28.2
Canada	9,156	72.5
China	1,155	5.6
Czech Republic	5,885	n.a.
France	6,285	81.6
Germany	4,737	51.8
India	813	n.a.
Indonesia	2,762	n.a.
Iran	423	n.a.
Japan	705	6.9
Malaysia	n.a.	78.8
Mexico	6,638	52.8
Russia	5,935	n.a.
South Korea	945	6.6
Spain	6,279	57.3
Thailand	4,012	9.1
Turkey	4,421	n.a.
United Kingdom	10,853	86.0
United States	5,897	48.6

n.a. = not available

Notes: Figures for auto parts imports per vehicle are calculated using total imported auto parts divided by the number of vehicles produced in each country. For Germany, Thailand, and Argentina, assembled auto imports are calculated as follows: imports = sales – (production – exports). For Germany, sales figures are the number of registered new cars. For the United Kingdom and Mexico, assembled auto imports are calculated as follows: imports = domestic sales – production for home sales.

Sources: Production figures are from International Organization of Motor Vehicle Manufacturers, Production Statistics, http://oica.net/category/production-statistics (accessed on May 12, 2012); trade figures are from UN Comtrade database, http://comtrade.un.org/db; for Germany, Spain, Thailand, Argentina, Australia, Canada, and Mexico, production, sales, and trade figures are from JETRO (2012b); for Mexico, sales and imports figures are from export.gov, available at http://export.gov/mexico/leadingindustrysectors/eg_mx_042754.asp (accessed on May 31, 2012).

half of total sales. In Thailand, Japan, Korea, and China, the share of imported car sales is less than 10 percent. These patterns may be explained largely by Ricardian comparative advantage, but it seems likely that trade and investment barriers also play a role.

China has revised many of its laws and regulations to conform to its WTO commitments. Yet some measures continue to raise concerns, especially those that encourage technology transfers into China. Encouragement may not amount to a formal requirement, but foreign companies worry that, in

Figure 6.4 Imported auto parts per vehicle, selected countries, 2011

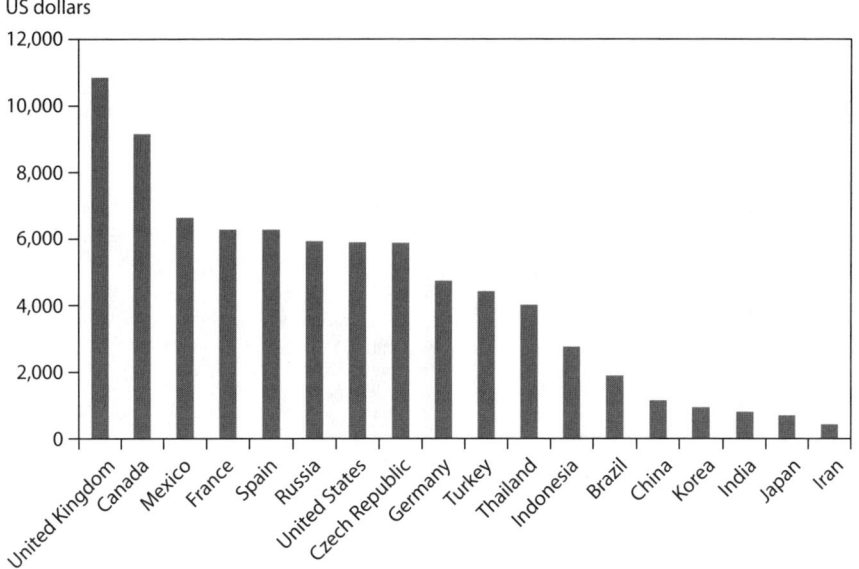

Note: Figures calculated by dividing total imported auto parts by the number of vehicles produced in each country.

Sources: International Organization of Motor Vehicle Manufacturers, Production Statistics, http://oica.net/category/production-statistics (accessed on May 12, 2012); UN Comtrade database, http://comtrade.un.org/db.

practice, encouragement can become obligatory, particularly given the high degree of discretion enjoyed by Chinese officials when reviewing investment applications. Similarly, some laws and regulations encourage firms to use local content. According to US companies, Chinese officials may consider factors such as export performance and local content use when deciding whether to approve an investment or recommend a Chinese bank loan.

Another concern relates to a series of antidumping orders imposed by China. Starting in December 2011, China imposed antidumping and countervailing duties on US auto exports. The penalty tariffs ranged from 2.9 to 8.9 percent on US-made sport utility vehicles (SUVs) with engines larger than 2.5 liters; according to US officials, the penalty tariffs cover about 80 percent of US autos exported to China in 2011, about $5.4 billion.[10] In July 2012, the United States requested consultations with China under WTO auspices, with the expressed hope that China would drop the duties. The

10. Carole E. Lee, Jared A. Favole, and Tom Barkley, "Obama Hits China over Auto Duties," *Wall Street Journal*, July 5, 2012, http://online.wsj.com/article/SB100014240527023039623045775083 61840692508.html (accessed on July 12, 2012).

Figure 6.5   Assembled auto imports as a share of total sales, selected countries, 2011

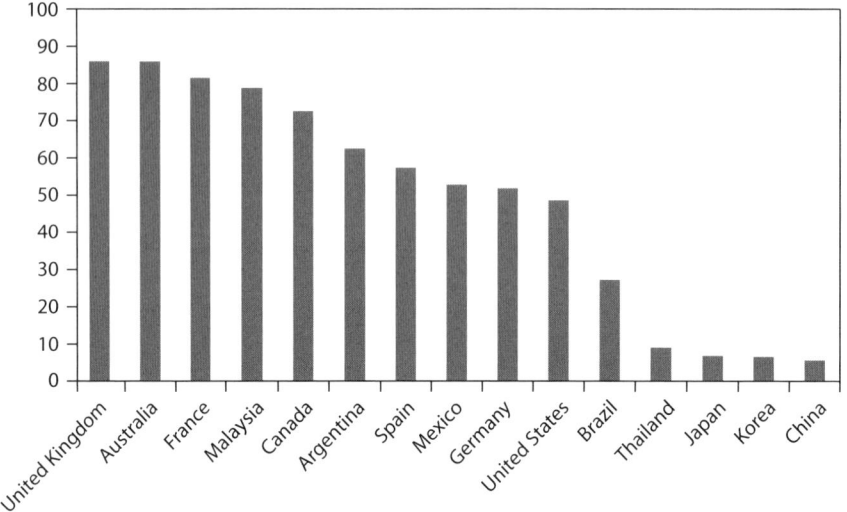

percent share of total sales

Notes: For Germany, Thailand, and Argentina, import figures are calculated as sales minus (production minus exports). For Germany, sales are the number of new cars registered. For the United Kingdom and Mexico, import figures are calculated as domestic sales minus production for home sales.

Sources: Production figures are from International Organization of Motor Vehicle Manufacturers, Production Statistics, http://oica.net/category/production-statistics (accessed on May 12, 2012); trade figures from UN Comtrade database, http://comtrade.un.org/db; all figures for Germany, Spain, Thailand, Argentina, Australia, Canada, and Mexico are from JETRO (2012b); sales and import figures for Mexico are from export.gov, http://export.gov/mexico/leadingindustry sectors/eg_mx_042754.asp (accessed on May 31, 2012).

central motivation for China's imposition of penalty tariffs seems to have been retaliation for trade remedy cases brought by the United States against Chinese products. However, it is probably not an accident that the penalty tariffs reinforce China's localization policies with respect to the automotive industry.

Automobile Prices

The average price of Chinese automobiles is probably higher as a result of LCRs and related policies. To estimate the impact, we compared the 2010 prices of four popular models (the Toyota Yaris, the Ford Focus, the VW Passat, and the Mercedes Benz E-class) in four countries (China, the United States, Japan, and the United Kingdom) (table 6.4). In 2010, the market exchange rate was RMB6.36 per dollar. In the same year, the fundamental equilibrium exchange rate (FEER) was RMB5.50 per dollar (Cline and Wil-

Table 6.4 Retail car prices, selected countries, 2010 (US dollars)

Model	Exchange rate	China			United States			Japan			United Kingdom		
		Low	High	Average	Low	High	Average	Low	High	Average	Low	High	Average
Toyota Yaris	Market[a]	13,671	19,642	16,657	14,158	15,541	14,850	13,200	22,471	17,835	17,584	24,105	20,844
	FEER[b]	15,818	22,727	19,273	14,416	15,824	15,120	12,310	20,956	16,633	17,121	23,470	20,295
Ford Focus[c]	Market[a]	16,468	23,382	19,925	17,600	23,901	20,750	12,603	22,565	17,584	26,211	43,402	34,806
	FEER[b]	19,055	27,055	23,055	17,920	24,336	21,128	11,753	21,044	16,399	25,520	42,259	33,890
VW Passat	Market[a]	34,382	48,839	41,610	28,472	30,014	29,243	40,825	47,126	43,975	30,941	42,616	36,778
	FEER[b]	39,782	56,509	48,145	28,991	30,560	29,775	10,008	43,950	26,979	30,126	41,494	35,810
Mercedes Benz E-Class	Market[a]	73,070	111,569	92,319	50,583	89,883	70,233	79,905	136,114	108,009	47,377	124,485	85,931
	FEER[b]	84,545	129,091	106,818	51,504	91,520	71,512	74,519	126,940	100,730	46,130	121,207	83,668

FEER = fundamental equilibrium exchange rate

a. For market exchange rate figures, original figures in renminbi were converted using the foreign exchange rate of 6.363 RMB/US dollar.
b. For FEER, 2010 FEER of 5.50 RMB/US dollar was used.
c. In our judgment, the high quoted prices for the Ford Focus in the United Kingdom reflect sharply different model characteristics and are not relevant for an international comparison.

Note: The prices listed are the manufacturer's suggested retail prices.

Sources: Gasgoo, Global Auto Sources, "Analysis: Car Price Comparison between China and the Rest of the World," http://autonews.gasgoo.com/AutoNews/Auto-biz_print.aspx?id=1019860 (accessed on June 15, 2012); market exchange rate from World Bank, World Development Indicators database, http://data.worldbank.org/indicator; FEER data from Cline and Williamson (2010).

liamson 2010).[11] We focus on the FEER because it is calculated to bring the traded sector of the Chinese economy roughly into balance with the rest of the world (in other words, at the FEER, Chinese exports of traded goods and services roughly equal Chinese imports of traded goods and services).

The fact that in 2010 the value of the renminbi was about 14 percent higher at the FEER than at the market exchange rate reflects an important reality. When Chinese prices are translated into dollars at the market exchange rate, most traded goods sold in China are considerably cheaper than comparable goods sold in other countries. This advantage is the reason why China has persistently run a large merchandise trade surplus. But, as the data in table 6.4 show, this is not generally true of automobiles. For the four representative models, at the market exchange rate of RMB6.36 per dollar, average Chinese prices are about the same as prices in the United States, the United Kingdom, and Japan. (In our judgment, the high quoted prices for the Ford Focus in the United Kingdom reflect sharply different model characteristics and are not relevant for an international comparison.) However, at the FEER of RMB5.50 per dollar, in most cases Chinese auto prices are considerably higher than prices in the other countries.

A thought experiment illustrates the benefits of free trade for China. Suppose that open trade and free competition in China reduced Chinese auto prices, expressed in renminbi, by half the amount of appreciation implied by the FEER exchange rate. For example, at the market exchange rate of RMB6.36 per dollar, the average Chinese price of the Toyota Yaris in 2010 was RMB106,000 (table 6.5). The thought experiment envisages that the renminbi price would drop by 7 percent, to RMB98,834, in the wake of open competition in the auto sector and appreciation of the renminbi by 14 percent. Expressed in the jargon of economists, the thought experiment assumes that the pass-through coefficient from the exchange rate to local prices in the auto sector is 0.5 (0.5 × 14 percent = 7 percent). As table 6.4 shows, before any Chinese price response, 2010 Chinese auto prices expressed in dollars would have been somewhat higher than the prices then prevailing in the other three countries. In our thought experiment, if China both liberalized its auto policies and allowed the exchange rate to appreciate, Chinese auto prices expressed in renminbi would eventually drop by 7 percent on average. Not only would Chinese consumers benefit but also China would soon become a major exporter of assembled autos and auto parts, as Chinese auto firms would be forced to increase their productivity.

---

11. Cline and Williamson (2010, 2) define the FEER as "an exchange rate that is expected to be indefinitely sustainable on the basis of existing policies. It should therefore be one that is expected to generate a current account surplus or deficit that matches the country's underlying capital flow over the cycle, assuming that the country is pursuing internal balance as well as it can and that it is not restricting trade for balance-of-payments reasons."

Table 6.5   Market and thought experiment Chinese retail car prices in 2010 (Chinese renminbi)

Model	Exchange rate[a]	Low	High	Average
Toyota Yaris	Market	87,000	125,000	106,000
	PIIE thought experiment	81,119	116,550	98,834
Ford Focus	Market	104,800	148,800	126,799
	PIIE thought experiment	97,716	138,741	118,227
VW Passat	Market	218,800	310,800	264,800
	PIIE thought experiment	204,009	289,790	246,900
Mercedes Benz E-Class	Market	465,000	710,000	587,500
	PIIE thought experiment	433,566	662,004	547,785

a. The Peterson Institute for International Economics (PIIE) thought experiment assumes that Chinese auto prices drop 7 percent in the wake of open competition in the auto sector and appreciation of the renminbi by 14 percent.

Sources: Gasgoo, Global Auto Sources, "Analysis: Car Price Comparison between China and the Rest of the World," http://autonews.gasgoo.com/AutoNews/Autobiz_print.aspx?id=1019860 (accessed on June 15, 2012); market exchange rate from World Bank, *World Development Indicators* database, http://data.worldbank.org/indicator; fundamental equilibrium exchange rate (FEER) data from Cline and Williamson (2010).

Effect of Trade Barriers on Productivity

LCRs and related barriers have stifled productivity in the Chinese auto industry. To compare productivity levels, we estimate how many cars the average worker produces in a year (total number of cars produced in the year divided by the labor force in the industry). Chinese productivity in 2007 was about four automobiles per worker—roughly the level of Japan in 1965.[12] In 2011, US productivity was about 13 automobiles a year and Japanese productivity about 11.[13] China's productivity thus appears to be about one-third that of the United States or Japan.

One of the biggest differences between Chinese assembly plants and plants in Japan and the United States is the extent of automation. To take advantage of relatively cheap labor, Chinese assembly plants are fairly labor intensive. The Nissan Kyushu plant uses about 430 robots for welding, and about 92 percent of the assembly process has been automated. By contrast, the

---

12. Shinichi Seki, "China's Auto Industry Seeking to Adjust for Environment," *Asia Monthly*, August 1, 2011 (in Japanese), www.jri.co.jp/page.jsp?id=20007 (accessed on August 6, 2012).

13. These calculations were made by the authors. Labor data are from the Bureau of Labor Statistics for the United States and METI Industrial Statistics Analysis for Japan. The lower productivity measured for Japan probably reflects less reliance by Japan on imported auto parts.

Shanghai VW Passat plant has just 63 welding robots, and only 25 percent of the assembly process is automated.[14]

The productivity of assembly plants strongly correlates with their size. According to Shinichi Seki, an expert on the Chinese economy at the Japan Research Institute, when a plant increases the annual number of cars produced from 100,000 to 200,000, the cost per unit decreases by about 8 percent; when annual production increases from 200,000 to 300,000, the cost per unit decreases by another 11 percent. Thus, if China reformed its trade and investment barriers and assembly plants consolidated to larger scale, the productivity of the industry could increase substantially.

Alternatives to LCRs

In the decade since China acceded to the WTO, its automobile industry has undergone massive expansion. Foreign auto firms, which aggressively entered the Chinese market through joint ventures, have been an important factor. In 2011, foreign joint venture automakers produced about 58 percent of all automobiles made in China. China has created a first-class automotive industry that ably serves domestic buyers. The logical next step for China is to sell autos abroad in volume.

All in all, it is fair to say that China's auto policy has accomplished its mission. But could China have achieved its current status as the world's largest auto producer with a different array of policies? Before China entered the WTO, it imposed tariffs of 52 percent on assembled auto imports and 15 to 46 percent on auto parts. In the process of accession, it lowered its tariffs to 25 percent on assembled automobiles and 10 percent on auto parts. Around the same time, LCR policies shifted from explicit to implicit measures. In retrospect, it would have been more transparent if China had initially retained its preaccession tariff levels, phasing them down over 15 years, while abolishing formal and informal LCRs and opening the procurement practices of auto SOEs. It cannot be stated with confidence that an array of policies along these lines would have led to a better outcome. However, the suggested array would have enabled the authorities to better evaluate the costs and benefits of their auto promotion policies.

Our thought experiment suggests that Chinese auto prices may be 7 percent higher today than they would be with reformed policies and an appreciated exchange rate. Productivity in China's automobile assembly industry is about one-third of US and Japanese levels. The time may have come to phase out the array of informal LCR policies and preferential SOE procurement practices. The potential gains to China and its trading partners from two-way specialization in autos and parts could be substantial.

---

14. Seki, "China's Auto Industry Seeking to Adjust for Environment."

7

Solar Cells and Modules in India

Most G-20 countries subsidize renewable energy in support of policies related to climate change, the environment, and energy security. The official goals of India's solar subsidy program are set out in a 2009 statement by the Ministry of Natural Resources and Environment describing the Jawaharlal Nehru National Solar Mission (JNNSM) (Government of India 2009). The program seeks to promote ecologically sustainable growth and energy security; empower people through decentralized energy generation, especially in rural areas; and establish India as a global leader in solar energy. India's solar policies aim to increase installed capacity, reduce costs, establish India as a manufacturing hub, and spur research and development. Embedded in these goals is India's effort to become a world leader in the rapidly evolving solar cell industry.

Through local content requirements (LCRs) and other policies, India may become a low-cost producer of solar cells. The United States is concerned that India is violating its national treatment obligation under the General Agreement on Tariffs and Trade (GATT) Article III and has asked for consultations under World Trade Organization (WTO) auspices.[1]

To achieve solar capacity and cost targets, the JNNSM auctions power purchase agreements to solar developers at a premium over the cost of coal-fired electricity. To ensure that the installation of capacity creates domestic

This chapter was written by Meera Fickling, former research analyst at the Peterson Institute, now a graduate student at Duke University.

1. "U.S. Seeks WTO Consultations with India over Solar LCRs, Subsidies," *Inside US Trade*, February 7, 2013, www.insidetrade.com (accessed on May 15, 2013).

Figure 7.1   Solar photovoltaic value chain (crystalline silicon)

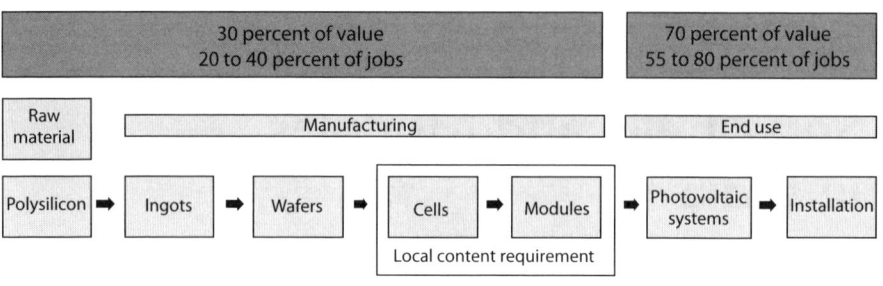

Source: Value added and jobs figures are from the Natural Resources Defense Council (NRDC 2012).

solar manufacturing, the program includes an LCR: developers must use cells and modules manufactured in India. Cells and modules are the main building blocks of solar photovoltaic (PV) systems, which are used to generate electricity (figure 7.1). However, the LCR requirement makes an exception for solar PV developers using thin film technologies, which may be imported. Accordingly, the vast majority of solar developers in India use imported thin film modules, which are less expensive than domestically produced modules.

The LCR seems to have substantially distorted the Indian module market. Globally, only 11 percent of PV deployment is in thin film; 89 percent is in crystalline silicon (CSi), the dominant technology.[2] In contrast, more than 70 percent of Indian PV capacity subsidized through the latest batch of JNNSM auctions was imported thin film (Bridge to India 2012).

The LCR has thus failed to accomplish its goal. By shifting market share from CSi to thin film, it has slightly increased the cost of PV systems, without creating very much domestic manufacturing. Absent the LCR, developers would have the option of using imported CSi modules, the price of which has plummeted over the past three years. Instead, if they wish to import, they must use thin film, which, despite low spot prices, adds costs because of its low efficiency. The LCR has spurred only modest growth in domestic modules, which we estimate capture 3 to 7 percent more market share than they would have without the LCR.

A main reason for reliance on imported thin film is that Indian manufacturers have so far failed to keep up with the demand from Indian solar developers for inexpensive modules. The lack of manufacturing competitiveness will likely worsen as global prices fall further; continuation of the LCR policy could hamper India's ability to meet its deployment targets for solar capacity. India needs better policies to ensure robust domestic solar manufacturing and to ensure the viability of its goals for solar electricity development.

---

2. M. J. Shiao, "Thin Film Manufacturing Prospects in the Sub-Dollar-Per-Watt Market," *Greentech Solar,* June 21, 2012, www.greentechmedia.com/articles/read/thin-film-manufacturing-prospects-in-the-sub-dollar-per-watt-market (accessed on November 24, 2012).

Demand for Energy in India

Energy security and expansion of energy access to the rural poor are primary motivators for India's solar program. Despite a rapidly growing economy, India's electricity infrastructure remains woefully inadequate: 300 million people continue to lack power. Energy supplies from existing resources have failed to keep up with rising demand for electricity. As a result, India suffered the worst blackout in its history in the summer of 2012. Part of the planned remedy is to establish India as a leader in solar energy manufacturing and deployment.

Although the high cost of solar power has prevented widespread commercial deployment to date, the industry is rapidly growing in many countries, thanks to generous government incentives. Feed-in tariffs for solar power are now available in about 50 countries, along with capital subsidies, production tax credits, and other incentives (Baziliana et al. 2012).

The International Energy Agency projects explosive growth (albeit from a very low base) in solar energy and other renewables over the next two decades (IEA 2012). Solar PV generation provided 32 terawatt hours of electricity globally in 2010 (table 7.1). If current policies are extended, this number will grow by a factor of almost 9 by the end of the decade and by a factor of 16 by 2035. With more aggressive policies in place, global solar PV generation could grow by a factor of 10 by the end of the decade and by a factor of 26 by 2035. Projections for concentrated solar power are even more impressive, with output growing 20-fold over the next decade and 70-fold by 2035 under current policies.[3]

Despite robust growth rates, solar power will provide only a modest percentage of renewable generation and total electricity generation over the coming decades. In total, solar power provided only 0.8 percent of renewable electricity generation and 0.2 percent of total global electricity generation in 2010 (table 7.2). Under current policies, it is expected to provide only 6.9 percent of renewable generation and 1.7 percent of total electricity generation in 2035.

Subsidies to the Solar Industry

Subsidies such as those provided by India's JNNSM are the single-largest driver of the growth in the solar industry. Almost 100 percent of expected solar PV generation over the coming decades will be subsidized (figure 7.2). Unlike biomass, wind, and hydro, solar power is not expected to gain a market foothold without subsidies.

The global solar industry receives a disproportionate amount of subsidies given its market share. In 2011, solar received $25 billion, more than any other form of renewable electricity (figure 7.3). This figure represented almost 30 percent of total global subsidies for renewable energy and nearly 40 percent of total global subsidies for renewable electricity. Though solar may not continue

---

3. These projections are subject to some uncertainty, as solar power is dependent on subsidies; if countries permanently remove or reduce subsidies because of worsening fiscal crises, the growth of solar power could stall.

Table 7.1 Renewable electricity generation by source in terawatt hours

Energy type	2010	New policies		Current policies	
		2020	2035	2020	2035
Solar photovoltaic	32	332	846	282	524
Concentrated solar power	2	50	278	39	141
Bioenergy	331	696	1,487	668	1,212
Hydro	3,431	4,513	5,677	4,390	5,350
Wind	342	1,272	2,681	1,148	2,151
Geothermal	68	131	315	118	217
Marine	1	5	57	3	32
Total from renewables	4,206	6,999	11,342	6,648	9,627

Source: World Energy Outlook 2012 © OECD/IEA, 2012, table 7.1, page 215, as modified by authors, www.worldenergyoutlook.org/media/weowebsite/2012/WEO2012_Renewables.pdf.

to receive such an outsize share of subsidies, funding will likely increase in absolute terms. The IEA (2012) expects solar subsidies to peak at $77 billion in 2027, before falling to $58 billion in 2035.

Most G-20 countries offer some form of subsidy for renewables, especially in the wake of the global recession. These subsidies apply largely to the installation of solar capacity and the generation of solar electricity rather than to the manufacture of components. Electricity is not widely traded across international borders, and subsidies limited to electricity generation itself are less likely to face WTO challenge. However, several subsidies, including India's JNNSM, aim to tie subsidies for the final product to the creation of a domestic manufacturing sector for intermediate components such as cells and modules.

LCRs are significant because solar PV systems are largely undifferentiated goods with low transportation costs. Although various technologies are available, they are substitutes for one another. PV systems compete primarily on the basis of cost; economies of scale are therefore crucial to maintaining market share (Platzer 2012). LCRs can help nascent domestic solar industries achieve economies of scale.

From India's perspective, LCRs are necessary to establish a manufacturing capacity in renewables; some would also argue that domestic manufacturing is necessary for energy security (for an example of this argument, see Jha 2011). Before the JNNSM, the Indian solar manufacturing sector was very small and largely dependent on export markets. Manufacturers exported 70 percent of cells and 80 percent of modules to Europe, the United States, Japan, and Australia (Jha 2011).

Barriers to Competitiveness

Several barriers prevent the Indian solar manufacturing sector from being competitive in international markets (Johnson 2013). First, financing is difficult, because Indian banks continue to perceive "significant risks" in solar

Table 7.2 Renewable electricity generation by source in percent

Energy type	2010		New policies 2020		New policies 2035		Current policies 2020		Current policies 2035	
	Percent of total renewable generation	Percent of total electricity generation	Percent of total renewable generation	Percent of total electricity generation	Percent of total renewable generation	Percent of total electricity generation	Percent of total renewable generation	Percent of total electricity generation	Percent of total renewable generation	Percent of total electricity generation
Solar photovoltaic	0.8	0.2	4.7	1.2	7.5	2.3	4.2	1.0	5.4	1.0
Concentrated solar power	0	0	0.7	0.2	2.5	0.8	0.6	0.1	1.5	0.1
Bioenergy	7.9	1.6	9.9	2.5	13.1	4.1	10.0	2.3	12.6	2.3
Hydro	81.6	16.3	64.5	16.1	50.1	15.5	66.0	15.2	55.6	15.2
Wind	8.1	1.6	18.2	4.5	23.6	7.3	17.3	4.0	22.3	4.0
Geothermal	1.6	0.3	1.9	0.5	2.8	0.9	1.8	0.4	2.3	0.4
Marine	0	0	0.1	0	0.5	0.2	0	0	0.3	0
Total from renewable sources	100.0	20.0	100.0	25.0	100.0	31.0	100.0	23.0	100.0	23.0

Source: World Energy Outlook 2012 © OECD/IEA, 2012, table 7.2, page 216, as modified by authors, www.worldenergyoutlook.org/media/weowebsite/2012/WEO2012_Renewables.pdf.

Figure 7.2　Subsidized and unsubsidized generation by source, 2011–35

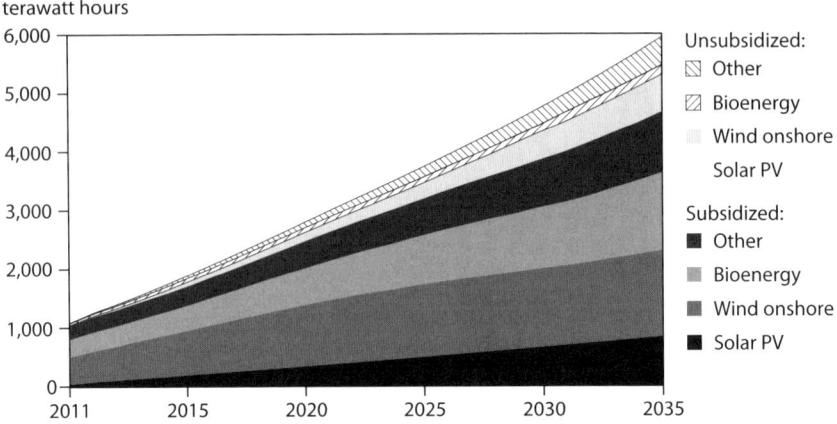

terawatt hours

PV = photovoltaic

Note: Other includes concentrating solar power, geothermal, marine energy, small hydro, and wind offshore.

Source: World Energy Outlook 2012 © OECD/IEA 2012, figure 7.11, page 235, as modified by authors, www.worldenergyoutlook.org/media/weowebsite/2012/WEO2012_Renewables.pdf.

Figure 7.3　Projected renewable energy subsidies by source, 2007–35

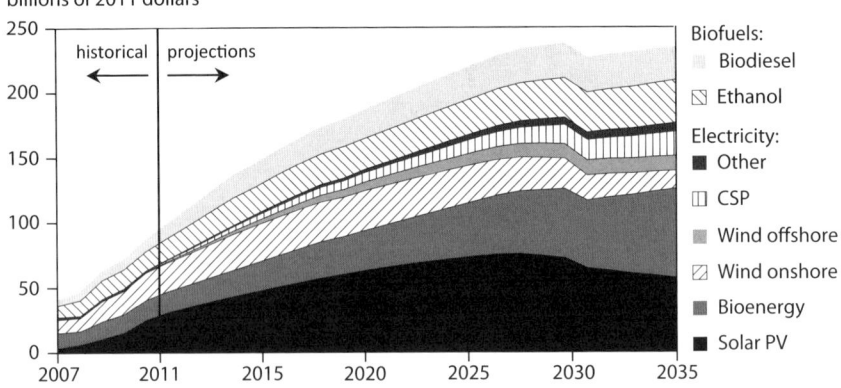

billions of 2011 dollars

CSP = concentrating solar power; PV = photovoltaic

Note: Other includes geothermal, marine, and small hydro.

Source: World Energy Outlook 2012 © OECD/IEA 2012, figure 7.10, page 234, as modified by authors, www.worldenergyoutlook.org/media/weowebsite/2012/WEO2012_Renewables.pdf.

energy, and international lenders doubt that projects will be completed, especially at low bid prices. There is also some uncertainty as to whether India will maintain its solar incentives over time (Jha 2011).

Second, Indian manufacturers lack economies of scale. Internationally, module manufacturing lines usually produce 75 megawatts (MW) of capacity per line. In contrast, Indian lines average about 10 to 20 MW. As a result, Indian firms not only are operating below the optimum size but also have little bargaining power for raw material purchases. Moreover, as Debasish Paul Choudhury, president of SEMI India, observes, Indian firms are limited to cell and module manufacturing.[4] Vertical integration is nearly absent: India lacks upstream production of silicon, wafers, and materials and downstream production of inverters and storage. Indigenous thin film producers are also notably missing, despite the technology's dominance in Indian solar electricity production downstream. Fragmentation of production leads to higher costs.

Third, Indian manufacturers do not employ cutting-edge technology. They lag far behind competitors in China, Taiwan, and Malaysia. Firms require additional training, manpower, and skilled technical workers. Indian manufacturing in general is also hampered by a lack of basic infrastructure (power, water, and roads).

Fourth, Indian manufacturers argue that they are disadvantaged by the subsidies offered by other countries.[5] In addition to LCRs in China, Brazil, and South Africa, export financing can play a significant role. The US Export-Import Bank offers US PV exporters such as First Solar an interest rate of 9 percent as opposed to the 13 percent rate offered locally to Indian manufacturers.[6]

By protecting indigenous firms, the LCR arguably gives Indian firms space to overcome these obstacles. Access to a growing domestic market shielded from international competition may in time enable domestic firms to develop economies of scale and technological capacity. As domestic solar firms become more established, their finance costs may also decrease. In the meantime, the downside to LCRs is higher costs for PV modules, which are passed on to power consumers.

Overview of the Jawaharlal Nehru National Solar Mission

The goal of the JNNSM is to install 20 gigawatts (GW) of solar capacity in India by 2022, in three phases:

- Phase 1, 2010–13 (11th Plan): 1,000 MW by the end of 2013
- Phase 2, 2013–17 (12th Plan): additional 3,000 MW by end of 2017
- Phase 3, 2017–22 (13th Plan): additional 16,000 MW by end of 2022

---

4. "In Conversation: Debasish Paul Choudhury," *Energy Next,* August 2011, www.pvgroup.org/sites/pvgroup.org/files/In_Conversation_Debasish_Paul_Choudhury%5B1%5D.pdf (accessed on November 18, 2012).

5. See, for example, the article by the Centre for Science and Environment, an Indian think tank, "The US Is Using Climate Finance to Kill the Indian Solar Industry," August 17, 2012, www.cseindia.org/content/us-using-climate-finance-kill-indian-solar-panel-industry-cse (accessed on November 24, 2012).

6. Natalie Obiko Pearson, "India May Join US–China Trade Spat to Prevent Solar Disaster," *Bloomberg Businessweek,* December 19, 2011, www.businessweek.com/news/2011-12-24/india-may-join-u-s-china-trade-spat-to-prevent-solar-disaster-.html (accessed on November 24, 2012).

The 2003 Electricity Act calls on state electricity regulatory commissions to establish minimum purchase requirements for renewable energy, starting at 0.25 percent of total procurement in Phase 1 and increasing to 3 percent by the end of Phase 3 (Gangania 2012). The JNNSM adds a reverse auction scheme to the mix. During each auction period, or batch, the government agrees to support a specified amount of solar generation. Firms submit bids specifying the lowest price at which they are willing to generate. The government awards power purchase agreements to the lowest bidders. This electricity is bundled with conventional generation and sold to utilities. Because the national government is the main procurer of thermal generation in India, it has sufficient market power to force the utilities to buy the bundles at a slight premium.[7]

Two auctions have taken place so far under this system. Batch I pledged government support to 140 MW of solar PV capacity and 470 MW of concentrated solar power. Batch II supported about 300 MW of PV capacity. As of April 2013, 130 MW of the 140 MW of capacity auctioned during Batch I had been commissioned (Government of India 2012).

The JNNSM has spawned similar state-level policies in about 13 different states, which are either developing policies or have put them into place. Of these, Gujarat, Karnataka, and Rajasthan have already accepted more than 200 MW each in bids.[8]

Overall, national and state policies have spurred rapid growth in solar electricity. Indian solar capacity ballooned from 18 MW in 2010 to 507 MW in March 2012. The JNNSM and other central government schemes directly commissioned 203 MW of this capacity, and an additional 800 MW of capacity is expected to come on line by 2013 as a direct result of the JNNSM auctions (NRDC 2012).

The JNNSM required CSi-based solar PV projects selected during Batch I (FY2010–11) to use modules manufactured in India. During Batch II (FY2011–12), all projects were required to use cells and modules manufactured in India, with the exception of thin film modules and concentrator PV cells, which could be sourced anywhere (Government of India 2011). For concentrated solar power projects, 30 percent of equipment had to be sourced from India.

There are indications that the LCR will be continued and expanded after Phase I. Officials have explored the possibility of including inverters in the requirement.[9] The requirement will likely become more technology neutral in the future by prohibiting (or limiting) imports of thin film in addition to CSi.[10]

---

7. Phone conversation with Arunabha Ghosh, CEO of the Council on Energy, Environment, and Water, New Delhi, India, October 15, 2012.

8. Raj Prabhu, "Project Due Dates Pass—How Many Were Successfully Completed? Indian Solar Market Update—Fourth Quarter 2011," Mercom Capital Group, 2012, www.mercomcapital.com/india-its-time-for-results (accessed on November 24, 2012).

9. Pearson, "India May Join US-China Trade Spat to Prevent Solar Disaster."

10. Phone conversation with Arunabha Ghosh, CEO of the Council on Energy, Environment, and Water, New Delhi, India, October 15, 2012.

Effects of LCRs

Ample evidence indicates that the LCR has distorted the cell and module market in India. The strongest indicator is the distribution of CSi versus thin film modules in JNNSM projects. Under the JNNSM, thin film modules may be imported, whereas CSi modules must be produced domestically. More than 70 percent of Indian PV capacity is in imported thin film (Bridge to India 2012). In contrast, about 11 percent of global PV deployment is in thin film and 89 percent is in CSi.[11] Although thin film modules are a bit less expensive, developers usually prefer CSi modules because they attain much higher efficiencies (12 to 24 percent, compared with thin film efficiencies of 4 to 12 percent).[12] In addition, very low polysilicon prices are allowing CSi modules to close the price gap with thin film.

Three main explanations have been offered for the disparity in usage of thin film between India and global norms.[13] The first is that thin film panels perform better in hot climates. However, the climate alone cannot explain thin film's enormous market share in India, as the efficiency advantage it provides is not enough to erase the initial efficiency gap between thin film and CSi.[14] Studies have shown that hot temperatures have only a modest effect on panel efficiency relative to baseline (Huld et al. 2009). Moreover, India is not the only tropical country with a large PV market—Brazil is also growing its solar industry. Yet India is the only major PV market in the world where thin film dominates.[15]

The second explanation is low-cost US Export-Import (Ex-Im) Bank finance for US thin film exporters. The Ex-Im Bank lent $248 million in 2010 and 2011 to Indian firms that purchased modules from Arizona-based First Solar and the now bankrupt Abound Solar. So far, the Ex-Im Bank has approved seven projects for loans.[16] The majority of these projects are small, 20 MW or less; together they total 130 MW. These loans, among others issued by foreign lenders, make foreign modules more attractive, given high domestic interest rates for solar

---

11. Shiao, "Thin Film Manufacturing Prospects in the Sub-Dollar-Per-Watt Market."

12. "Thin Film vs. Crystalline Solar Panels," *CivicSolar*, November 16, 2010, www.civicsolar. com/resource/thin-film-vs-crystalline-silicon-pv-modules (accessed on November 24, 2012); Mat Dirjish, "What's the Difference between Thin Film and Crystalline Silicon Solar Panels?" *Electronic Design*, May 16, 2012, http://electronicdesign.com/article/components/whats-difference-thinfilm-crystallinesilicon-solar-panels-73937 (accessed on November 24, 2012).

13. Jason Deign, "What Is behind India's Love Affair with Thin Film?" *PV Insider*, February 14, 2012, http://news.pv-insider.com/thin-film-pv/what-behind-india%E2%80%99s-love-affair-thin-film (accessed on November 24, 2012).

14. Phone conversation with Arunabha Ghosh, CEO of the Council on Energy, Environment, and Water, New Delhi, India, October 15, 2012.

15. Deign, "What Is behind India's Love Affair with Thin Film?"

16. The loan recipients are Azure Power Rajasthan (5 MW, 2011); Punj Lloyd (5 MW, 2011); Tatith Energies (5 MW, 2011); Dalmia (10 MW, 2011); ACME (15 MW, 2011); Dahanu Solar Power (40 MW, 2011); Mahindra Surya Prakash (20 MW and 10 MW, 2012); and Solar Field Energy Two (20 MW, 2012).

projects. Without the LCR, however, the US Ex-Im Bank funding might have been used to support purchases from US CSi-based module manufacturers instead of thin film, and the Export-Import Bank of China, which dominates the market for CSi, might have become more involved in India. The role of Ex-Im Bank lending thus helps explain the large market share of US exporters in the Indian market but does not explain thin film's disproportionate share.

The third explanation for this distortion is the LCR. Given current market shares in India, the LCR appears to have done more to encourage thin film module production abroad than to promote module manufacturing at home. The question is what effect this encouragement has had on prices and the feasibility of meeting India's goals for solar electricity production.

The best information available about the price of solar electricity in India comes from JNNSM bid data, which are published online (table 7.3). India's feed-in tariff started at $0.37 per kilowatt hour (kWh), but the first round of bidding posted prices of $0.22 to $0.26. Projects have achieved high commissioning rates at these prices, suggesting that they accurately represent the cost of solar power.[17] As previously mentioned, of the 140 MW of solar PV capacity auctioned during Batch I of Phase I, 130 MW have been commissioned to date, according to the website of the Ministry of New and Renewable Energy (Government of India 2012).

The subsequent bidding round achieved even more dramatic price reductions. Batch II bids ranged from $0.15 and $0.19 per kWh. The Central Electricity Regulatory Commission (CERC) predicts that Phase II bids will be even lower ($0.10 to $0.11 per kWh). There was some uncertainty as to whether developers could really deliver at these low prices.[18] But latest figures show that of the 340 MW of solar capacity auctioned during Batch II of Phase I, 300 MW have been commissioned as of May 2013 (Government of India 2013).

It is difficult to determine an "international" or "world" price for solar electricity delivered to homes and businesses, because electricity is generally produced entirely within national borders and every country provides different incentives for solar electricity production. Because solar power is seldom viable without subsidies, solar electricity markets in all countries are somewhat distorted. Nevertheless, it is fair to say that the solar electricity prices achieved through Batch I of India's reverse auction mechanism are comparable to prices that are seen internationally, and prices in Batch II are, if

---

17. Prices achieved through reverse auction subsidies frequently lowball the true cost of production, as suggested by the fact that reverse auction subsidy winners often have trouble delivering. Firms that are overoptimistic about how much prices will fall by the commissioning deadline might bid low to win the contract, then fail to deliver. Reverse auction subsidies in California and the United Kingdom in the 1990s and early 2000s achieved commissioning rates of only 25 to 40 percent.

18. A report by CRISIL Research casts doubt on developers' ability to deliver at prices under Rs. 9 ($0.17) per kWh. See "Solar Power Bids below Rs. 9 per Unit Risky," press release, June 7, 2012, http://crisil.com/Ratings/Brochureware/News/CRISIL%20Research_pr_Solar_07Jun2012.pdf?cn=null.

Table 7.3 Summary of JNNSM auction results

Policy	Year	Type	Bids (US dollars per kilowatt hour)			
			Feed-in tariff/starting	Highest	Average	Lowest
JNNSM – Migration	2009–10	Feed-in tariff	0.37	n.a.	n.a.	n.a.
JNNSM – Batch I	2010–11	Bidding	0.37	0.26	0.25	0.22
JNNSM – Batch II	2011–12	Bidding	0.31	0.19	0.18	0.15
CERC (proposed tariff), phase II	2013–14	Bidding	0.18	0.12	0.11	0.1

JNNSM = Jawaharlal Nehru National Solar Mission; CERC = Central Electricity Regulatory Commission
n.a. = not applicable.

Note: Rupees are converted to US dollars using an exchange rate of 49 rupees to 1 dollar.

Source: Raj Prabhu, "The Next Phase—Indian Solar Market Update for 3rd Quarter 2012," Mercom Capital Group, www.mercomcapital.com/indian-solar-market-update-3rd-quarter-2012 (accessed on December 21, 2012).

anything, on the low end of solar prices in other countries. The feed-in tariff in Germany, by comparison, is $0.23 per kWh, although Germany has installed much more solar electricity (25,000 MW as of 2011).[19] The US Energy Information Administration predicts that solar electricity costs in the United States will range from $0.11 to $0.24 per kWh by 2017 (EIA 2012a).

Taking module efficiency into account, however, Indian developers might be paying a premium for PV systems. Thin film modules have historically been slightly less expensive on a per watt basis, but CSi modules have nearly closed the price gap over the past year, and forecasters expect the price of CSi modules to continue to decline (figure 7.4).

If thin film modules are cheaper than CSi on a per watt basis, then why has CSi captured the lion's share of the global PV market? Part of the answer is that thin film's lower efficiency imposes a so-called balance of system penalty on developers. The "balance of system" refers to nonmodule system costs, such as land, installation, and inverters (which change a direct current [DC] to an alternating current [AC]). These costs fall with rising efficiency. Even with a lower module price per kWh, thin film modules may impose a higher overall cost when their lower efficiency is taken into account. The balance of system penalty reflects how much cheaper thin film modules must be than CSi modules in order to be competitive in the global market.

According to analysis by Eric Wesoff and M. J. Shiao, the balance of system penalty for thin film panels varies by the type used: $0.12 per watt for CIGS, $0.18 per watt for CdTe, and up to $0.91 per watt for a-Si panels.[20] Figure 7.5 imposes a $0.21 balance of system penalty on the thin film spot price and a weighted average of penalties on the three types. With this balance of system penalty, the effective thin film spot price approached the CSi spot price at the end of 2010, as thin film's share plummeted, exceeding the price of CSi in late 2011.

Subtropical countries such as India have an advantage when it comes to thin film, however, because thin film is more efficient in hot weather. Moreover, it performs better in low-light conditions. Adjusting for both factors reduces the balance of system penalty to $0.12 per watt, a weighted average of balance of system penalties calculated by Wesoff and Shiao for hot and humid climates (figure 7.6).[21] Thin film maintains a small price advantage until 2012, when the spot price of CSi falls below that of thin film.

Adjusted for efficiency and performance, thin film currently costs about $0.08 per watt more than CSi, on average. The difference implies that solar developers importing thin film panels in 2012—that is, the majority of developers

---

19. Prabhu, "Project Due Dates Pass—How Many Were Successfully Completed?"

20. The acronyms refer to the semiconductor used in thin film PV technologies: CIGS stands for copper indium gallium selenide, CdTe stands for cadmium telluride, and a-Si refers to amorphous silicon. See Eric Wesoff and M. J. Shiao, "Is Thin Film Solar Dead?" *Greentech Media*, April 27, 2012, www.greentechmedia.com/articles/read/Slide-Show-Is-Thin-Film-Solar-Dead (accessed on December 5, 2012).

21. Wesoff and Shiao, "Is Thin Film Solar Dead?"

Figure 7.4 Crystalline silicon versus thin film module spot prices, 2010–12

dollars per watt

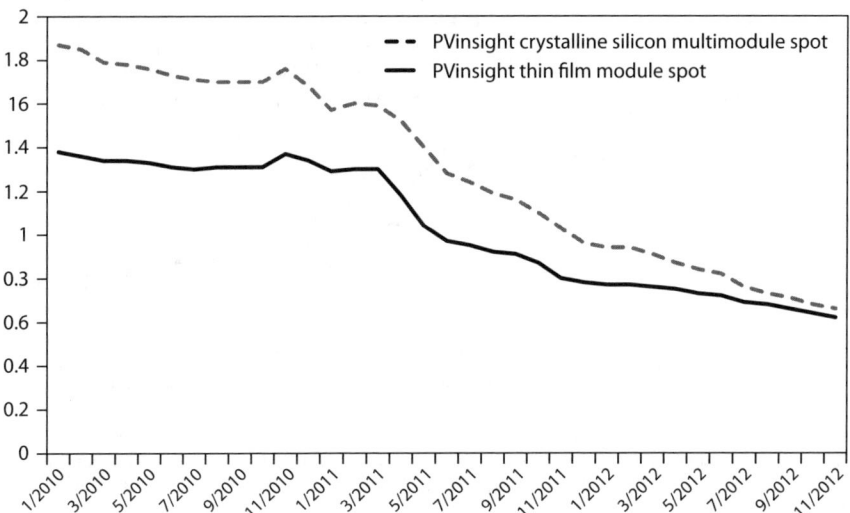

Source: Bloomberg New Energy Finance, 2012, accessed through the Bloomberg Professional database, Perkins Library, Duke University.

Figure 7.5 Crystalline silicon versus thin film module spot prices, adjusted for balance of system penalty, 2010–12

dollars per watt

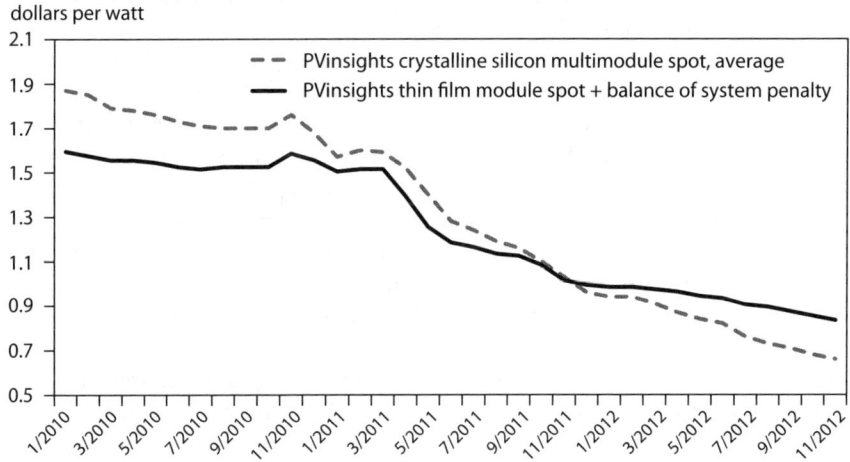

Source: Authors' calculations based on data from Eric Wesoff and M. J. Shiao, "Is Thin Film Solar Dead?" Greentech Media, April 27, 2012, www.greentechmedia.com/articles/read/Slide-Show-Is-Thin-Film-Solar-Dead (accessed on December 5, 2012); Bloomberg New Energy Finance, 2012, accessed through the Bloomberg Professional database, Perkins Library, Duke University.

Figure 7.6   Crystalline silicon versus thin film module spot prices, adjusted for balance of system penalty and climate, 2010–12

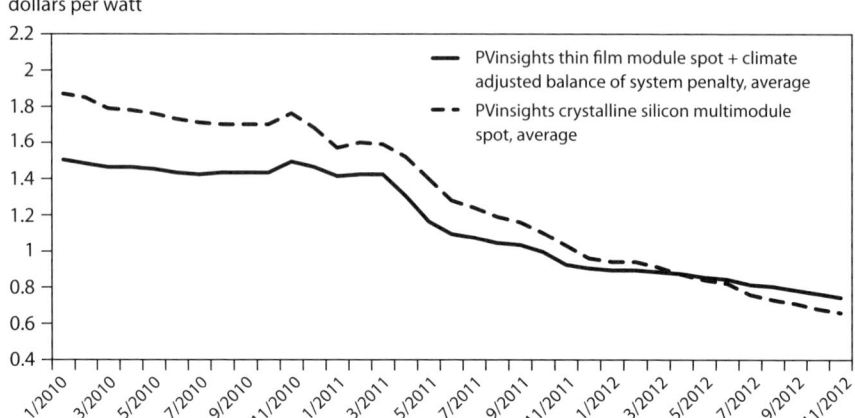

Source: Authors' calculations based on data from Eric Wesoff and M. J. Shiao, "Is Thin Film Solar Dead?" *Greentech Media*, April 27, 2012, www.greentechmedia.com/articles/read/Slide-Show-Is-Thin-Film-Solar-Dead (accessed on December 5, 2012); Bloomberg New Energy Finance, 2012, accessed through the Bloomberg Professional database, Perkins Library, Duke University.

in India—are effectively paying up to 12 percent more for solar PV modules than they would without the LCR. Assuming a total system cost of $2.50 to $3.00 per watt, developers are paying up to 3 percent more for PV systems than they would without the LCR.

The LCR is likely responsible for some of the growth in India's domestic CSi manufacturing: Assuming that today's prices do not change, domestic manufacturing of PV modules is at most 12 percent higher than it would be without the LCR.[22] Assuming a higher price elasticity of 2.7—the price elasticity of supply for renewable energy estimated by Erik Johnson (2011)—domestic manufacturing of PV modules might be up to 32 percent higher than it would be without the LCR. Because the market share of domestic panels is low to begin with, however, the increase does not correspond to a large change in absolute terms. The LCR has allowed domestic manufacturers to capture an additional 3 to 7 percent of the overall domestic solar market, given about a 30 percent share of domestic modules in Batch II.

There is some uncertainty surrounding these estimates. Although global average spot prices for CSi and thin film remain stable from week to week, there is about a $0.40 per watt spread between the highest and lowest quote offered in the market at any given time (figure 7.7).[23] If either thin film or CSi

---

22. A study of Chinese solar tariffs by the Brattle Group also uses 1 as a lower bound and 2.7 as an upper bound for the price elasticity of supply of PV modules (Berkman, Cameron, and Chang 2012).

23. Low quotes tend to be within $.010 per watt of the global average; the highest quotes offered tend to be about $0.30 per watt higher than the global average.

Figure 7.7 Crystalline silicon versus thin film module spot prices, adjusted for balance of system penalty and climate, with highest and lowest observed quotes, 2010–12

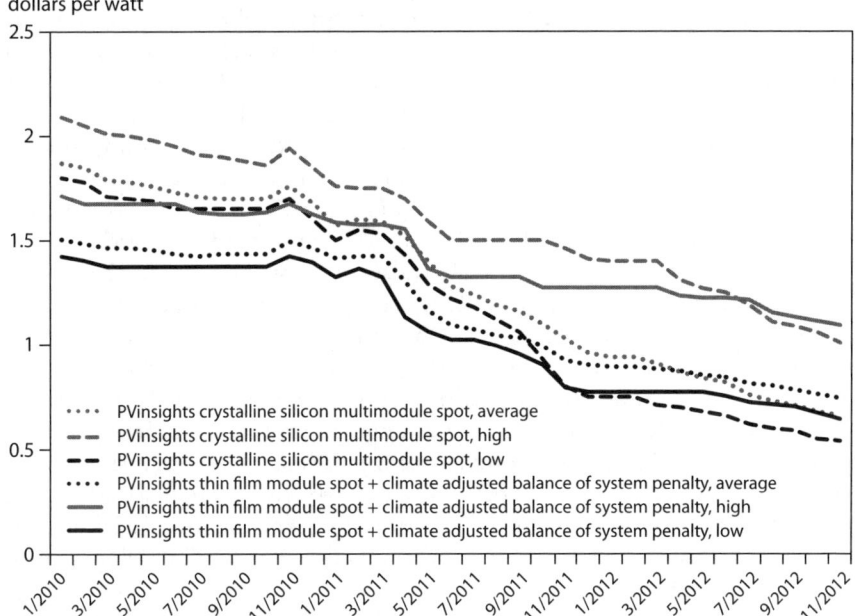

dollars per watt

···· PVinsights crystalline silicon multimodule spot, average
- - PVinsights crystalline silicon multimodule spot, high
- - PVinsights crystalline silicon multimodule spot, low
···· PVinsights thin film module spot + climate adjusted balance of system penalty, average
— PVinsights thin film module spot + climate adjusted balance of system penalty, high
— PVinsights thin film module spot + climate adjusted balance of system penalty, low

Source: Authors' calculations based on data from Eric Wesoff and M. J. Shiao, "Is Thin Film Solar Dead?" *Greentech Media,* April 27, 2012, www.greentechmedia.com/articles/read/Slide-Show-Is-Thin-Film-Solar-Dead (accessed on December 5, 2012); Bloomberg New Energy Finance, 2012, accessed through the Bloomberg Professional database, Perkins Library, Duke University.

prices in India fail to reflect global averages, and instead are skewed in one direction or another, our estimates could be off the mark.

Another issue to bear in mind is that prices are not static. As the market for PV modules consolidates, increasing market share is expected to go to low-cost Chinese manufacturers. The prices of CSi modules will likely fall further relative to thin film, leaving only a handful of thin film manufacturers standing.[24] As a result, the LCR will likely bite a little more in 2013 than in 2012, pushing prices up even further relative to a scenario without a LCR and encouraging additional domestic manufacturing. More than half of the solar PV capacity auctioned through the JNNSM (340 MW) was to have been commissioned in early 2013.[25]

24. Shyam Mehta, "PV Module Consolidation in 2013–2014: What to Expect," *Greentech Media,* October 18, 2012, www.greentechmedia.com/articles/read/pv-module-consolidation-in-2013-2014-what-to-expect (accessed on December 23, 2012).

25. Raj Prabhu, "The Next Phase—Indian Solar Market Update for 3rd Quarter 2012," Mercom Capital Group, www.mercomcapital.com/the-next-phase-indian-solar-market-update-for-3rd-quarter-2012 (accessed on December 21, 2012).

Alternatives to LCRs

Because it places no limit on imported thin film, the LCR has stimulated far less domestic manufacturing than the Indian government envisioned. Instead, it has mainly shifted the market from one imported technology to another. It has likely caused modest increases in the cost of PV systems in India, of up to $0.08 per watt—a 12 percent increase over the average global CSi module spot price and a 3 percent increase in the price of the whole PV system.

The LCR has also caused small increases in domestic manufacturing: Domestic module manufacturers have captured an estimated additional 3 to 7 percent of the domestic market as a result of the LCR. As the price of CSi falls further relative to thin film, these effects will increase going forward.

Although the current LCR likely causes modest increases in the cost of solar electricity relative to a no-LCR scenario, it should not keep India from meeting its solar deployment goals. However, the government is considering expanding the LCR to cover all technologies. Such a move could cause prices to increase more dramatically and might endanger those goals. Expanding the scope of LCRs will not solve the range of problems hindering India's solar manufacturing sector. Moreover, across the solar electricity value chain, manufacturing creates only 25 percent of jobs; the rest are in installation and sales (NRDC 2012). Even if the LCR creates domestic manufacturing jobs, it threatens far more jobs downstream if it impedes the overall development of solar installations.

Evidence suggests that the current LCR distorts the market for cells and modules without creating a robust domestic industry in return. India should look beyond its narrow focus on protecting domestic manufacturers of cells and modules through LCRs and instead work to create favorable conditions across the entire value chain for solar energy. If the United States launches a full-blown WTO complaint against Indian LCRs, the WTO Dispute Settlement Body is likely to find India in violation of its obligations, just as it did in the Canada wind turbines case.

Regardless of its policy toward LCRs, India should tackle the underlying causes of the lagging competitiveness of its solar manufacturers. Economies of scale in solar manufacturing are necessary but not sufficient. Manufacturers and developers need better financing options. The private sector in India seems unwilling to provide competitive financing on its own; government-subsidized financing such as loan guarantees could help domestic manufacturers succeed.[26] Joint ventures with foreign solar firms should be encouraged. Better infrastructure and training programs for domestic workers are also necessary.

---

26. An Asian Development Bank project is doing just this, offering to guarantee a maximum of $150 million in loans to Indian solar developers. See "India Solar Generation Guarantee Facility," www.adb.org/site/private-sector-financing/india-solar-generation-guarantee-facility (accessed on December 5, 2012).

8

Oil and Gas Industry in Nigeria

Nigeria's local content regime centers on procurement and employment by the oil and gas industry, which is controlled largely by foreign multinationals. The overt goal is to encourage the creation of a domestic oil and gas industry and to ensure the employment of Nigerian nationals. Because Nigeria is a developing country, and the oil and gas industry basically stands apart from the World Trade Organization (WTO) framework, there is no apparent conflict between the WTO rulebook and Nigeria's local content requirement (LCR) policies.

The Nigerian Oil and Gas Content Development Act explicitly states that "independent operators [namely, Nigerian firms] shall be given first consideration in the award of oil blocks, oil field licenses, oil lifting licenses and in all projects for which contract is to be awarded in the Nigerian oil and gas industry." The law also claims that "there shall be exclusive consideration to Nigerian indigenous service companies which demonstrate ownership of equipment, Nigerian personnel and capacity to execute such work." It states that a "Nigerian indigenous company . . . shall not be disqualified exclusively on the basis that it is not the lowest financial bidder, provided the value does not exceed the lowest bid price by 10 percent." This language implies that "exclusive consideration" in favor of a Nigerian company can be overcome by a sufficiently large difference in costs. In reality, the local Nigerian market simply does not offer many of the products and services needed to maintain and further develop Nigeria's oil and gas resources. Thus, in practice, the law creates an environment that encourages corruption—because of administrative ambiguities—with few, if any, gains to domestic firms. The estimated loss of government tax revenue, via decreased overall production, is substantial.

Human Development and Security Conditions in Nigeria

Despite—or perhaps because of—Nigeria's abundance of natural resources, its economic indicators are weak. The World Bank classifies Nigeria as a lower-middle-income country. More than half the country lives below the poverty line of less than $1.25 a day, and income is only $1,200 per capita. Only 43 percent of the rural population has easy access to water. The literacy rate is 65 percent, less than half the population goes beyond primary education, and even fewer students complete secondary education. Public expenditure on education is less than 0.5 percent of GDP.

The Niger Delta—the region richest in oil—is rudimentary and violent. The region faces constant pressure from militants, who siphon off oil, either directly through vandalism or indirectly through corruption. Vandalism seemed to have subsided after hitting a high in 2006, with more than 3,000 reported cases of broken pipelines. However, recent figures remain substantial: In 2011, 2,768 cases were reported, an increase of 224 percent over the previous year.[1] The government has taken steps to reduce violence, including by offering amnesty and cash for weapons; in 2009 it announced the Niger Delta Amnesty. Despite these efforts, Nigeria ranks 143rd on Transparency International's 2011 Corruption Perceptions Index, far down the list of 182 countries.[2]

Importance of the Industry and Role of Foreign Firms

The oil and gas industry plays a critical role in Nigeria's economy. Nigeria has estimated oil reserves of more than 36 billion barrels—the second largest in Africa after Libya. Average daily production of 2.45 million barrels makes it the largest oil producer in Africa.

The Nigerian National Petroleum Corporation (NNPC) claims that total crude oil and condensate production was 896 million barrels in 2010.[3] Less than 4 percent of this production (34 million barrels) was refined domestically; 96 percent (865 million barrels) was exported. Oil and gas exports represented 87 percent of total Nigerian exports by value; of this total, crude oil accounted for 70 percent, valued at $61 billion.[4] The United States was the largest destination market for Nigerian crude (38 percent of exports), fol-

---

1. Nigerian National Petroleum Corporation (NNPC), *2006 Annual Statistical Bulletin* and *2011 Annual Statistical Bulletin*, www.nnpcgroup.com/PublicRelations/OilandGasStatistics/Annual StatisticsBulletin/MonthlyPerformance.aspx.

2. Transparency International, Corruption Perceptions Index, http://cpi.transparency.org/cpi2011/results.

3. NNPC, *2010 Annual Statistical Bulletin*, www.nnpcgroup.com/PublicRelations/OilandGas Statistics/AnnualStatisticsBulletin/MonthlyPerformance.aspx.

4. Gas exports—classified under Harmonized System (HS) heading 2711—accounted for 5 percent of exports. Other noncrude exports (e.g., gasoline and kerosene)—classified under HS heading 2710—accounted for 11 percent of exports.

Table 8.1 Top destinations for Nigerian exports of crude oil, 2010

Country	Value (millions of US dollars)	Barrels (millions)	Share of exports (percent)
United States	23.2	313.2	38.0
India	6.9	110.3	11.3
Brazil	4.5	71.1	7.4
Netherlands	3.3	44.1	5.4
Equatorial Guinea	2.7	36.4	4.4
Canada	2.5	39.1	4.1
Spain	2.5	41.2	4.1
France	2.1	25.6	3.5
Italy	1.8	29.2	3.0
South Africa	1.6	28.6	2.6
World	60.9	738.8	—

Source: Barrels of oil data are from Nigerian National Petroleum Company, *2010 Annual Statistical Bulletin*, Table 7: Crude Oil Exports by Destination, www.nnpcgroup.com/Portals/0/Monthly%20 Performance/2010%20ASB%201st%20edition.pdf; trade value data are from World Bank, World Intergrated Trade Solution (WITS), http://wits.worldbank.org/wits.

lowed by India (11 percent), Brazil (7 percent), and the Netherlands (5 percent) (table 8.1).

Nigeria's oil earnings account for about 70 percent of government revenue, according to the International Monetary Fund (IMF 2013). Under the Nigerian constitution, all levels of government share in oil revenues. Revenues first flow into the Federation Account, where all revenues collected by the government are credited and allocated. From there, the first cut (13 percent) goes to oil-producing states as "derivation grants." The remaining 87 percent is split among the federal government (52.7 percent), the state government (26.7 percent), and local governments (20.6 percent).

The oil and gas industry includes joint venture companies, production-sharing companies, service contractors, and independents/sole risk firms. In 2010, joint venture companies (typically referred to as IOCs [international oil companies]) accounted for 83.9 percent of crude production, and production-sharing companies accounted for another 14.3 percent.

Foreign firms seeking to do business in Nigeria must establish themselves as either joint venture or production-sharing companies. Foreign ownership in both types is limited to 49 percent. The largest IOCs (measured by 2010 crude production) are ExxonMobil (28 percent), the Shell Petroleum Development Company (SPDC) (24 percent), and Chevron (16 percent). Independent/sole risk firms are solely domestic firms; they account for less than 2 percent of production (table 8.2).

The industry is regulated by the NNPC, which also plays an active role in the sector. For example, the NNPC is the majority shareholder (55 percent) in SPDC (Shell has a 30 percent stake).

Table 8.2   Breakdown of crude oil production in Nigeria by company type, 2010

Company	Number of wells	Annual barrels (millions)	Daily average (thousands of barrels)	Share of total (percent)
Joint ventures				
ExxonMobil	219	166	454	28
Shell Petroleum Development Company of Nigeria Ltd.	n.a.	143	391	24
Chevron	331	95	259	16
Total-Elf	143	51	141	9
Agip	211	41	114	7
Texaco	25	4	11	1
Pan-Ocean	12	3	8	0
Subtotal	941	503	1,378	84
Production-sharing				
Addax	90	30	83	5
Esso	10	56	153	9
Subtotal	100	86	235	14
Service				
Agip Energy and Natural Resources	6	2	5	0
Independent				
Nigerian National Petroleum Corporation	7	9	25	2
Total	1,054	600	1,643	100

n.a. = not available

Source: Nigerian National Petroleum Company, *2010 Annual Statistical Bulletin,* Table 3: Non-Fiscalized Crude Oil Production By Company, www.nnpcgroup.com/Portals/0/Monthly%20Performance/2010%20ASB%201st%20edition.pdf.

Nigeria's oil and gas industry depends on a mix of imports and services for its upstream, midstream, and downstream activities. According to Ugwushi Bellema Ihua, Chris Ajayi, and Kamdi Nnanna Eloji (2009), Nigeria spends about $8 billion annually to service the industry (this figure includes construction, engineering, machine fabrication, seismic studies, and other services). Some estimates suggest that this figure will rise to $15 billion in the next few years.

By value, in 2010, Nigeria's largest nonautomotive import at the 4-digit level of the Harmonized System (HS) was "taps, cocks, valves and similar appliances, for pipes boiler shells, tanks, vats or the like" (heading 8481)—essentially oil field supplies (table 8.3). More than half of these imports came from the United States. The next largest nonautomotive import categories were telephone equipment (8517) and projectors/monitors (8525). Imports of these products were dominated by the United States and China (table 8.4).

Table 8.3   Top Nigerian nonautomotive imports by value, 2010

HS heading	6-digit HS description	Value of imports (millions of US dollars)
100190	Wheat other than durum wheat; meslin	795
850410	Ballasts for discharge lamps/tubes	647
560391	Nonwovens, whether or not impregnated, coated, covered or laminated, of man-made filaments, weighing not more than 25 g/m2	593
401691	Floor coverings and mats of vulcanized rubber other than hard rubber	461
252329	Portlant cement (excluding white cement, whether or not artificially coloured), whether or not colored	451
848180	Taps, cocks, valves and similar appliances for pipes, boiler shells, tanks, vats or the like, including thermostatically controlled valves, not elsewhere specified in 84.81	428
30379	Fish (excluding 0303.71-0303.78), not elsewhere specified, frozen (excluding fillets or other meat of 03.04 or livers and roes)	415
100630	Semi-milled or wholly milled rice, whether or not polished or glazed	404
852872	Other color reception apparatus for television, whether or not incorporating radio-broadcast receivers, sound, or video recording or reproducing apparatus	394
690790	Unglazed ceramic flags and paving, hearth, or wall tiles (excluding 6907.10); unglazed ceramic mosaic cubes and the like, whether or not on a backing	378
390110	Polyethylene having a specific gravity of less than 0.95, in primary forms	376
271019	Petroleum oils and oils obtained from bituminous minerals (other than crude) and preparations not elsewhere specified or included, containing by weight 70 percent or more of petroleum oils or of oils obtained from bituminous minerals, these oils being the basic constituents	347
170111	Cane sugar, raw, in solid form, not containing added flavoring or coloring matter	344
847330	Parts and accessories of the machines of heading 84.71	316
852352	Semiconductor media, smart cards for the recording of sound or of other phenomena, but excluding products of Chapter 37	309
732690	Articles of iron or steel, not elsewhere specified	306
851761	Base stations for transmission or reception of voice, images or other data, including apparatus for communication in a wired or wireless network (such as a local or wide area network)	295
401693	Gaskets, washers and other seals of vulcanized rubber other than hard rubber	287
730830	Doors, windows and their frames, and thresholds for doors, of iron or steel	285
730890	Structures (excluding prefabricated buildings of heading 94.06) and parts of structures (e.g., bridges and bridge sections, lock-gates, towers, lattice masts, roofs, roofing frame-works, doors and windows and their frames and thresholds for doors, shutters, balustrades	280

HS = Harmonized System

Source: World Bank, World Integrated Trade Solution (WITS), http://wits.worldbank.org/wits.

Table 8.4 Source markets for top Nigerian nonautomotive imports, 2010

HS code	HS description	Country	Value (millions of US dollars)	Share of imports (percent)
8481	Taps, cocks, valves and similar appliances, for pipes, boiler shells, tanks, vats or the like	United States	457	51
		Barbados[a]	119	13
		France	117	13
		China	41	5
		United Kingdom	38	4
		World	896	n.a.
8528	Transmission apparatus for radio broadcasting or television, whether or not incorporating reception apparatus or sound recording or reproducing apparatus; television cameras, digital cameras, and video camera recorders	United States	12	34
		China	9	26
		India	2	6
		South Africa	2	6
		Israel	2	6
		World	35	n.a.
8517	Telephone sets, including telephones for cellular networks or for other wireless networks; other apparatus for the transmission or reception of voice, images or other data, including apparatus for communication in a wired or wireless network (such as a local or wide area network)	China	242	36
		Singapore	89	13
		France	84	13
		United Arab Emirates	83	13
		Sweden	32	5
		World	664	n.a.
8414	Air or vacuum pumps, air or other gas compressors and fans; ventilating or recycling hoods incorporating a fan	United States	262	57
		France	58	13
		China	50	11
		India	10	2
		Algeria	9	2
		World	462	n.a.

n.a. = not applicable
HS = Harmonized System

a. Barbados is an intermediate shipping point for these products.

Source: World Bank, World Intergrated Trade Solution (WITS), http:/wits.worldbank.org/wits.

The government of Nigeria reports that in recent years the oil and gas sector imports more than 95 percent of industry needs.

Relations between foreign firms and their Nigerian counterparts have a long and storied history, dating back to British colonial rule. Nigerian policymakers walk a delicate line between capturing maximum rents from Nigeria's abundant natural resources and attracting foreign capital and expertise to extract and distribute those resources. The government's approach to this balance has varied over time. As one example, more than 95 percent of the 4,500 employees of SPDC are locals.

The government has long tried to encourage domestic production by restricting imports, with little success. According to Ademola Oyejide, A. Ogunkola, and A. Bankole (2005, 438), "from the mid-1970s onwards, Nigeria's main trade policy instruments shifted markedly away from tariffs to quantitative import restrictions, particularly import prohibition and import licensing."

The Nigerian Oil and Gas Content Development Act

On April 22, 2010, the government passed the Nigerian Oil and Gas Content Development Act (CDA). (The complete text of the CDA is available at www.ncdmb.gov.ng.) It is the most recent heavy-handed attempt to enforce local content requirements, or "Nigerianization." The CDA was broadly worded to cover "all matters pertaining to Nigerian content in respect of all operations or transactions carried out in or connected with the Nigerian oil and gas industry." Specifically, it covers "all regulatory authorities, operators, contractors, subcontractors, alliance partners and other entities involved in any project, operation, activity or transaction in the Nigerian oil and gas industry." With this wording, the legislature gave the regulators extensive flexibility and power to enforce the various provisions. Broadly, the CDA's 106 provisions outline three main policies: those that promote "first consideration" of Nigerian content, those that outline reporting requirements for companies ("operators" in the language of the CDA), and those that create a regulatory body to oversee these provisions. Additionally, the CDA sets out a host of detailed obligations on oil and gas industry companies. Implementation of the law has been slow, nontransparent, and inconsistent.

"First Consideration" for Nigerian Content

The CDA explicitly states that "first consideration" must be given to Nigerian content in all oil and gas industry operations. First consideration is not clearly defined, but various provisions provide some illumination. The act applies the first consideration principle to hiring of employees, procurement of goods and services, and contract bidding and selection procedure.

In addition to giving first consideration to locals for employment, the CDA explicitly requires that all junior and intermediate positions be held by

Nigerians (provision 35). In fact, operators may hire expatriates for a maximum of only 5 percent of positions; foreigners must be managers, hired to "take care of investor interests" (provision 36). Non-Nigerians can hold positions for a maximum of four years, after which the position must be "Nigerianized" (provision 32).

For contract bidding, "the award of contract shall not be solely based on the principle of the lowest bidder where a Nigerian indigenous company has capacity to execute such job and the company shall not be disqualified exclusively on the basis that it is not the lowest financial bidder, provided the value does not exceed the lowest bid price by 10 percent." Additionally, if a contract bid contains 5 percent more Nigerian content than its closest competitor, it will be selected, as long as the bids are within 1 percent of each other (provisions 14 and 15).

The CDA's most specific provisions apply to the procurement of goods and services. The CDA includes a schedule that outlines the "minimum Nigerian content in any project" (appendix table 8A.1). This schedule outlines the specific levels of "Nigerian content" for a variety of goods and services in the oil and gas industry. It requires, for example, that "all fabrication and welding activities" must occur in Nigeria. Accordingly, the schedule requires 100 percent Nigerian content for pipeline systems, risers, steel pipes, and steel plates, among many other products. The CDA grants exceptions to the schedule only when there is "inadequate capacity." In these cases, the Minister of Petroleum Resources may authorize the continued importation of relevant items for a maximum of three years.

Reporting and Planning Requirements

The CDA sets the bar extremely high in a variety of industries. In financial services, for example, 100 percent of "general banking services" must be local. The law's drafters likely realized that implementation of these measures would prove extremely difficult, as local suppliers often have "inadequate capacity." In order to further the "Nigerianization" of these tasks, the CDA stipulates that foreign operators themselves must come up with specific plans that accomplish certain levels of local content. The most significant requirement is an annual plan that each operator must submit to the Nigerian Content Development and Monitoring Board (discussed below). Specifically, "within 60 days of the beginning of each year, each operator shall submit to the Board their annual Nigerian Content Performance Report covering all its projects and activities for the year under review." In addition to an annual report, operators are required to submit plans for employment and training (provision 29), research and development (provision 39), technology transfer (provisions 43 and 44), legal services (provision 51), financial services (provision 52) and insurance services (provision 49). These plans require operators to report the current levels of their Nigerian content in all of the corresponding services and goods and, in cases where required local levels are not met, outline a timeline for reaching the target levels.

Nigerian Content Development and Monitoring Board

The CDA creates and funds the Nigerian Content Development and Monitoring Board (NCDMB), which is empowered to "guide, monitor, coordinate, and implement" CDA provisions. The board is funded by a 1 percent tax on all industry contracts that flow into the Nigerian Content Development Fund. It is granted broad authority in implementing these provisions. Specifically, the board appraises, evaluates, and approves all required plans from foreign operators. It oversees the awarding of certificates of authorization for operators and is empowered to host a variety of content promotion efforts, such as conferences, studies, workshops, seminars, and training.

An Example: Subsea Systems

Two-thirds of Nigeria's oil reserves are located offshore. Offshore oil drilling requires highly technical design, construction, management, and maintenance of subsea systems. The interaction between CDA provisions and technical realities illustrates the unrealistic design and questionable implementation of Nigeria's LCR program and the difficult legal position created for foreign multinational corporations.

The CDA specifically outlines the LCRs for virtually all of the steps entailed in subsea systems. To begin with, it requires that 80 percent of labor for "Front-End Engineering Design (FEED) and detailed engineering on deep offshore facilities" be local. It also requires that 60 percent of the construction of a subsea system (measured by tonnage) be local. During installation, 60 percent of the labor must be local. Once the offshore well is up and running, 75 percent of the management and 55 percent of "protection services" must be local. Throughout this process, if consulting expertise is required, 45 percent of consulting expenses must be local. Ongoing maintenance must be 75 percent local.

The FEED process is typically split into three front-end loading activities (FEL). During FEL-1, an "energy balance" of a proposed drill site must be submitted, which requires the expertise, for example, of hydrogeologists. FEL-2 typically involves the identification of all the equipment required for drilling. A subsea system typically includes a production platform (oil rig), drilling equipment, centrifugal pumps, control systems for informatics, hydraulic power, a hyperbaric chamber, and remotely operated underwater vehicles, to list just a few components. FEL-3 finalizes the FEED process with highly sophisticated 3D modeling of the actual system, to ensure that it will meet health, environmental, and safety standards; 80 percent of the labor in this process must be local. These three steps typically require the expertise of geologists, engineers, and biologists, among other technical specialists. Given the limitations of Nigeria's education system, which cannot meet the demand for these professionals, it is not feasible to employ 80 percent Nigerian labor in subsea systems, despite sincere efforts by foreign multinational corporations.

Once the FEED process is complete, the Nigerian local market continues to come up short in supplying the equipment needed for a subsea system. In March 2012, the subsidiary of ExxonMobil—Mobil Producing Nigeria—"pioneered" the production of just three platforms in a Nigeria.[5] These platforms, however, are onshore platforms, not offshore platforms, which are significantly more complicated. More recently, the NCDMB touted that "history was made" when "Cameron Offshore Systems Nigeria unveiled the first made in Nigeria Subsea Christmas Tree at the Onne oil and gas free zone," according to Ernest Nwapa, the executive director of the NCDMB. He predicts that in "the next 3 to 5 years, Nigeria will have over 25 globally recognized Original Equipment Manufacturers making their equipment or major components here, either directly or using their Nigerian representatives."[6] The NCDMB has touted both these instances as major wins for the domestic industry.

Although these cases may be successes for the CDA, they are small relative to the industry as a whole. In the short term, Nigerianization cannot supply the industry demand for specialized equipment, although in the medium and long term, the 25 original equipment manufacturers may be able to supply the industry with a considerable amount of equipment. However, the CDA requirements are not being phased in; in principle, they are implemented immediately. Moreover, the government's proclaimed goal of producing 4 million barrels of oil a day will remain out of reach without the support of foreign companies.

Protection services, which have a relatively low content requirement, are one of the few industries that have flourished in Nigeria. But prosperity points to an unfortunate reality: Implementation of CDA provisions increases corruption more than local content. According to the *Wall Street Journal*, as part of its 2009 Niger Delta Amnesty program, the government now pays former bandits to protect the pipelines they once attacked.[7] In addition, "Nigeria will spend about $450 million on its amnesty program, according to the government's 2012 budget, more than what it spends to deliver basic education to children."

---

5. "Mobil, NNPC Complete Fabrication of Three Platforms," *Business Day Online*, March 16, 2012, www.businessdayonline.com/NG/index.php/oil/34534-mobil-nnpc-complete-fabrication-of-three-platforms (accessed on September 13, 2012).

6. "Cameron Offshore makes first Nigerian Christmas Tree," *NOGintelligence*, Issue 20, October 2012, www.nigeriaoilandgasintelligence.com/cameron-offshore-makes-first-nigerian-christmas-tree (accessed on October 22, 2012).

7. Drew Hinshaw, "Nigeria's Former Oil Bandits Now Collect Government Cash," *Wall Street Journal*, August 22, 2012, http://online.wsj.com/article/SB1000142405270230401940457742016 0886588518.html (accessed on September 13, 2012).

This brief overview of a subsea system makes clear that the LCRs outlined in the CDA defy implementation and that the 10 percent cost difference provision provides little practical relief. In the short term, impractical standards virtually require multinational corporations to obtain waivers for a whole host of purchases and services. A foreign multinational hoping to invest in an offshore site needs to obtain a waiver for essentially all of the design and equipment procurement as well as most of the construction work and site management. Obtaining a waiver entails a new and demanding set of obstacles. In the medium and long term, however, there is some room for optimism that the domestic market will supply some of the industry's needs for equipment, construction, and management.

Popularity of and Legal Challenges to the Content Development Act

Regardless of its impact, the CDA is popular with Nigerians, a fact President Goodluck Jonathan often mentions. The local press has begun to support the expansion of the CDA to other industries, notably the information and communications technology (ICT) industry, which has annual revenues of about $8 billion. One industry executive expressed a common view when he suggested "what is good for the petroleum industry is also good for the ICT industry."[8] Such support for LCRs is also spreading beyond Nigeria. Ghana, as part of its official industrial policy, claims it will pass a local content law, though specifics have not yet been released.[9]

To date, neither the United States nor other countries whose companies provide significant support to the Nigerian oil and gas industry have raised legal challenges. Although CDA implementation is expected to increase their costs, the IOCs have avoided fighting Nigerian plans. Instead, they have focused their lobbying efforts on the proposed Petroleum Industry Bill (PIB), which would restructure the entire industry. In its 2011 report on foreign trade barriers, the US Trade Representative (USTR) points out that "investment in the oil and gas sector remains strictly limited to existing joint ventures or production-sharing agreements. A proposed PIB would change the way Nigeria's oil and gas sector is regulated and funded. The PIB could increase taxes and royalties to the government, at least in the short term, and make it unprofitable to invest in Nigeria's deepwater fields" (USTR 2011, 266). With regard to the CDA, the USTR notes only that "according to industry representatives" the CDA "will adversely affect a diverse range of actors, which include industry operators, contractors, subcontractors, and service providers." Facing a barrage of bad policies, the IOCs are focusing on the laws that affect them

8. "Economy Loses N18bn FDI to Foreigners in Telecoms," *Business Day Online*, June 5, 2012, www.businessdayonline.com/NG/index.php/news/76-hot-topic/38997-economy-loses-n18bn-fdi-to-foreigners-in-telecoms (accessed on October 22, 2012).

9. See the government of Ghana's official industrial policy, section 3.1.4, www.ghana.gov.gh/index.php/information/policy-documents/6108-ghana-industrial-policy.

most directly. Service providers such as Halliburton and Schlumberger are strongly opposed to the CDA, which affects them most directly.

In the medium or long term, the CDA may succeed in developing a domestic industry capable of supplying drilling equipment. However, once foreign competitors begin to lose out on contracts, their motivation to pursue legal challenges will increase significantly. If the law spreads to other industries or countries, it is likely that other service provides will increase the pressure on their own governments to challenge Nigeria's laws. Given the overt domestic preferences in these laws, their consistency with WTO obligations is highly suspect. The CDA includes numerous provisions that likely violate Nigeria's WTO obligations under Articles III and XI of the General Agreement on Tariffs and Trade (GATT) 1994, Article 2.1 of the WTO Agreement on Trade-Related Investment Measures (TRIMs), and the WTO Agreement on Subsidies and Countervailing Measures (ASCM). Likewise, the local sourcing requirements for services in the CDA suggest possible violations of Nigeria's market access and national treatment obligations under the General Agreement on Trade in Services (GATS) Articles XVI and XVII.

Reinforcement of Negative Trends

Assessing the efficacy and costs of LCRs in the oil and gas industry is difficult given the high levels of corruption and vandalism in the industry and the absence of statistics from international organizations. The Nigerian government has been pushing local production in various forms for many decades, with varying degrees of success. The CDA toggles between codifying current business practices (i.e., the 95 percent Nigerian employment requirement) and creating impossible standards for foreign companies. A general appraisal of the law is therefore difficult, though it seems to reinforce two negative trends within the Nigerian economy: decreasing investment and increasing corruption.

Moreover, the government often proclaims a goal of producing 4 million barrels a day. Most recently, the NNPC reiterated this target, stating that it is achievable by 2020.[10] We use that goal as a baseline to estimate the cost of this law on government revenue. The costs are substantial and will only grow over time.

Effect on Investment

The CDA may or may not succeed in encouraging local industry; it has certainly succeeded in discouraging foreign investment. According to the USTR

---

10. Chineme Okafor, "Nigeria: Crude Oil Production Drops to 2.4 Million Barrels per Day," *AllAfrica*, October 8, 2012, http://allafrica.com/stories/201210080115.html (accessed on November 1, 2012).

(2012, 282), "the international oil companies (IOCs) have approved no major investments in the oil and gas sector since the first quarter of 2009." This discouraging picture is not related to the CDA but rather to the PIB, which has been pending for years. But the CDA continues to reinforce Nigeria's generally unfriendly attitude toward foreign investment. As one consequence, the IOCs are divesting their mature onshore oil fields. These fields require less capital and expertise to manage and are thus more realistic projects for local operators. Meanwhile, the IOCs are focusing their strategies on offshore, deepwater wells, which require more technical expertise and so far have stayed out of reach of vandals. About two-thirds of Nigeria's reserves lie in these hard-to-reach places. But the government's long-proclaimed goal of producing 4 million barrels of oil a day also remains out of reach without the support of foreign companies. A bifurcated approach that distinguishes between onshore and offshore investments could have avoided this outcome; the law makes no such distinction.

Divestment by foreign operators of onshore fields has created a window for local operators. The Nigerian National Petroleum Corporation recently released its "draft" production estimates for 2011—the first full year in which the law was in place. It shows little to no increase by local small and medium enterprises, suggesting that the CDA has had limited impact on crude production. A special report by the *Financial Times* on the industry points to some bright spots, quoting a local CEO who believes local production will "quadruple" by the end of 2013.[11] For now, however, local production remains at just 100,000 barrels a day (less than 5 percent) and much of that is in fields operated by large foreign companies.

Effect on Corruption

The board responsible for implementing the CDA has not been active in a public fashion, doing little more than issue a few press releases on "successful" cases. It has not released its annual report, despite a statutory requirement to do so. Its website (www.ncdmb.gov.ng) provides minimal guidelines for the industry, aside from those related to the 1 percent payment to the fund and legal and technology services plans. If the board has been active in other ways, it has done so behind the scenes, working directly with operators. Its website makes no mention of certificates of authorization and presents no industry-wide statistics.

The very nature of the board raises red flags, given Nigeria's history of corruption. Although Nigerian regulators have already begun to request waivers from foreign firms, the board has not published the process or costs of obtaining a waiver. Without a transparent process for obtaining a waiver, US

---

11. "Nigeria: Oil and Gas 2012," *Financial Times*, Special Report, July 2012, www.ft.com/intl/nigeria-oil-gas-2012 (accessed on August 1, 2012).

multinational corporations cannot make payments without raising serious concerns about violations of the US Foreign Corrupt Practices Act, which outlaws bribery of foreign officials. Unbelievably, the CDA explicitly states that board members may receive "gifts" from the industry, specifically allowing the board to raise funds "by way of donations, gifts, grants, and endowments" (provision 90(2)(b)).

Effect on Government Revenue

The Nigerian government at all levels depends heavily on taxes from oil revenue. In 2011, crude oil production averaged close to 2.13 million barrels a day, up from 2.05 million the previous year, an annual growth rate of about 4 percent. In order to reach daily production of 4 million barrels by 2020, Nigeria would need to increase production by 190,000 barrels a day, or 7 percent, every year between 2010 and 2020. It is not currently on track to do so. Although other factors are at play—notably the lack of clarity on a clear investment framework via the pending PIB—the CDA is playing a significant part in preventing Nigeria from accomplish its targets. Most analysts do not anticipate much growth in production in the next few years.

We generously assume that Nigeria will maintain its 2011 growth rate until 2020. Next, we accept the government's assertion that Nigeria could, with the proper regulatory environment, produce 4 million barrels a day by 2020. Table 8.5 quantifies the losses in government revenue created by the production gap between Nigeria's potential and its projected path. The results are substantial. By 2020, poor policy choices, including the CDA, will cost the government $59 billion in forgone tax revenue. The average annual loss between 2011 and 2020 is $5.9 billion. In 2011, that figure amounted to nearly 10 percent of total government revenue.

Of course, if Nigeria does not pump this oil in the next decade, the oil will remain under the seabed for future extraction. The tax revenue cost calculated at $59 billion over a decade therefore overstates the loss of economic value to Nigeria. Assuming the oil in question will be recovered between 2021 and 2030, and discounting each year's forgone revenue between 2011 and 2020 (namely $5.9 billion a year) by 6 percent compounded for 10 years, the lost economic value is $33 billion—a smaller but still considerable sum.

Alternatives to LCRs

The NCDMB is still working on how it will develop and enforce the CDA requirements, even though the laws came into force immediately. It is still finding its bark and bite. Once it does, it envisages imposing fines of up to 5 percent of the value of the noncompliant transaction. These fines could be significant, given that individual contracts and transactions are often worth more than $100 million.

Table 8.5 Estimated impact of CDA on Nigerian government tax revenue, 2010–20

Year	Crude oil production (barrels per day)[a]	Potential production (barrels per day)[b]	Estimated loss in production (barrels per day)	Annualized loss (millions of barrels)	IMF budget reference oil price (US dollars)[c]	Estimated government revenue per barrel (US dollars)[d]	Estimated losses in government revenue (millions of US dollars)
2010	2.1	2.1	0.0	0.0	70.0	35.0	0
2011	2.1	2.2	0.1	23.2	70.0	35.0	811
2012	2.2	2.3	0.1	48.9	70.0	35.0	1,711
2013	2.3	2.5	0.2	77.3	70.0	35.0	2,706
2014	2.4	2.7	0.3	108.7	70.0	35.0	3,806
2015	2.5	2.9	0.4	143.4	70.0	35.0	5,018
2016	2.6	3.1	0.5	181.5	75.0	35.0	6,805
2017	2.7	3.3	0.6	223.3	75.0	37.5	8,375
2018	2.8	3.5	0.7	269.3	75.0	37.5	10,097
2019	2.9	3.8	0.9	319.6	75.0	37.5	11,985
2020	3.0	4.0	1.0	374.7	75.0	37.5	14,050
					Total costs in 2010–20 (11 years)		65,364
					Average annual costs in 2010–20 (11 years)		5,942

CDA = Content Development Act; IMF = International Monetary Fund

a. Assumes annual production growth rate of 3.9 percent.
b. Assumes annual production growth rate of 7 percent, the required growth needed to accomplish the Nigerian government's goal of 4 million barrels per day by 2020.
c. Based on IMF's budget forecast for Nigeria for 2010–15. Based on Nigerian parliament's estimates used in budget forecast for 2015–20.
d. Assumes Nigerian government retains 50 percent of revenue per barrel sold. Historically, this figure has ranged from 50 to 75 percent.

Sources: Budgetary data are from IMF (2012); oil production data from EIA (2012b); authors' calculations.

The NCDMB has already collected $100 million.[12] Like other aspects of this case, the way in which it plans to spend its cash remains vague. Whatever fines may be collected and however they are disbursed, the CDA is likely to impose a substantial cost on the Nigerian economy over the next decade, conservatively estimated at $3.3 billion a year.

Alternative policies that might have created a domestic oil and gas industry are not evident. State-owned oil and gas firms in developing countries have a long and troubled history of political patronage and corruption. To Nigeria's credit, it has relied largely on foreign oil companies to develop its resources.

Nigeria might have greater success in creating a cadre of skilled Nigerian technicians and managers if it insisted on serious training programs run by foreign multinationals. For several years, the graduates would choose to work for those companies. However, over time, some of them might launch their own onshore and offshore drilling companies, as well as ancillary service firms. Nigeria might learn a great deal by consulting with Aramco over its extensive history from a joint venture of oil majors to a company fully owned by Saudi Arabia.

---

12. "Nigerian Content Fund gets $100m from oil firms," *The Nation,* September 24, 2012 http://thenationonlineng.net/new/nigerian-content-fund-gets-100m-from-oil-firms (accessed on July 16, 2013).

Appendix 8A

Table 8A.1 Industry-specific schedule of the Nigerian Oil and Gas Content Development Act

Industry description	Nigerian content requirement (percent)	Unit of measure for Nigerian content
Front-end engineering design (FEED) and detailed engineering and other engineering service		
FEED and detailed engineering on onshore facilities	90	Labor
FEED and detailed engineering on offshore facilities, shallow water	90	Labor
FEED and detailed engineering on liquefied natural gas facility	50	Labor
FEED and detailed engineering on gas gathering facilities	90	Labor
FEED and detailed engineering on deep offshore facilities, hull and topside modules	80	Labor
FEED and detailed engineering on deep offshore floating concrete structure	80	Labor
Fabrication and construction		
Terminal/oil movement systems	80	Volume
Drilling modules/packages	75	Tonnage
Piles, anchors, buoys, jackets, bridges, flares, booms, storage tanks, pressure vessels	80	Tonnage
Umbilical	60	Tonnage
Topside module (process modules and storage modules)	50	Tonnage
Accommodation module	70	Tonnage
Subsea systems	60	Tonnage
Pipeline systems	100	Tonnage
Risers	100	Tonnage
Utilities module/packages	50	Tonnage
Materials and procurement		
Steel plates, flat sheets, sections	100	Tonnage
Steel pipes	100	Tonnage
Low voltage cables	90	Length
High voltage cables	45	Length
Valves	60	Number
Drilling mud-baryte, bentonite	60	Tonnage
Cement (portland)	80	Tonnage
Cement (hydraulic)	60	Tonnage
Heat exchangers	50	Number
Steel ropes	60	Tonnage
Protective paints	60	Liters
Glass reinforced epoxy (GRE) pipes	60	Tonnage

(continued on next page)

Table 8A.1 Industry-specific schedule of the Nigerian Oil and Gas Content Development Act *(continued)*

Industry description	Nigerian content requirement (percent)	Unit of measure for Nigerian content
Well and drilling services/petroleum technology		
Reservoir services	75	Expenditure
Well completion services (permanent gauges and intelligent wells)	80	Expenditure
Wire line services (electric open holes, electric cased hole, slickline)	45	Expenditure
Logging while drilling (LWD) services	75	Labor
Measurement while drilling (MWD) (direction and inclination/gamma ray)	90	Labor
Production drilling service	85	Labor
Performance services (temperature and pressure)	90	Labor
2D seismic data acquisition services	85	Length
Well overhauling/stimulation services	85	Labor
Wellhead services	85	Labor
Directional surveying services	100	Labor
Cutting injections/cutting disposal services	100	Labor
Recutting inspection services	85	Labor
Cased hole logging services (gyro, perforation, gauges, production logging tools)	90	Labor
Well watch services	70	Labor
Cement service	75	Labor
Coiled tubing services	75	Labor
Pumping services	95	Labor
Fluid/bottom hole sampling services	80	Labor
Cleaning, hardbanding, recutting, rethreading, storage	95	Labor
Well crisis management services	90	Labor
Directional drilling services	90	Labor
Other drilling services	80	Labor
Petrophysical interpretation services	75	Volume/labor
Extended well test/early production services including provision of floating or jackup production unit	50	Expenditure
Provision of all catering, cleaning, office and security service at location/platform	80	Expenditure
Rental of drill pipe	75	Expenditure
Electric open hole	45	Expenditure
Electric ceased holes	100	Expenditure
Slickline	100	Expenditure
Well head safety panels	100	Expenditure
Chemical: drilling, process, maintenance	90	Expenditure

(continued on next page)

**Table 8A.1   Industry-specific schedule of the Nigerian Oil and Gas
Content Development Act** *(continued)*

Industry description	Nigerian content requirement (percent)	Unit of measure for Nigerian content
Research and development services		
Engineering studies—reservoir, facilities, drilling, etc.	60	Expenditure
Geological and geophysical services	80	Expenditure
Safety and environmental studies	75	Expenditure
Local materials substitution studies	75	Expenditure
Exploration, subsurface, petroleum engineering and seismic		
3D seismic data acquisition services	100	Expenditure
4D seismic data processing services	55	Expenditure
2D seismic data processing services	100	Expenditure
Geophysical interpretation services	90	Expenditure
Geological evaluation services (organic geochemistry, petrology, digenesis, biostratigraphy, fluid characterization, PVT, core analysis, flooding)	80	Expenditure
Mud logging services	90	Expenditure
Coring services	90	Expenditure
Well testing service	55	Expenditure
Drilling rigs (swamp)	60	Labor
Drilling rigs (semi-submersibles/jack ups/others)	55	Labor
Drilling rigs (land)	70	Labor
Work-over rigs (swamp)	70	Expenditure
Snubbing services	80	Expenditure
Linger float, hangers and running equipment services	55	Expenditure
Field development plan	100	Expenditure
2D seismic data interpretation services	100	Expenditure
3D seismic data interpretation services	100	Expenditure
4D seismic data interpretation services	55	Expenditure
Drilling rigs (land)	70	Labor
Transportation/supply/disposal services		
Tugs, remotely operated vehicle (ROV) support/ diving support vessels	65	Expenditure
Barges	95	Expenditure
Accommodation platforms/vessels	90	Expenditure
Disposal/distribution and water transport services	100	Expenditure
Rental of cranes and special vehicles	75	Expenditure
Freight forwarding/logistics management services	65	Expenditure
Supply base/warehouse/storage services	70	Expenditure

(continued on next page)

Table 8A.1 Industry-specific schedule of the Nigerian Oil and Gas Content Development Act *(continued)*

Industry description	Nigerian content requirement (percent)	Unit of measure for Nigerian content
Truck package/product transportation services	100	Expenditure
Health, safety, and environment		
Site clean up service	100	Labor
Pollution control	45	Expenditure
Waste water treatment services	65	Labor
Fire and gas protection system services	50	Labor
Ventilation/heating/sanitary services	85	Labor
Waste disposal/drainage services	100	Labor
Industrial cleaning services	100	Labor
Disposal/distribution and waste transport services etc.	100	Expenditure
Safety/protection/security/firefighting system services	90	Labor
Preservation of mechanical and electrical components services	95	Labor
Equipment brokerage services	75	Expenditure
Temporary accommodation/camp services	80	Expenditure
Catering services	100	Expenditure
Cleaning and laundry services	100	Expenditure
Security services	95	Expenditure
Medical services	60	Expenditure
Equipment brokerage services	75	Expenditure
Other supporting services	85	Expenditure
Pollution control	90	Labor/ expenditure
Information systems/information technology/communication services		
Network installation/support services	85	Expenditure
Software development and support services	45	Expenditure
Computer based modeling services	51	Expenditure
Computer based simulation/training programs services	51	Expenditure
CAL/CAP services	51	Expenditure
Hardware installation support services	50	Expenditure
Operating system installation/support services	50	Expenditure
User support/help desk services	60	Expenditure
Library services	70	Expenditure
IT management consultancy services	50	Expenditure
Data management services	50	Expenditure
Telecommunication installation/support services	60	Expenditure
Data and message transmitting services	60	Expenditure
Rental of telecommunication lines	75	Expenditure

(continued on next page)

Table 8A.1 Industry-specific schedule of the Nigerian Oil and Gas Content Development Act *(continued)*

Industry description	Nigerian content requirement (percent)	Unit of measure for Nigerian content
Telecommunication subscription services	85	Expenditure
Public address system services	95	Expenditure
Other information systems (IS)/information technology (IT) services	75	Expenditure
Marine operations and logistics services		
Telecommunication services	90	Labor
Supply of crew men for domestic coastal services	80	Number
Diving/ROV/submersible operations	70	Labor
Hook-up and commissioning including marine installation services	75	Labor
Dredging service	55	Labor/ expenditure
Gravel and rock dumping service	65	Labor
Floating storage units (FSU)	45	Labor
Subsea pipeline protection services	55	Labor
Installation of subsea package	60	Labor
Mooring system services	50	Labor
Ship chandler service	90	Expenditure
Moving services	100	Labor/ expenditure
Supply vessels	45	Labor/ expenditure
Stand-by vessels	55	Expenditure
Domestic clearing of cargos	30	Expenditure
Bunkering services	60	Expenditure
Marine insurance	40	Expenditure
Marine consulting	40	Expenditure
Marine logistic	30	Expenditure
Finance and insurance		
General banking services	100	Usage
Monetary intermediation services	70	Usage
Credit granting services	50	Loan amount
Security broking and fund management services	100	Expenditure
Financial management consultancy services	70	Expenditure
Accounting services	70	Labor
Auditing services	100	Expenditure
Life insurance services	100	Expenditure
Pension funding services	100	Expenditure
Non-life insurance services	70	Expenditure
Insurance broking services	100	Expenditure

(continued on next page)

Table 8A.1   Industry-specific schedule of the Nigerian Oil and Gas Content Development Act *(continued)*

Industry description	Nigerian content requirement (percent)	Unit of measure for Nigerian content
Installation, hookup, and commissioning		
Surface treatment, sandblasting, painting, coating, and fire proofing services	80	Labor
Subsea construction services	45	Labor
Hookup and commissioning including marine installation services	75	Labor
Installation of subsea packages	45	Labor
Electrical/instrument services	45	Labor
Insulation services	50	Labor
Diving/ROV/submersible operations	75	Labor
Subsea construction services	45	Labor
Pipe cutting and bending services	100	Labor
Catalyst handling/regeneration services	85	Labor
Bolt tensioning services	75	Labor
Rope access services	70	Labor
Welding and jointing services	60	Labor
Maintenance and modification of pumps and rotating equipment	65	Labor
Heat treating and demagnetising services	80	Labor
Tank bottom sludge treatment services	85	Labor
Valve management services including testing and repair	85	Labor
Crane management services	80	Labor/rate
Other construction/maintenance services	80	Labor/ tonnage/rate
Pipe laying/cable laying services	50	Labor
Trenching and excavation services	100	Labor
Cranes/crane barges/heavy lift vessels	100	Labor
Marine services	65	Labor/ expenditure
Subsea services	45	Labor/ expenditure
Well services	70	Labor/ expenditure
Cutting services	75	Labor/ expenditure
Site services	85	Labor/ expenditure
Other decommissioning and abandonment services	90	Labor/ expenditure
Service station tank maintenance/services	75	Expenditure
Electrical/electronic systems integration	55	Expenditure
Process testing including helium and nitrogen services	65	Expenditure

(continued on next page)

Table 8A.1   Industry-specific schedule of the Nigerian Oil and Gas Content Development Act *(continued)*

Industry description	Nigerian content requirement (percent)	Unit of measure for Nigerian content
Inspection/testing/certification		
Material technology/anti-corrosion/surface protection services	85	Labor
Non-destructive testing (NDT) services	60	Labor
Pipeline flushing, external/internal inspection, pigging services	85	Labor/rate
Surface treatment inspection services	90	Labor
Pressure testing services	90	Labor
Instrument testing/calibration services	85	Labor
Load testing services	75	Labor
Diving/ROV operations	65	Labor
Laboratory testing services	55	Labor
Dimensional control/verification services	45	Labor
Third party measurement services	45	Labor
Other inspection services	45	Labor
Quality management systems certificate	55	Number of certifications obtained
Environmental management systems certificate	45	Number of certifications obtained
Safety management system certification	45	Number of certifications obtained
Information security management systems certificate	45	Number of certifications obtained
Certification of welders	50	Number of certifications obtained
Certification by NDT personnel	45	Labor
Certification of machinery and equipment	45	Number of certifications obtained
Certification on NDT personnel	50	Number of certifications obtained
Certificate of machinery	50	Number of certifications obtained
Certification of cranes and lifting appliances	45	Number of certifications obtained

(continued on next page)

Table 8A.1   Industry-specific schedule of the Nigerian Oil and Gas Content Development Act *(continued)*

Industry description	Nigerian content requirement (percent)	Unit of measure for Nigerian content
Certification of pressurized equipment	45	Number of certifications obtained
Evaluation and certification of software and electronics (IT)	45	Number of certifications obtained
Notified body for machinery	45	Number of certifications obtained
Notified body for simple pressure vessels	45	Number of certifications obtained
Notified body for telecommunication terminal equipment	50	Number of certifications obtained
Notified body for personal protection equipment	45	Number of certifications obtained
Notified body for lifts	50	Number of certifications obtained
Notified body for pressure containing equipment	45	Number of certifications obtained
Integrity management services	50	Number of certifications obtained
Other certification services	50	Number of certifications obtained
Other testing services	49	Labor
Project management/consulting services		
Construction management and supervision services	80	Labor
Project administration services/project management	80	Labor
Quality assurance QA/QC consultancy	45	Labor
Safety, health and environment consultancy	45	Labor
Risk analysis consultancy	45	Labor
Personnel/training system consultancy (for training courses select 3.99.13)	45	Labor
Legal consultancy	50	Contracts
Cost and planning consultancy	75	Labor
Material administration consultancy	75	Labor

(continued on next page)

Table 8A.1 Industry-specific schedule of the Nigerian Oil and Gas Content Development Act *(continued)*

Industry description	Nigerian content requirement (percent)	Unit of measure for Nigerian content
Technical documentation/document control consultancy	85	Labor
Advertising/public affairs/public relations consultancy	80	Labor
Marketing and market research consultancy	75	Labor
Translation and manual writing consultancy	45	Labor
Welding and jointing consultancy	45	Labor
Warranty surveyors	45	Labor
Third party evaluation/verification consultancy	50	Expenditure
Energy conservation consultancy	65	Expenditure
Decommissioning and abandonment consultancy	90	Expenditure
Meteorological consultancy	55	Expenditure
Staff search/selection consultancy	80	Expenditure
Sub-surface consultancy (geological, geophysical, reservoir)	90	Expenditure
Design consultancy (industrial design, web design etc.)	85	Labor
Marine consultancy	50	Expenditure
Subsea consultancy	45	Expenditure
Career/outplacement consultancy	70	Expenditure
General management and business development consultancy	80	Expenditure
Other consultancy services	55	Expenditure
Pollution and pollution control works and consultancy	65	Expenditure
Surveying/positioning services		
Soil investigation services	80	Expenditure
Navigation/positioning services	50	Expenditure
Geotechnical services	60	Expenditure
Geophysical and hydrographic site survey	100	Expenditure
Oceanographic services	60	Expenditure
Rig positioning services	65	Expenditure
Photogrammetric surveying services	45	Expenditure
Chart and map production services	45	Expenditure
Rental of surveying/positioning equipment services	45	Expenditure
Survey and positioning support services	75	Expenditure
Aeromagnetic survey	45	Area
Modification and maintenance		
Canopy equipment maintenance/services	90	Expenditure
Dredging services	90	Expenditure
Signs and accessories maintenance/services	55	Expenditure

(continued on next page)

Table 8A.1   Industry-specific schedule of the Nigerian Oil and Gas Content Development Act *(continued)*

Industry description	Nigerian content requirement (percent)	Unit of measure for Nigerian content
Service station pumps maintenance/services	80	Expenditure
Payment terminal maintenance/services	65	Expenditure
Service station tanks maintenance/services	80	Expenditure
Subsea systems	75	Expenditure
Pipeline systems	45	Expenditure
Risers	60	Expenditure
Umbilicals	49	Tonnage
Terminal/oil movement systems	51	Tonnage
Accommodation/office/workshop/storage modules	70	Volume
Process modules/packages	80	Expenditure
Utilities modules/packages	65	Tonnage
Drilling modules/packages	80	Tonnage
Building including service stations	70	Tonnage
Shipping		
Domestic coastal carriage of petroleum products	60	Expenditure
Tow of oil and gas infrastructure and vessels conveying oil and gas products from or to any port or point in Nigerian waters	90	Expenditure
Supply of very large crude carriers (VLCC)	90	Expenditure

Source: Nigerian Oil and Gas Content Development Act, www.ncdmb.gov.ng/images/DOWN-LOADS/NC-ACT/NC_ACT.pdf.

9

Not Buying It:
Buy American/Buy America

American politicians have often invoked populist rhetoric to justify protection during periods of economic hardship. Tariff bills in the 19th and early 20th centuries were replete with this spirit. The most comprehensive local content requirement (LCR)—the original Buy American bill—was enacted in the Great Depression, shortly after the Smoot-Hawley tariff.

With the Great Recession of 2008-09, politicians rediscovered the Buy America mood, flooding Congress with proposals and enacting a few. As in the Great Depression, the overriding argument for Buy America during the Great Recession was to ensure that federal stimulus spending created jobs at home, not abroad.

LCRs in the United States have singled out government procurement and, more recently, government-financed projects. Listening to powerful domestic interests, legislators focused on the sourcing of iron and steel products. Purchases by the Department of Defense and the Department of Transportation have long been favorite targets. More recently, the Environmental Protection Agency (EPA) has drawn congressional attention.

This case study sketches the history of LCRs in the United States. It then examines their impact on highway, water, and sewer projects.

History of LCRs in the United States

The Buy American Act of 1933

In 1933 the US Congress passed, and President Hoover signed (on his last day in office), the Buy American Act, which granted a preference to domestic products in all federal government purchases. This act was the landmark local content initiative in the United States. Like most LCRs, the law intended to protect domestic labor. Significantly, it defined nationality based on location, not on the nationality of the contractor or the type of service provided. Buy American defined products as domestic if "substantially all" of the materials originated in the United States. Subsequent regulations defined "substantially all" to mean that the cost of foreign components does not exceed 50 percent of the cost of all components (Luckey 2012). The original act enumerated the primary exceptions to the LCR rule: when its application is inconsistent with the public interest, when costs are unreasonable, when procurement takes place outside US territory, when domestic production is not available in commercial quantity or quality, and when the value of the procured good or service is less than $3,000.

The Berry Amendment

In 1941, under the pretext of protecting the US industrial base during wartime, Congress added the Berry Amendment to legislation that funded the Department of Defense (then the Department of War). The amendment requires that certain purchases (military clothing and specialty items) be 100 percent domestic origin.

Surface Transportation Assistance Act

In 1982 President Ronald Reagan pushed the Surface Transportation Assistance Act through Congress. Along with its companion funding bill, the act was a major transportation initiative, providing federal funds for the construction and repair of America's interstate highways and bridges. Section 165 included various provisions that became known as "Buy America."[1] These provisions greatly extended the reach of LCRs beyond the previous limit (government procurement) to new areas (government financing). Since then, these provisions have applied to various transportation funds, including the following:

- Federal Transit Administration funds (49 USC 5323 (j)),
- Federal Highway Administration funds (23 USC 313),
- AMTRAK funds (49 USC 24305),
- Federal Railroad Administration High Speed Rail Program funds (49 USC 24405), and
- Federal Aviation Administration funds (49 USC 50101 and 50103).

---

1. Media sources often confuse the terms Buy American and Buy America. Properly used, Buy American refers to the original Buy American Act of 1933 and relates to direct government procurement. Buy America refers to provisions that require US-made products for government-financed projects.

The specific amount of required content and waiver eligibility varies across these programs. Domestic content requirements range from 50 to 100 percent. These thresholds are higher than the typical rule of origin threshold in most US free trade agreements, which are typically closer to 40 percent and permit the inclusion of labor costs (e.g., for handling and shipping) as domestic components. However, the Buy America waivers usually enable exceptions for the public interest, for unavailability of a component in the domestic market, and for low-value purchases.

The American Recovery and Reinvestment Act

In response to the Great Recession, President Barack Obama pushed the American Recovery and Reinvestment Act of 2009 (ARRA, usually referred to as the stimulus bill), which included $787 billion mix of tax cuts and expenditures. Sections 1512(c), 1605(a), and 1606 outline the LCRs of the act. They specify that "none of the funds appropriated or otherwise made available by this Act may be used for a project for the construction, alteration, maintenance, or repair of a public building or public work unless all of the iron, steel, and manufactured goods used in the project are produced in the United States" and provide for standard waiver exceptions. In addition to the standard waivers from the older templates, new waivers are granted for components sourced from signatories of the World Trade Organization (WTO) Government Procurement Agreement and US partners in free trade agreements. The Obama administration thereby made an effort to observe the country's international obligations. However, the largest US trading partners have expressed considerable frustration with ARRA provisions, as discussed later in this chapter.

The application of ARRA provisions is clarified in Title 2, Part 176 of the Code of Federal Regulations.[2] It states that a waiver applies if the "inclusion of iron, steel, or manufactured goods produced in the United States will increase the cost of the overall project by more than 25 percent."

In a comprehensive review of the LCR provisions (Hufbauer and Schott 2009, 8), we conclude that they "damage the United States' reputation, with very little impact on US jobs." Moreover, following enactment of ARRA, more reputational damage has been done by "me-too" rhetoric and proposals.

Recent Rhetoric and Proposals

Since the Great Recession and ARRA, a robust recovery has eluded the United States, and economic concerns remain at the top of public consciousness. Politicians have responded with more Buy America rhetoric, though

---

2. The Electronic Code of Federal Regulations is available at www.ecfr.gov/cgi-bin/ECFR?page=browse.

few measures have actually been enacted. According to the Global Trade Alert (www.globaltradealert.org)—which tracks new protectionist measures, including LCRs, around the world—no additional measures have become law in the United States. However, legislators have offered up fresh proposals:

- The House of Representatives' version of the National Defense Authorization Act for FY2010 included Buy American requirements. The proposals, which related to procurement of small arms and uniforms, limited the number of foreign workers on construction projects designed to relocate facilities to Guam. Most of these provisions were stripped after reconciliation with the Senate version of the bill; a weaker provision, relating to procurement of small arms from the "production industrial base," passed.

- On September 29, 2010, the House of Representatives approved the All-American Flag Act (HR 2853), requiring that all American flags used by any agency of the federal government be made using exclusively US-derived materials and be manufactured in the United States. The bill remains in committee.

- The Buy American at the Smithsonian Act of 2011 (HR 983), introduced in the US House of Representatives on March 9, 2011, would generally prohibit the Smithsonian Institution from either using non-US materials in construction projects or selling items in its gift shops that are not made in the United States. The bill remains in subcommittee; however, administrators of one Smithsonian gift shop have discontinued purchases of goods not made in the United States.

- On May 15, 2013, the Senate approved the Water Resources Development Act (S 601), which authorizes the Army Corps of Engineers to contract for water resources development, conservation, and other construction projects. An amendment to the bill (SA 866) mandates the use of American iron, steel, and manufactured goods "for the construction, alteration, maintenance, or repair" of any project but allows for exceptions in cases where US-sourced goods are not sufficiently available, overall project costs would increase by more than 25 percent, or using US-made materials is deemed "inconsistent with the public interest."

These measures—which so far have been applied only in a limited way—hinder the ability of US diplomats to negotiate international disciplines on LCR practices. Canada, the most important US trade partner, has repeatedly expressed concerns. These concerns are well founded. Although it is impossible to draw a tight causal connection between the global spread of LCRs and the assorted US proposals, the term Buy America stands out as a protectionist rallying cry. This turn of phrase is highly familiar to trade negotiators around the globe.

The WTO Government Procurement Agreement and Free Trade Agreements

Many critics claim that Buy American/Buy America mandates violate WTO and other US international agreements. Technically, the mandates are not violations because of the flexible nature of the relevant WTO provisions and trade agreements. The Government Procurement Agreement (GPA) is a plurilateral agreement that was negotiated during the Uruguay Round and entered into force on January 1, 1996. Current members of the GPA are Armenia, Canada, the 27 member states of the European Union, Hong Kong, Iceland, Israel, Japan, Korea, Liechtenstein, the Netherlands with respect to Aruba, Norway, Singapore, Switzerland, Taiwan, and the United States. The point of the GPA is to open procurement to competition from firms based in the signatory countries—but not to firms based in other WTO members, such as Brazil, China, India, Mexico, and Russia, which together accounted for about 40 percent of US iron and steel imports in 2006.

According to the WTO, "the Agreement does not automatically apply to all government procurement of the Parties. Rather, the coverage of the Agreement is determined with regard to each Party in Appendix I Annexes." Appendix I contains four annexes, covering central government entities; subcentral government entities; all other entities; services, whether listed positively or negatively, covered by the agreement; and construction services.

In essence, the GPA gives member states easy avenues to appease protectionist pressures by allowing exceptions for highly specific projects and agency funds. The US annexes listed well over 50 entities that dole out billions of dollars in government procurement. Because of exceptions, however, much of their expenditure is excluded from GPA coverage.

Modern free trade agreements—typically negotiated bilaterally—provide more depth than WTO agreements, which are negotiated at the multilateral level. Thus, partners in US trade agreements naturally raised an eyebrow when Buy America provisions were included in ARRA. Canada has long been the United States' most important trading partner; the North American Free Trade Agreement (NAFTA) provides a comprehensive framework for this partnership. Buy America provisions clearly fly in the face of NAFTA, a chapter of which is dedicated to government procurement. Equally important, these provisions clearly violate the national treatment and nondiscrimination principles on which robust international trade relies.

Legal Gap for Stimulus Measures

Well aware that Buy America poised numerous legal issues with regard to US international obligations—most importantly, the WTO GPA and NAFTA—US trade negotiators got to work. Instead of adjusting domestic policy, they were able to create a temporary gap and capitalize on the slow-moving pace at which international trade disputes are resolved.

More than any other trade partner, the Canadian business community was outraged by the steel provisions of ARRA and pushed for a retaliatory response from the Canadian government. The outcome of this trade battle came on February 12, 2010, in the form of a new agreement between the United States and Canada. This one-off agreement—simply titled Agreement between the Government of United States of America and the Government of Canada on Government Procurement—modified various parts of both Canadian and US Appendices I to the GPA, which enumerate exceptions and exclusions from the GPA and other agreements. Specifically, the US Annex 3 of Appendix I was modified to read:

> List C–Point 7: US Environmental Protection Agency, *Clean Water and Drinking Water State Revolving Funds,* for projects funded by reallocated ARRA funds where the contracts are signed after 17 February 2010 (Note 3)...

> ... (Note 3) For the programs listed in List C, entities shall not impose, through 30 September 2011, the domestic purchasing requirement of section 1605(a) of the *American Recovery and Reinvestment Act of 2009* (ARRA) as a condition of ARRA financing of those programs with respect to Canadian iron, steel, or manufactured goods in procurement above the threshold for construction applicable to this Annex. The United States undertakes no other commitments with respect to these programs.

On the surface, this decision looks like a win for free trade and Canadian policymakers. However, the administration simply side-stepped the issue by getting all projects "under contract" during the one-year window it created—between February 17, 2009 (when the stimulus law was signed) and February 16, 2010 (when the new agreement came into force). To add further insult to injury, the US federal government created a parallel deadline—February 17, 2010—for US states. States were required to place funds "under contract" by the deadline or the funds would be reallocated to states with surplus projects. The majority of states rushed to comply. A review of annual appropriations clearly demonstrates why the Canadians were so upset. In 2009—during the legal gap created by the United States—EPA doled out more than twice as much funding as it did in any other year (table 9.1). Similar measures were taken for other industries and other trade agreements. Given the importance of Canada as a trade partner, this record is egregious.[3]

The debate is far from over. Concerns of US trading partners over Buy America provisions have recently resurfaced in the negotiations between the United States and European Union over the Transatlantic Trade and Investment Partnership (TTIP). The European Union has long wanted to improve access to the US government procurement market at both the subfederal level and for specific sectors like public utilities. The European Union's draft

---

3. Recently, Canada raised its remaining grievances over Buy America restrictions in the Trans-Pacific Partnership talks, suggesting new procurement rules that would help avoid what has been a "persistent irritant for Canadian companies." See "In TPP, Canada May Seek Bilateral Deals with U.S. on Procurement, Visas," *Inside US Trade*, March 13, 2013, www.insidetrade.com (accessed on May 2, 2013).

Table 9.1 Environmental Protection Agency water infrastructure funding, 2001–12
(millions of US dollars)

Fiscal year	President's request	Total appropriation
2001	1,753	2,621
2002	2,233	2,660
2003	2,185	2,599
2004	1,798	2,610
2005	1,794	2,335
2006	1,649	2,006
2007	1,570	2,005
2008	1,553	1,695
2009	1,397	7,702
2010	3,920	3,674
2011	3,307	2,505
2012	2,560	2,385
Total	55,746	69,214

Source: Copeland (2012, table 1).

mandate for the US-EU trade pact implicitly references US Buy America provisions, noting that a transatlantic free trade agreement should include "rules and disciplines to address barriers having a negative impact on each other's public procurement markets, including localization requirements."[4] The immediate concern is that EU firms (as well as firms based in other GPA members) could still face Buy America restrictions in cases in which US federal funding is allocated to states or municipalities not covered under the GPA and cases in which US federal funding is attached to highway and mass transit projects in states that are covered under the GPA, as a result of a specific exception under Annex 2 of the GPA.[5,6] Although limiting the scope of Buy America requirements within the Trans-Pacific Partnership or TTIP may be a tough sell, doing so may be an essential US "concession" to conclude the two superregional agreements.

Transportation and Water Infrastructure

Investments in transportation and water infrastructure have long been viewed as a means of both stimulating immediate labor demand and, over the longer term, raising productivity (see Copeland, Levine, and Mallett 2011). Conditioning appropriations on Buy America provisions was intended to create jobs and promote US industry. A study by the Federal Highway Administration

---

4. "EU Objectives on Procurement in U.S. Deal Reflect Longstanding Issues," *Inside US Trade,* April 11, 2013, www.insidetrade.com (accessed on May 5, 2013).

5. "EU Objectives on Procurement in U.S. Deal Reflect Longstanding Issues."

6. The GPA agreement currently covers some procurement in 37 of the 50 US states.

summarizes the perceived objectives of ARRA's LCR provisions (drawn from GAO 2008):

- boost domestic employment through infrastructure spending,
- stimulate economic growth,
- protect against unfair competition from foreign firms that receive government subsidies, and
- strengthen national security by promoting the iron and steel industries.

The ARRA package included $62 billion for spending on transportation and water infrastructure. The Congressional Budget Office reports that $4.4 billion of ARRA funds were allocated to transportation and water infrastructure outlays in 2009 but that cumulative ARRA spending would amount to an estimated $54 billion by 2013 (CBO 2010). Of that amount, $39 billion would be spent on surface transportation (with $28 billion allocated to highways), $6 billion on water resources, and $8 billion on water and wastewater treatment.[7]

Buy America was a questionable blessing for the US water/wastewater equipment and pipe sector, which relies heavily on exports that have driven its impressive growth rates in recent years. According to the US Water and Wastewater Equipment Manufacturers Association, 30 percent of US production in this field is typically exported. Total US exports of these goods almost doubled between 1998 and 2008, from $13.3 billion to $24.9 billion. During the same period, US exports to Canada grew from $3.7 billion to $6.2 billion, representing 25 percent of total US exports of these goods. The next largest markets (in order) are Mexico, China, the United Kingdom, Germany, and Japan. For the water/wastewater sector, Buy America raised the risk of "me-too" LCR measures abroad that could hamper US exports.[8]

Clean Water and Drinking Water State Revolving Funds

Congress created the Clean Water State Revolving Fund (CWSRF) program in 1987 to serve as a long-term funding source for projects that protect and restore the nation's waters. During the last two decades, the CWSRF has provided low-interest loans targeting a wide range of projects in areas such as wastewater treatment, nonpoint source pollution control, estuary management, and a host of projects focusing on water quality. It is the largest federal funding program for wastewater infrastructure projects across the country.

---

7. These initial estimates were generally consistent with actual spending reported. For details, see "Actual ARRA Spending over the 2009–2011 Period Quite Close to CBO's Original Estimate," January 5, 2012, www.cbo.gov (accessed on April 20, 2013).

8. In June 2013 a number of trade associations, including the Water and Wastewater Equipment Manufacturers Association (WWEMA), voiced such concerns in a letter to the US Congress. See "Business Groups Urge Congress to Oppose Wave of Buy American Bills," *Inside US Trade,* June 14, 2013, www.insidetrade.com (accessed on June 18, 2013).

Under ARRA, EPA received $4 billion for the CWSRF.[9] The water and wastewater equipment and pipe sector relies heavily on steel.

The Safe Drinking Water Act, as amended in 1996, established the Drinking Water State Revolving Fund (DWSRF) to make funds available to drinking water systems to finance infrastructure improvements. Under ARRA, EPA received $2 billion for the DWSRF, with up to 1 percent of funds reserved for federal management and oversight and 1.5 percent for Indian tribes. The program emphasizes the provision of funds to small and disadvantaged communities and to programs that encourage pollution prevention as a tool for ensuring safe drinking water. It provides funds to states to establish state loan revolving funds that finance infrastructure improvements for public and private community water systems and not-for-profit noncommunity water systems, along with direct grants to Washington, DC, and US territories (e.g., the Virgin Islands).

In total, ARRA allocated $6 billion to the existing CWSRF. It allocated an additional $1.4 billion was to the Rural Utilities Services program of the Department of Agriculture for water and wastewater loans and grants.

Promoting sustainability and green jobs was a condition of ARRA fund allocation. States were required to allocate at least 20 percent of their grants to the Green Project Reserve, which is made up of projects related to green infrastructure, water and energy efficiency improvements, and environmental innovations (EPA 2011).

Section 1605 of ARRA extends the obligation to ensure that American steel is used, in compliance with the Buy America provisions to EPA. Its passage marked the first time either of these programs was subject to an LCR. The act took the LCRs to new heights in two key ways. First, it replaced the long-used "unreasonable cost" exception with an exception that allows for the use of foreign-made manufacturing goods only when the inclusion of domestic materials would increase the cost of the overall project by more than 25 percent. Second, it mandated that all domestic steel must be American. In other words, no imported pig iron ingots can be used to make finished pipe.

According to EPA's most recent quarterly report, released January 31, 2013, of the 3,367 projects that had started construction with stimulus funds under the CWSRF and the DWSRF, 70 percent had been completed as of the end of 2012 (EPA 2013). Nearly 1,000 projects remain to be completed. Despite these figures, the reality is that ARRA funding has been slow to translate into completed projects. Table 9.2 shows the value of projects started and completed. Although the target of $5.6 billion projects under contract and

---

9. In 2009 the CWSRF funded more than $5.2 billion in projects, about $430 million of it consisting of ARRA funds. Nearly $412 million of ARRA funds went toward publicly owned treatment works, consisting of sewer construction (60 percent) and secondary and advanced treatment facilities (40 percent); $14 million went toward nonpoint source projects, such as brownfield rehabilitation (EPA 2009).

Table 9.2   State Revolving Fund projects started and completed with ARRA funding, 2009–13 (billions of US dollars)

Fiscal year	Amount of projects under contract			Amount of projects that have started construction			Amount of projects that have completed construction		
	CWSRF	DWSRF	Total	CWSRF	DWSRF	Total	CWSRF	DWSRF	Total
2009	0.6	1.6	2.2	0.7	0.2	0.9	0.0	0.0	0.0
2010	3.8	1.8	5.6	3.8	1.8	5.6	0.2	0.1	0.3
2011	3.8	1.8	5.6	3.8	1.8	5.6	0.8	0.5	1.3
2012	3.8	1.8	5.6	3.8	1.8	5.6	1.6	0.8	2.4
2013[a]	3.8	1.8	5.6	3.8	1.8	5.6	1.8	0.9	2.7

ARRA = American Recovery and Reinvestment Act of 2009; CWSRF = Clean Water State Revolving Fund; DWSRF = Drinking Water State Revolving Fund

a. Results reported for FY2013 are as of first quarter.

Note: Projects indicated here are nontribal contracts and do not include tribal contracts.

Source: EPA (2013).

under construction has been reached, only $2.7 billion worth of projects have been completed, suggesting that nearly half of the funds have yet to be fully expended.

Steel Costs and Industry Delays

Steel is crucial to modern economies: buildings, automobiles, pipelines, and bridges are made of steel. However, steel manufacturing is highly capital intensive; the US steel industry employs only about 150,000 workers (North American Industrial Classification System Codes 3311 and 3312).

The key selling point for both the original and latter-day Buy America legislation was job creation. Politicians asserted that "not one dollar of the stimulus plan should be spent on foreign steel." In a time of crisis, this is a powerful argument. Blue-collar and white-collar jobs alike were shed at a terrifying pace in the Great Recession, including in the steel industry. Even before the financial crisis, the Bureau of Labor Statistics predicted that steel industry employment would decrease by 25 percent between 2006 and 2016. With the crisis, the drop came much sooner. US steel shipments plunged almost 40 percent in November 2008 year-on-year, with a quarter of that decrease occurring between October and November 2008. As the automobile sector collapsed, steel producers lost a large volume of sales. To compensate, the US steel industry hoped that strong Buy American provisions would lock in a stable customer, namely, the US public sector.

Many reports have estimated the overall effect of ARRA on employment in the United States; few have quantified the impact of Buy America provisions on US jobs. Estimates of job creation from infrastructure investment vary depending on the source but range from 7,000 to 10,000 direct jobs per billion dollars of spending.[10] Buy America provisions facilitate direct jobs by shifting federal procurement from foreign sources to domestic sources.

In Hufbauer and Schott (2009) we estimate that the additional steel production fostered by Buy America provisions could amount to 0.5 million metric tons, which would translate to about 1,000 jobs. In the US economy of roughly 140 million workers, 1,000 jobs is a very small number. Furthermore, if all manufactured goods used in projects were produced in the United States, an additional 9,000 jobs could be gained in the manufacturing industry (Hufbauer and Schott 2009).[11] Laura M. Baughman and Joseph F. Francoise (2009) estimate that a $3.2 billion shift in federal procurement from foreign to domestic sources could result in broader gains of about 24,000 jobs, but this figure includes both direct and indirect jobs.[12] Both studies conclude that any positive effect of ARRA on jobs could be outweighed if foreign governments emulate Buy American with their own LCR policies, thereby adversely affecting US exports and jobs.[13]

Whether the Buy America provisions of ARRA facilitated net US job growth is unclear.[14] Rather than revisit the employment debate, we consider the impact on project costs. The Government Accountability Office (GAO 2008) summarizes some of the challenges of complying with ARRA provisions in the case of federally funded transportation projects: higher iron and steel

---

10. The Federal Highway Administration estimates that in 2007 every $1 billion of expenditures on highway construction supported 30,000 jobs (10,300 direct jobs in construction; 4,675 jobs in supporting industries, such as steel; and 15,094 induced/indirect jobs). Based on labor productivity and employment requirements for 2008, the US Bureau of Labor Statistics estimates that $1 billion of expenditures in construction activities created 7,174 direct jobs and 4,091 indirect jobs (see Copeland, Levine, and Mallett 2011).

11. These figures are based on estimates from Romer and Bernstein (2009) that ARRA would directly create 1.5 million jobs in the US economy. Of these direct jobs, about 220,000 jobs would be in the manufacturing sector, calculated based on spending components of the recovery package for sectors including energy, infrastructure, healthcare, and education. As about 4 percent of US federal spending for the procurement of manufactures used in the United States is spent on manufacturing goods from foreign countries, the Buy America provisions might facilitate a switch of this "normal" 4 percent foreign purchases to domestic firms. Four percent of 220,000 is roughly 9,000.

12. Estimates are based on Bureau of Labor Statistics calculations of labor productivity in steel production. For details on the methodology used, see Baughman and Francoise (2009).

13. Hufbauer and Schott (2009) estimate that if US exports purchased by public entities abroad in 12 countries were at risk of an "echo effect" or outright retaliation, the job loss entailed could range between 6,500 and 65,000 jobs. Baughman and Francoise (2009) estimate that if 90 countries (including EU countries) included "buy national" requirements in stimulus bills that cut 1 percent of their spending on US entities, the job loss entailed could be as high as 170,000 jobs.

14. A study by the Political Economic Research Institute (Heintz, Pollin, and Garrett-Peltier 2009) claims that raising the requirement of domestically produced supplies to 100 percent (in other words, banning imports for infrastructure projects) could create 77,000 direct and indirect additional jobs in the United States, a 33 percent increase in employment in the manufacturing sector alone. This calculation is based on heroic assumptions and fails to take into account the impact on economywide costs, exports, and potential retaliation from US trading partners.

prices, higher overall project costs, reduced bidding competition, and project delays were among the most cited. In some cases, Buy America requirements influenced the ability to select or start projects and even the decision to use nonfederal funding in certain projects.[15] For example, Department of Transportation officials in Washington State reportedly opted out of ARRA funding and instead used nonfederal money for the Tacoma Narrows Bridge project. The project cost of almost $850 million included savings of $30 million to $35 million thanks to the use of lower-priced foreign steel.

There is evidence that the cost to the public of Buy America legislation was substantial. Here we walk through some arithmetic based on prices for US and imported steel. The average price of a metric ton of structural steel exported from the United States in 2011 was $3,450. Table 9.3 lists US imports of structural steel for selected countries. The average price per metric ton of structural steel imported into the United States was $2,870 from Canada, $2,240 from Mexico, $,2050 from China, and $1,690 from India.[16] The price of US steel is about $580 per metric ton higher than Canadian steel and about $1,450 higher than an average for Mexican, Chinese, and Indian steel.

Taking the average of these price differentials, as rough calculations we assume that imported structural steel costs about $1,000 per metric ton less than US steel. According to the Federal Highway Administration, a weighted average of 16.3 metric tons of structural steel was used per million dollars of highway construction expenditure between 2000 and 2003.[17] In 2009 the federal government spent $87 billion on transportation and water infrastructure, about $41 billion of it on highway infrastructure projects (CBO 2011). According to the Congressional Budget Office, in 2009 capital spending accounted for 95 percent (or $39 billion) of total federal spending on highway infrastructure (CBO 2011). ARRA provided funding of nearly $28 billion for highway projects (table 9.4).[18]

---

15. Five federal agencies (Commerce, Education, Homeland Security, Housing and Urban Development, and EPA), indicated that Buy America provisions affected their ability or the ability of their grantees to approve and start projects. For details, see GAO (2010).

16. These price estimates were calculated using the total value of exports divided by total quantity (in kilograms) of HS 7308, as reported in the UN Comtrade database. HS 7308 is the heading-level tariff classification of structures (excluding prefabricated buildings of heading 9406); parts of structures (e.g., bridges and bridge sections, lock gates, towers, lattice masts, roofs, roofing frameworks, doors and windows and their frames and thresholds for doors, shutters, balustrades, pillars and columns) of iron or steel; and plates, rods, angles, shapes, sections, tubes, and the like, prepared for use in structures of iron or steel.

17. This figure was converted into metric tons based on the original figure of 18 short tons per $1 million of spending on highway construction (FHWA 2004, table PT-4).

18. By the end of 2010, the Federal Highway Administration reported that ARRA had fully or partially funded more than 12,900 highway projects (FHWA 2013). Highway projects implemented with ARRA funds included pavement improvement (49 percent of ARRA projects), pavement widening (17 percent), new construction (7 percent), bridge replacement and improvement (9 percent), safety and traffic management (5 percent), and other projects. By the beginning of 2013, the number of projects funded rose to 13,375, with 85 percent reported completed (FHWA 2011).

Table 9.3   US structural steel imports from selected countries, 2011

	US imports	
Partner country	Value (billions of US dollars)	Percent of US imports from the world
Canada	530	20.5
China	846	32.8
India	48	1.9
Mexico	467	18.1
World	2,580	100.0

Note: Structural steel imports calculated from tariff heading HS 7308 classification: Structures (excluding prefabricated buildings) and parts of structures (e.g., bridges and bridge sections, lock gates, towers, lattice masts, roofs, roofing frameworks, pillars and columns) of iron or steel; plates, rods, angles, shapes, sections, tubes and the like, prepared for use in structures of iron or steel.

Sources: UN Comtrade database, http://comtrade.un.org/db; authors' calculations.

Table 9.4   ARRA funding distributed to highway construction by project type, May 2011

Project type	Amount (billions of dollars)	Percent of total funds
New bridge construction	0.5	2
Bridge improvement	1.2	5
Bridge replacement	1.4	5
New construction	1.8	7
Other	3.3	13
Pavement widening	4.7	18
Pavement improvement resurface	6.1	23
Pavement reconstruction/rehabilitation	7.1	27
Total	26.1	100

ARRA = American Recovery and Reinvestment Act of 2009

Note: These figures are for highway obligations, based on the amount allotted by the Federal Highway Administration for distribution to projects. In most cases, this amount was slightly less than the total ARRA funding received because some funds were set aside for administrative and oversight expenses, as allowed by the ARRA.

Source: GAO (2011, figure 2).

Assuming steel usage remained the same during the period of most ARRA expenditures (2009–11) and assuming federal highway outlays averaged about $40 billion annually, perhaps 652,000 metric tons of structural steel were used annually for federal highway construction during the ARRA era. Putting the figures together, the Buy America provision may have increased the cost of highway construction by $652 million annually ($1,000 per metric ton times 652,000 metric tons), or about $2.0 billion over three years. Federal spending on total highway construction and maintenance has been less than 30 percent of total highway spending; the rest represents state and local outlays, significantly supported by stimulus funds during the ARRA era. It seems likely that steel usage is about the same for state and local highways and roads. Doubling the figure calculated for federal costs, it seems plausible that the national cost of Buy America legislation for highway construction during the stimulus era was at least $3.9 billion.

Another large target of the Buy America requirement was water resources. Steel is used to construct water storage facilities such as reservoirs, tanks, and drums. The United States imports such products mainly from Canada, China, and Mexico (table 9.5).[19] On average, the price differential between the US steel and steel imported from these three countries is about 17 percent, or $80 per metric ton.[20] Annual US public spending on water resources—total spending by federal, state, and local governments, divided about equally between capital spending and spending on operations and maintenance—is about $8 billion.[21] Assuming that a fifth of capital spending goes to the purchase of steel, we can calculate that Buy America legislation increased the cost of water storage infrastructure by about $136 million annually, or about $400 million over the three-year ARRA era.

Buy America also affected purchases of steel pipe. In 2011, imported steel pipe was cheaper than US steel pipe by 30 to 50 percent, with an average of 37 percent. CBO budget outlay data show total public infrastructure spending on water supply and wastewater treatment averaging about $90 billion a year (CBO 2010). Capital spending accounts for about a third of public infrastructure spending on water supply and wastewater treatment, or about $30 billion a year. For rough calculations, we assume that only half of the projects (measured in terms of capital spending) during the three-year ARRA period were affected by the Buy America provisions, namely $15 billion a year.[22] Assuming that 10 percent of the affected outlays went to the purchase of steel pipe, steel expenditures would amount to $1.5 billion annually. If US steel pipe cost 30 percent more than the imported foreign alternative, Buy America added about $450 million a year to construction costs. Thus, the extra cost of Buy American legislation could be as much as $1.4 billion over the three-year ARRA era.

---

19. Imports calculated from the HS 7309 heading-level tariff classification include reservoirs, tanks, vats, and similar containers (other than compressed or liquefied gas) of iron or steel.

20. UN Comtrade data and authors' calculations.

21. Capital spending includes "purchases, construction, rehabilitation or improvement of physical assets, such as land, facilities, and equipment"; operations and maintenance includes spending on "current operations," investment in intangible assets such as R&D, and expenditures on administrative activities and public outreach (CBO 2010).

22. This approximation is rough, but it seems reasonable. According to EPA, by the end of 2011, more than 1,950 projects were administered under the CWSRF program with ARRA funding, nearly 40 percent of the 5,200 CWSRF wastewater assistance agreements from 2009 to 2011. Assuming similar figures for the DWSRF program yields an annual figure of $15 billion of capital spending.

Table 9.5 US steel imports from top countries for water resources, 2011

Partner country	Value (billions of dollars)	Percent of US imports from the world
Canada	122	39.6
China	38	12.2
Mexico	43	13.8
World	308	100.0

Note: Imports calculated from tariff heading HS 7309 classification: reservoirs, tanks, vats and similar containers (other than compressed or liquefied gas) of iron or steel.

Source: UN Comtrade database, http://comtrade.un.org/db; authors' calculations.

Adding the cost figures for the use of steel in highways, water resources, and water and wastewater construction, we calculate, very roughly, that the Buy America provision in ARRA may have cost the public about $5.7 billion over three years (table 9.6).

Alternatives to LCRs

The costs of Buy America provisions reported here are broad estimates. But the assessment captures only a portion of the story, the steel industry. Had we calculated the effect of ARRA on all manufactures, we might have concluded that costs were more than twice as great as our figure of $5.7 billion.

Despite the rapid commitment of money in 2009 and 2010, many projects were slow to get off the ground (as President Obama noted, "Shovel-ready was not as. . . uh. . . shovel-ready as we expected").[23] In reality, it seems that many projects were shovel ready but that the shovel was often made from Canadian steel, which ARRA prevented from crossing the border.

Probably the greatest damage from the Buy America eruption in ARRA was not higher project costs or project delays but rather the green light it gave to countries around the world to emulate the United States with their own LCRs. The LCR demonstration effect is impossible to quantify. Doubtless the sluggish world economy would have prompted many LCRs without any inspiration from the United States. Nevertheless, many US exporters and investors now find themselves confronting an array of LCRs that did not exist in 2008.

Two alternatives to LCRs should have been considered. First, given the political origins of Buy America in ARRA, it might have been possible—and it certainly would have been better—to have expressed the LCR as a bid

---

23. "Obama Jokes at Jobs Council: 'Shovel-Ready Was Not as Shovel-Ready as We Expected,'" FoxNews, June 13, 2011, http://nation.foxnews.com/president-obama/2011/06/13/obama-jokes-jobs-council-shovel-ready-was-not-shovel-ready-we-expected (accessed on January 28, 2013).

Table 9.6   Estimated costs of Buy America provisions from higher steel costs in infrastructure projects, 2009–11

Sector	Estimated cost over three-year ARRA period (billions of dollars)
Highway construction	3.9
Water resources	0.4
Water and wastewater construction	1.4
Total	5.7

ARRA = American Recovery and Reinvestment Act of 2009

Source: Authors' calculations.

preference solely for iron and steel, not as an escape clause if the overall project cost increased by more than 25 percent. A preference of 50 percent would have given ample protection to domestic steel firms while illuminating the costs to lawmakers and the public alike. Second, it would have been better to include a sunset clause on the Buy America provision, to emphasize that LCR protection was an emergency measure, not a semipermanent feature of US trade policy.

10

Conclusions and Recommendations

Local content requirements (LCRs) flourished in the wake of the Great Recession, but their use can be traced to the early annals of trade policy. Government procurement historically gave preferences to local suppliers, and free trade agreements customarily contain restrictive rules of origins. Many of the recent LCRs identified in our survey were inspired by three related factors: the political urgency to create jobs, the infant industry argument applied to renewable energy, and public outlays to boost the economy (stimulus spending).

The World Trade Organization (WTO) rulebook limits the scope of LCRs, as do some free trade agreements. The WTO rules are strongest when LCRs violate the obligation of national treatment, when a country has agreed to open procurement by certain of its agencies in the Government Procurement Agreement, and when a country offers incentives to spur investment. However, political energy is needed to launch a case in the WTO Dispute Settlement Body, technical escape hatches abound, case resolution often takes two or three years, and relief is always prospective, never retroactive. Not surprisingly, the number of new LCRs imposed since 2008 (117) vastly exceeds the handful of new WTO cases (3).

Classic LCRs, which give a bid preference to local suppliers (e.g., 25 percent on a construction project or a narrowly defined category of goods such as military uniforms) at least have the benefit of transparency. The cost of such LCRs can be easily calculated, their administration is relatively simple, and they are not prone to corruption. This type of LCR is the exception. Much more common are quantitative restrictions and opaque guidelines, which are highly objectionable on both economic and political grounds. From an economic standpoint, their cost is highly variable, depending both on underlying supply and demand conditions and administrative whims. Consequently, their effectiveness in supporting targeted jobs or growing an infant industry is hard to determine. From a political standpoint, nontransparency serves to insulate these LCRs from both domestic reform and international surveillance.

These same characteristics make LCRs highly attractive to their supporters. The costs are off-budget and can be dismissed in political debate. The benefits in terms of new jobs and new industries are easily exaggerated, but whether large or small, they are immediate.

Advice to Governments

Several alternative policies can deliver better results with less distortion and lower costs. They include measures to improve the business climate, corporate responsibility norms that encourage local suppliers without forcing localization, training programs that teach relevant skills, logistical upgrades that cut trade transaction costs, and infrastructure investments financed by user fees. Although the benefits of these measures may emerge only after three to five years, our strong recommendation for governments is to roll them out. With imagination, they can be displayed to the public with as much fanfare as a new set of LCRs.

For governments that urgently need immediate results—visible jobs—new tariffs can deliver just as quickly as new LCRs. Most developing countries have retained a degree—sometimes a large degree—of policy space between their tariff rates bound in the WTO schedules and their currently applied tariff rates. In these circumstances, it would be better to raise the tariff to the bound limit rather than impose an LCR on the same product. A tariff has the important advantages of transparency and simple administration. When the tariff is bound near the applied level, it is often better to raise it and then negotiate compensation with affected foreign suppliers.[1] Such a mechanism is transparent and simple. As part of the compensation, the government could commit to roll back the tariff within a reasonable period of time, rather than live indefinitely with a new LCR.

Governments that are determined to support an infant industry should design an appropriate mix of tariffs and subsidies rather than impose an LCR. The very fact that the subsidy component would entail a fiscal cost would force a periodic evaluation of costs and benefits. As for the tariff component, for the reasons already outlined, it is likely to have a shorter duration than the LCR.

Our final recommendations go to governments that are determined to impose new LCRs. We strongly recommend that the LCRs be expressed as classic price preferences on a narrow set of products or projects rather than

---

1. This approach can also be taken with free trade agreement partners, as most free trade agreements stipulate zero or very low tariffs.

as quantitative restrictions or discretionary guidelines. The LCRs should also include a time limit, expressed as a sunset clause.

Advice to Trade Officials and Negotiators

We offer just two recommendations to trade officials and negotiators. The first goes to WTO and regional free trade agreement secretariats, which should commission periodic reports that describe and analyze new (and perhaps preexisting) LCRs along with other new protective measures.[2] In the WTO, this "sunshine" function could be carried out by the Trade Policy Review Mechanism, provided that its staff is permitted to flag inconsistencies between the LCRs and WTO obligations. In established regional groups, like the North American Free Trade Agreement, Mercosur, the Association of Southeast Asian Nations, and the Pacific Alliance, the secretariats may not have the staff to carry out the "sunshine" function; these organizations might contract with independent bodies to prepare reports. The superregional groups now being formed—the Trans-Pacific Partnership, the Transatlantic Trade and Investment Partnership, and the Regional Comprehensive Economic Partnership—should build strong surveillance mechanisms into their pacts.

Our second recommendation calls upon trade negotiators to craft language that broadly penalizes any form of nontariff preference that has not been specifically scheduled on a "negative list." The penalty could take the form of a monetary payment or a countermeasure expressed in terms of trade or investment restrictions. We are not so lost in the ivory tower to imagine that such language could be inserted in established regional pacts, and it might be a distant aspiration for the WTO. However, we think that appropriate disciplines can and should be inserted in the superregional groups now being formed.

---

2. There is no reason to agonize over the dividing line between LCRs and other protective devices; if resources are available, all should be covered in the periodic reports.

Appendix A
Local Content Requirements
since 2008

This appendix attempts to identify all local content requirement (LCR) measures proposed or implemented since 2008 (see table A.1). Most of the cases are drawn from Global Trade Alerts (www.globaltradealert.org), a database established by the Center for Economic Policy Research. Other sources were also consulted.

Although policymakers avoided anything resembling an avalanche of protection, the list reveals disconcerting trends. Many of the new policies are opaque in nature, thus difficult to quantify. Several policies depart from the classic format of mandated purchases from domestic suppliers, instead mixing price and quantity signals. As discussed in the main text, we calculate that proposed and implemented LCRs may have affected 5 percent of world trade in goods and services in 2010, a significant amount. The LCR phenomenon requires greater attention in official circles.

Table A.1 New cases of local content requirements (post-2008)

Country and case number	Date announced; current status	Affected sectors	Size of affected domestic sectors	Estimated affected trade	Description of LCR measure
Argentina-1	2010; LCR remains in force	Agriculture and automotive		$9.0 billion in automobiles and auto parts imported in 2010	Owing to its radical debt restructuring policies, Argentina cannot access international credit markets. Thus it must maintain a trade surplus to pay for imports and build foreign exchange reserves. This has led to an overt policy of "import balancing," whereby companies are required to export $1 of a product from Argentina in order to import $1 of another product. Several auto and industrial manufacturers have become exporters of Argentine agricultural products to comply.
Argentina-2	February 2010; LCR remains in force	Transportation equipment	850,000 motorcycles were sold in Argentina in 2011	$379.8 million worth imported in 2010	The Local-Investment Incentives Regime for Motorcycles and Motorcycle Parts Manufacturing (Secretaria de Industria, Resolución 11/2010) in Argentina conditions tax credits on locally produced input purchases. The reduction of duties on imported inputs is conditioned on the applicant's pledge to invest in the facilities, machinery, and/or business of local suppliers.
Argentina-3	February 2011; LCR remains in force	Textiles, laptops, auto parts, plastics, toys, luggage, bicycles, machinery and tools, chemicals, and paper products		$18.3 billion in goods on nonautomatic import license list imported in 2010	Argentina's nonautomatic import license (NAL) list is expanded to cover 4,000 products in 600 Harmonized System (HS) lines, affecting a broad range of goods. NALs are permitted under the World Trade Organization (WTO), but only when licenses are processed within 60 days and are not trade distorting. In Argentina, licenses are seldom granted in less than 60 days unless affected companies meet unrelated government demands, such as agreeing to manufacture locally.

Argentina-4	September 2011; LCR remains in force	Reinsurance		Insurance 4.7 percent of commercial services imports or $687 million in 2010	The Argentine Superintendent of Insurance (SSN) has established a regulatory framework (SSN resolution no. 35.615/2011) that prohibits certain cross-border reinsurance operations. Prior to that regulation, overseas reinsurers were allowed to engage in reinsurance business from their home country, either upon registration with the regulator or via a broker authorized to operate in Argentina. The new regulation means that local insurance firms can only lay off reinsurance risks to locally based Argentine reinsurers, or Argentine subsidiaries or branches of foreign companies.
Argentina-5	October 2011; LCR remains in force	Insurance, mining, oil and gas	Mines and quarries $12.1 billion (3.4 percent of GDP), electricity, gas, and water supply $4.2 billion (1.2 percent of GDP) in 2010	Insurance 4.7 percent of commercial services imports or $687 million, diesel $1.8 billion, fuel $332 million, liquefied natural gas $443 million in 2010	To decrease the outflow of foreign currency reserves, Decree No. 1.722/2011 requires that all insurance, mining, and oil and gas companies must repatriate their foreign earnings. The decree requires that all export revenues be converted into pesos using the local foreign exchange market.
Argentina-6	January 2012; LCR remains in force	All imports, particularly information and communication technology (ICT) firms	Domestic telecom investment $104.6 billion (0.26 percent of GDP) in 2010, transport, storage and communication $27.3 billion (7.6 percent of GDP) in 2010	Computer, communications, and other services imports $4.5 billion, cell phone imports $627 million in 2010, telephone (land and cell) equipment imports $3.3 billion	As of February 2012, firms must submit a Declaración Jurada Anticipada de Importación for advance approval to import (Administración Federal de Ingresos Públicos General Resolution No. 3252 and 3255). Import approvals will take 3 to 18 days to process. To continue selling into the Argentine market, some foreign companies have set up assembly facilities within Argentina.

(continued on next page)

Table A.1 New cases of local content requirements (post-2008) *(continued)*

Country and case number	Date announced; current status	Affected sectors	Size of affected domestic sectors	Estimated affected trade	Description of LCR measure
Argentina-7	May 2012; LCR remains in force	Coal and lignite, uranium and thorium ores, metal ores, stone, sand and clay, other minerals	Mines and quarries $12.1 billion (3.4 percent of GDP)		Resolution no. 13/2012 introduced a number of measures for mining companies operating in Argentina. Companies are required to set up an import substitution department and to "respect the current norms of the Republic of Argentina in the design and completion of engineering projects," which means companies must prioritize local purchases and services. If companies are unable to set up this department, an import approval must be obtained from the mining ministry at least 120 days prior to the import.
Argentina-8	May 2012; LCR remains in force	Coal and lignite, uranium and thorium ores, metal ores, stone, sand and clay, other minerals; land, water, and air transport services	Mines and quarries $12.1 billion (3.4 percent of GDP)		Resolution no. 12/2012 requires mining companies with operations in Argentina to use local transport companies for the shipment of products.
Australia-1	June 2009; LCR rejected	Labor markets			The government of New South Wales included a Local Jobs First Plan in its stimulus package, providing a price preference for Australian and New Zealand content.

Australia-2	July 2009; LCR remains in force	Government procurement	A\$32.6 billion in total federal government procurement in 2010. Only \$2.1 million (A\$2.3 million) in federal procurement contracts awarded to overseas vendors in 2010	Australia provided \$2.5 million over four years to apply the National Framework of the Australian Industry Participation (AIP) to federal, state, and local governments. The AIP program requires applicants for government tenders to give details on the participation of Australian companies in projects exceeding threshold levels.
Australia-3	April 2010; LCR remains in force	Real estate		On April 24, 2010, the Australian government announced a major tightening of the foreign investment rules as they relate to residential real estate. The new rules: (1) require temporary residents to seek approval to acquire residential real estate in Australia, prevent foreign nonresidents from investing in Australian real estate if that investment does not add to the housing stock; (2) ensure that investments by temporary residents in established properties are only for their use whilst they live in Australia; and (3) if the investment concerns vacant land, foreigners are required to build within 24 months or resell the property.
Australia-4	October 2011; LCR remains in force	Government procurement		Prime Minister Julia Gillard announced a one-year extension of the AIP, expansion of the AIP to state and local governments, and a 5 percent import tariff tax credit law on federal and state projects of A\$20 million or more that entail major procurement contracts with Australian companies.

(continued on next page)

Table A.1 New cases of local content requirements (post-2008) *(continued)*

Country and case number	Date announced; current status	Affected sectors	Size of affected domestic sectors	Estimated affected trade	Description of LCR measure
Australia-5	March 2012; LCR implementation pending	Healthcare	In the 2009–10 financial year, healthcare business generated over $43 billion in income, spent over $32 billion on expenses. Payments to administrative businesses for support services is $1.4 billion or 13.9 percent of total healthcare expenditure		Section 77 of the Personally Controlled Electronic Health Record bill, proposed in the Australian parliament, would require local data centers to handle personal e-health records. No electronic health information could be held or processed outside of Australia.
Australia-6	November 2012; LCR remains in force	Postal and telecommunications services			In November 2011, Australia issued a media release "Government moves to ensure quality Australian content stays on Australian television," which outlines new regulations that aim to promote the production of local content. Specifically, commercial television broadcasters are required to air at least 730 hours of Australian content in 2013, 1,095 hours in 2014, and up to 1,460 hours in 2015.

Australia-7	2013; implemented mid-2013, in force by 2014	Manufacturing and all industries			In 2013, the Australian government released an Innovation and Industry Statement, which establishes the Australian Industry Participation Authority to coordinate the Buy Australian at Home and Abroad and Supplier Advocate initiatives and to review local content in AIP plans for large investment projects. Any project worth $500 million or more and projects with expenditures of $2 billion or more in all sectors of the economy must provide an AIP plan that indicates the use of local content. These efforts do not mandate LCRs but do intend to maximize the opportunities and funding for small and medium-sized enterprises, i.e, local manufacturers and help integrate them into global supply chains.
Azerbaijan-1	October 2010; LCR remains in force	Crude petroleum and gas, textiles, construction, computer and related services	Oil production 1.041 million barrels per day (2010 estimate); natural gas production 16.52 billion cubic meters (2009 estimate)	$346.7 million for construction and IT services in 2010, only 0.4 million in natural gas imports	Legislation on public procurement gives preference to products of local manufacturers listed in Azerbaijan's Catalogue of Industrial Enterprises & Item List of Industrial Products.
Botswana-1	February 2010; LCR remains in force	Basic metals, construction	Metals and mining approximately $5.2 billion (35 percent of GDP) in 2010	$33.7 million for construction services imported in 2010	The 2010/2011 Botswana national budget encouraged public works projects to target local contractors and use locally sourced building and raw materials.

(continued on next page)

Table A.1   New cases of local content requirements (post-2008) *(continued)*

Country and case number	Date announced; current status	Affected sectors	Size of affected domestic sectors	Estimated affected trade	Description of LCR measure
Brazil-1	September 2009; LCR remains in force	Information and communication technology (ICT)		$7.1 billion in telecommunications equipment imported in 2010	Brazil's National Telecommunications Regulatory Agency (ANATEL) does not accept test data generated outside Brazil, except in cases where the equipment is too large or too costly to transport. Foreign suppliers of cellphones and terminal access stations and radio base station transceivers must submit virtually all of their information technology and telecommunications equipment for testing to laboratories located in Brazil before that equipment can be placed on the Brazilian market. This requirement results in redundant testing, and consequently, higher costs and delayed time to market in Brazil.
Brazil-2	2010; LCR remains in force	Public procurement			Procurement law no. 12.349/2010 establishes a 25 percent margin of preference for manufactured goods and national services in compliance with Brazilian technical standards.
Brazil-3	July 2010; LCR remains in force	Construction	$3.68 billion		President Lula da Silva's "Medida Provisória nº 497" included a program of incentives for capital goods and civil construction associated with soccer stadiums (RECOM). RECOM grants fiscal benefits until June 2014 for the local acquisition or importation of equipment and building materials.

Brazil-4	July 2010; LCR remains in force	Public procurement, ICT	The Buy Brazil Act (law no. 12.349/2010) establishes preferences for Brazilian goods and services in government contracts, to be determined by the president, though not in excess of 25 percent above the price of foreign goods and services. For strategic IT and communications technology contracts, tenders will be restricted to goods and services developed with national technology. The procurement rules were further tightened as part of the Brasil Maior plan.
Brazil-5	November 2010; LCR remains in force	Manufacturing and all industries	Brazilian Development Bank (BNDES) financing (up to 100 percent for small and medium enterprises and up to 80 percent for larger companies) requires new capital goods (machinery and equipment) to meet national content indexes, in weight and value, equal to or greater than 60 percent, to follow the Basic Production Process (Processo Produtivo Básico), which entails a minimum set of operations necessary to certify the end product is Brazilian-made. Among other features, this requires that certain components be acquired from local manufacturers. Circular No. 55/2010 prohibited BNDES financing for the acquisition of airplanes; it also changed the financing system for the acquisition of new capital goods.
Brazil-6	December 2010; LCR remains in force	Insurance	US companies seeking to enter Brazil's insurance and reinsurance market must establish a subsidiary, enter into a joint venture, or acquire or partner with a local company. Market entry for banks is subject to case-by-case approval. The Brazilian reinsurance market was opened to competition in 2007. However, in December 2010 and March 2011, the Brazilian National Council on Private Insurance (CNSP) effectively rolled back market liberalization through the issuance of Resolutions 225

(continued on next page)

Table A.1   New cases of local content requirements (post-2008) *(continued)*

Country and case number	Date announced; current status	Affected sectors	Size of affected domestic sectors	Estimated affected trade	Description of LCR measure
					and 232, which disproportionately affect foreign insurers operating in the Brazilian market. Resolution 225 requires that 40 percent of all reinsurance risk be placed with Brazilian companies. In addition, Resolution 232 allows insurance companies to place only 20 percent of risk with affiliated reinsurance companies.
Brazil-7	2011; LCR remains in force	ICT, media		$957 million in audiovisual and related services (film, television, radio, music, etc.) imported in 2010	Brazil's "new" media law (Law 12.485) requires all channels to retransmit 3.5 hours of Brazilian content per week in primetime, half of which must be produced by Brazilian independent producers. It also requires the direct participation of a Brazilian advertising agency. Additionally, the draft regulations require hiring personnel through a Brazilian company located in Brazilian territory, and permitting Brazilian producers to own their creation of audiovisual products and derivative products, as well as the licensing rights. Revisions to these regulations are under consideration for 2013.
Brazil-8	August 2011; LCR remains in force	All industries		$46.5 billion in products directly affected by the Reintegra Program exported annually	The Brasil Maior ("Greater Brazil") policy offers an additional variety of tax, tariff, and financing incentives to encourage local production for export. The Reintegra Program, launched in December 2011 as part of Brasil Maior, exempts exports of goods covering 8,630 tariff codes, representing R$80 billion (approximately $46.5 billion) of exports, from certain taxes and introduces a tax credit for exporters of industrialized goods equal to 3 percent of the value of their exports. To qualify, the imported content of the exported goods must not exceed

	Date; status	Sector	Trade affected	Description
Brazil-9	September 2011; LCR remains in force but set to expire December 2012	ICT	$6.4 billion in various motor vehicles exported in 2010	Decree No. 7.567/11 reduced Brazil's internal industrial tax (Imposto sobre Produtos Industrializados, or IPI) by about 5.5 percent on certain items of the car industry (i.e., cars, lorries, and commercial trucks) for companies fulfilling specific requirements on local content (at least 65 percent) and investment provisions (invest at least 0.5 percent of after-tax income in R&D in Brazil). Manufacturers have two months to prove that they produce 65 percent or more of their components in Brazil or to adjust their production chain and assembly operations. The decree also established higher IPI rates (ranging from 30 to 55 percent) applicable until December 31, 2012, on vehicles.
Brazil-10	September 2011; LCR remains in force	Transport equipment	$10.5 billion in various motor vehicles imported in 2010	Increases by 25 to 30 percent on Brazil's tax for imports of motor vehicles, tractors, buses, trucks and light commercial vehicles, in force until December 31, 2012, unless the vehicles meet rules of origin standards related to Mercosur members or Mexico.
Brazil-11	December 2011; LCR remains in force	Agriculture		On December 9, 2011, the National Land Reform and Settlement Institute (INCRA) published new rules covering the purchase of Brazilian agricultural land by foreigners. These rules follow Legal Opinion CGU/AGU N° 01/2008 - RVJ, released by the attorney general in August 2010, that limited foreign agricultural ownership in Brazil. Under the new rules, the area bought or

The first paragraph (continuing from previous page):

40 percent, except in the case of high-technology goods such as pharmaceuticals, electronics, and aircraft and parts, which are permitted to have imported content of up to 65 percent. Government procurement laws were revised to provide preferences for local producers.

(continued on next page)

Table A.1 New cases of local content requirements (post-2008) *(continued)*

Country and case number	Date announced; current status	Affected sectors	Size of affected domestic sectors	Estimated affected trade	Description of LCR measure
					leased by foreigners cannot account for more than 25 percent of the overall area in its respective municipal district. Additionally, no more than 10 percent of the land in any given municipal district may be owned or leased by foreign nationals from the same country. Congressional approval is required before large plots of land can be purchased by foreigners, foreign companies, or Brazilian companies with a majority of foreign shareholders. These restrictions and the accompanying uncertainty as to how they will be applied may discourage FDI in Brazilian agricultural land.
Brazil-12	2012; LCR remains in force	Healthcare			The Brazilian healthcare program will have two main components: government procurement through the Unified Health System (SUS), launched in early 2012, and a fiscal support plan expected to be launched during the second half of 2012. The procurement plan will establish up to 25 percent preferences for Brazilian medical technologies or medications in government contracts, in an effort to support indigenous industry.
Brazil-13	2012; LCR pending approval	Manufacturing			This measure if enacted will provide tax benefits to locally manufactured and locally developed technologies used in Brazil's national broadband plan.
Brazil-14	January 2012; LCR remains in force	ICT			The tender proposal (Edital de 2,5 GHz e 450 MHz CP 4/2012) approved by the Brazilian Agency of Telecommunications (ANATEL) for the sale of 450 MHz and 2.5 GHz frequencies increases the requirements for national content, raising the minimum level of Brazilian telecommunications equipment in public procurement to 60 percent between 2012 and 2014: 50 percent in products

Brazil-15	February 2012; Rules drafted; LCR in effect April 2013	Oil and gas, mining	$31.1 billion in various mineral exports in 2010	that meet the Basic Production Process and 10 percent in investment in technology developed in Brazil. During 2015–16, the overall level of national content required in the development of 4G telecommunications networks is scheduled to jump to 65 percent (including 15 percent investment in Brazilian technology) and from 2017 onward the level jumps to 70 percent (including 20 percent investment in Brazilian technology).

President Dilma Rousseff is deciding the local content percentage that the Brazilian government will require companies exploring and producing minerals to spend with local businesses. Brazil's LCRs for equipment such as oil platforms could affect the pace of development of Brazil's subsalt fields, as the LCR could exceed the capacity of Brazilian industry to provide the goods and services necessary for a large investment project. A new LCR went into full effect in Brazil's 11th licensing round for oil and gas in April 2013; bids are assessed based on the following criteria: signature bonus (40 percent), the mandatory exploration program (40 percent), and the minimum local content requirement (20 percent) of each bidder. |
| **Canada-1** | January 2009; LCR remains in force | Transport equipment | $143.8 million (C$175 million) | The Government of Canada provided $C175 million to the Canadian Coast Guard for the purchase of new vessels and improvements to existing vessels, requiring work to be done by shipyards within the regions of the vessel's homeport. |

(continued on next page)

Table A.1 New cases of local content requirements (post-2008) *(continued)*

Country and case number	Date announced; current status	Affected sectors	Size of affected domestic sectors	Estimated affected trade	Description of LCR measure
Canada-2	February 2009; LCR rejected	All government procurement	$195 billion federal government procurement market in 2008. $20 billion (C$20.4 billion) in federal contracts awarded by Canadian government in 2009		The Canadian Products Promotion Act (CPPA) would alter public procurement decisions to favor goods that contain at least 50 percent Candian content (except for natural resources, for which the test is 75 percent Canadian content) and limits the percentage of provincial purchases from abroad to no more than 50 percent of the total amount spent on Canadian products in a given fiscal year. Products from NAFTA countries are not counted as imports under these spending caps.
Canada-3	October 2009; LCR remains in force	Electrical machinery		$1.0 billion in provincial imports in 2010	Ontario's feed-in tariff program requires developers to acquire a certain percentage of their project costs come from Ontario goods and labor. The local content requirements differ by technology, project size and project timing. For wind projects over 10 MW, the LCR is 25 percent for a commercial operating date (COD) before January 2012, and 50 percent with COD after January 2012; for solar projects over 10 kW and less than 10 MW, the LCR is 50 percent for a COD before January 2011, and 60 percent with a COD after January 2011.
Canada-4	February 2012; LCR remains in force	ICT			British Columbia's amendments to the Freedom of Information and Protection Of Privacy Act require that personal information collected by public sector agencies in Canada must be stored or accessed only in Canada, and the service provider must report any foreign demands for data disclosure.

Canada-5	February 2012; LCR remains in force	ICT		Nova Scotia's and British Columbia's amendments to the Personal Information International Disclosure Act require that personal information collected in Canada must be stored or accessed only in Canada, but a public body may override the rules where storage or access outside of the respective province is essential.
China-1	October 2009; LCR remains in force	Wind turbines	$5.2 million in 2010	At the 20th US-China Joint Commission on Commerce and Trade meeting in October 2009, the Chinese government agreed to drop its local content requirement for wind turbines. Previous to the agreement, the Chinese government demanded that local governments to source more than 70 percent from domestic sources when planning wind power projects. However, China requires wind turbine imports to meet local test certification by the National Energy Administration.
China-2	November 2008; LCR in force	Energy	$11.5 million in imports in 2010	In November 2008, China implemented a $586 billion economic stimulus package, allocating a major portion of the government spending to renewable energy projects. A circular jointly released by nine government organizations requires that preference be given to domestic products. This combination of measures virtually ensures a massive volume of sales of domestically manufactured renewable energy equipment.

(continued on next page)

Table A.1   New cases of local content requirements (post-2008) *(continued)*

Country and case number	Date announced; current status	Affected sectors	Size of affected domestic sectors	Estimated affected trade	Description of LCR measure
China-3	May 2009; LCR remains in force	Metal ores, textiles, basic chemicals, basic metals, fabricated metal products, machinery, office equipment, electrical machinery, communication equipment, precision instruments, transport equipment		$11 billion in imports in 2010	The Ministry of Information Industry's Planning Release entitled "Restructuring and Revitalization of Planning for the Equipment Manufacturing Industry" encourages state bodies to ensure that domestic industries meet the requirements of the national market, particularly with respect to power generation and capital equipment. The ministry recommends measures that encourage the use of Chinese-made equipment, including insurance policies that favor local technologies and equipment. The release also calls for an increase in the export-tax rebates granted to producers of high-technology and high-value added equipment and the abolition of import tariffs on key components of these technologies and on related raw materials.
China-4	May 2009; LCR remains in force	Public procurement	Approximately $127.6 billion in central government procurement in 2010		The National Development and Reform Commission (NDRC) implemented measures to ensure that local content would be prioritized in government contracts. The extent to which the Government Procurement Law governs procurement of renewable energy services and equipment by state-owned enterprises (SOEs) is ambiguous. By its terms the law applies to purchases of goods and services by numerous SOEs; the firms reportedly apply LCR principles when making procurement decisions. The buy national principles set forth in the Government Procurement Law are most rigorously applied to procurement of equipment for projects that are funded by government investments. Projects requiring imported products need prior approval from relevant government authorities.

China-5	October 2009; LCR rejected	Machinery, office equipment	Approximately $514 million in central government procurement in 2009	The Ministry of Science and Technology, National Development and Reform Commission, and Ministry of Finance released a joint directive entitled "Notification Regarding the Launch of National Indigenous Innovation Product Accreditation Work for 2009," which aims to promote the use of Chinese products. The directory of accredited products that are eligible for government procurement contracts, discriminates against foreign firms not located in China when they seek to supply the listed products. These policies were abandoned after many foreign companies complained that they would be discriminatory.
China-6	January 2010; LCR remains in force	Entertainment	$371 million in audiovisual and related services (film, television, radio, music, etc.) imported in 2010	Measures to promote the domestic film industry include preferential taxes and two-thirds of screen time reserved for local films (applicable since 2001) under the Guiding Opinions on Promotion of Prosperous Development of the Film Industry of January 21, 2010.
China-7	March 2011; LCR remains in force	Basic chemicals, scraps	$38.5 billion	China set strict conditions for companies within the magnesium industry. These accelerate industry restructuring, regulate investment, prevent redundant construction, and enhance environmental protection. Many enterprises may not be able to meet these standards, thus allowing large SOEs to dominate the magnesium market.
China-8	April 2011; LCR remains in force	High-tech, agriculture, forestry, husbandry, computer and related services	Approximately $1.1 billion, maximum	High-tech enterprises in Guangdong Province may receive favorable tax treatment related to their income, research and development costs, depreciation deductions, land use, income from technology transfer, etc.

(continued on next page)

Table A.1   New cases of local content requirements (post-2008) *(continued)*

Country and case number	Date announced; current status	Affected sectors	Size of affected domestic sectors	Estimated affected trade	Description of LCR measure
China-9	2012; provisional LCR remains in force	ICT			Provisional telecom laws require all foreign firms that provide telecom services to enter a joint venture with a Chinese firm. This would also apply to data centers and cloud computing.
China-10	2012; LCR remains in force	Government automotive procurement		$2.9 billion in cars imported by the Chinese government in 2010	The government issues public procurement preference procedures for a list of 412 locally produced Chinese car models. Government car purchases are estimated to be 10 percent of the total automotive market in China.
Egypt-1	January 2012; LCR announced	Industrial engineering equipment		$6.9 billion imported in industrial engineering equipment in 2010	Egyptian Minister of Industry Mahmoud Eissa said he will ban imports of industrial engineering equipment, a policy that he believes will encourage domestic production, increase youth employment, and attract foreign investment.
France-1	February 2010; LCR rejected by firm	Transport equipment	About 10,000 electric cars sold in France in 2010		The French government offered automaker Renault a 100 million euro state loan for electric vehicles in return for the company's pledge to increase local content from 40 to 70 percent and to maintain employment. Renault declined the offer after the European Commission began an inquiry questioning whether the loan was an infringement of EU Single Market rules.

France-2	June 2011; LCR remains in force	ICT	The draft decree amending an article of the Code of Electronic Communications related to lawful interceptions includes a "territorial" restriction requiring that the systems for interception of electronic communications must be established in France, and encrypted with state-approved technology if data is transmitted outside the jurisdiction. Only employees entrusted by the state have access to the systems required for interception and the data produced by these systems. When technical obstacles warrant, derogations from the draft's restrictions can be granted on agreement with the State.
Greece-1	February 2011; LCR remains in force	ICT	Article 6 of Greek law no. 3917/2011 establishes a data residency requirement, potentially in violation of the principle of free flow of data as set out in article 16 (2) of the 2010 Treaty on the Functioning of the European Union (EU): "Any obligation imposed by a Member State for the data to be retained on its own territory, is a restriction to the principle of free flow of data within the EU."
India-1	August 2009; LCR remains in force	Energy	$295 million in wind turbines exported in 2010; $426.9 million imported	To introduce newer wind turbine models (or to modify existing models), the new models have to be registered with the Centre for Wind Energy Technology (C-WET), which requires establishing an assembly facility in India. Third-party certification is required in addition to the design assessment. State agencies require C-WET certification for allowing connection to the grid.

(continued on next page)

Table A.1 New cases of local content requirements (post-2008) *(continued)*

Country and case number	Date announced; current status	Affected sectors	Size of affected domestic sectors	Estimated affected trade	Description of LCR measure
India-2	December 2009; LCR implementation suspended	ICT		$12.5 billion in telecommunication equipment imported in 2010	India's Department of Telecommunications issued licensing amendments adopted in December 2009 and March 2010 and a "template agreement for security and business continuity" issued in July 2010. Under these measures, any vendor seeking to sell foreign manufactured telecom equipment and products to Indian telecom service providers was required to: (1) deposit its source codes with an escrow agency; (2) transfer its technology to Indian companies; and (3) meet burdensome testing and certification requirements. These requirements were mandatory for all private commercial contracts between foreign telecommunications service providers and vendors of foreign telecommunications-related equipment, products, and services in India. In response to US concerns, India suspended the "template agreement" and agreed to review its security regulations.
India-3	January 2010; LCR remains in force	Fabricated metal products, machinery		$4.9 billion in power-generating equipment imported in 2010	India decided to bar imports of certain equipment used in electricity generation on January 20, 2010. Ultra mega power projects (UMPP) are no longer allowed to source equipment from abroad, but are required to source domestically. In a related move, the Central Electrical Authority asked all state and central utilities to include an "indigenous manufacturing clause" in their equipment contracts. Likewise, other public utilities are asked to source their equipment from domestic providers.

India-4	May 2011; LCR remains in force	ICT	$597 million in telecommunications services imported in 2010	India issued revised telecom security regulations. The new regulations require all imported information and communications technology equipment to be tested in Indian laboratories. Vendors fear that they could be wrongly blacklisted because the regulations do not provide judicial rights and appeal procedures.
India-5	June 2011; LCR was a nonbinding recommendation	ICT		New guidelines from India's Ministry of Communication and IT regulating government purchases include Made in India clause requirements and grant price preferences (up to 30 percent) for locally manufactured electronic equipment and IT products.
India-6	October 2011; LCR remains in force	Energy, electrical machinery, radio, television and communication equipment	$672.3 million in semiconductor devices used to generate solar power imported in 2010	India's Ministry of New and Renewable Energy released guidelines that project developers "are expected to procure their project components from domestic manufacturers, as far as possible" as part of the country's Jawaharal Nehru National Solar Mission (JNNSM). For photovoltaic projects based on crystalline silicon technology, the guidelines require that all project developers use modules manufactured in India; for such projects selected in FY2011–12, developers must use both modules and cells manufactured in India. For projects based on solar thermal technology, the guidelines require 30 percent local content in all plants and installations (under the JNNSM Batches I and II).
India-7	January 2012; LCR remains in force	Retail trade services	$392.6 billion in retail trade sales in 2011	India announced intentions to increase the foreign direct investment caps on foreign-owned stores, allowing up to 100 percent ownership for single-brand stores (typically flagship stores of consumer goods producers) and a maximum stake of 51 percent by foreigners in multibrand stores (general retail). However, the government also included several safeguards, which it may

(continued on next page)

Table A.1 New cases of local content requirements (post-2008) *(continued)*

Country and case number	Date announced; current status	Affected sectors	Size of affected domestic sectors	Estimated affected trade	Description of LCR measure
					impose in the future. The safeguards under consideration include numerous LCRs, such as: (1) at least 50 percent of the jobs in the retail outlet could be reserved for rural youth and a certain amount of farm produce could be required to be procured from poor farmers, (2) a minimum percentage of manufactured products could be required to be sourced from the small and medium enterprise (SME) sector in India, and (3) the government may reserve the right to procure a certain amount of food grains to ensure that the public distribution system and the Indian food security system is not weakened.
India-8	January 2012; LCR under consideration	ICT			India proposed a privacy act that puts the onus on certain companies to locate part of their information technology infrastructure within the country to enable investigative agencies ready access to encrypted data. This act will also require that data on Indian citizens, government organizations and firms hosted on the servers not be moved out of the country. Companies found in violation of data leakage will be liable as having committed a criminal offense and officials will face prosecution. Currently, the servers of all service providers are located outside the country and data can transmit freely to the respective client country. If servers or similar facilities are located in India, then data exchanges would stay within India, with huge implications for India's software industry.

India-9	February 2012; LCR remains in force	Electronics, manufacturing		The Indian cabinet approved new rules requiring that all electronic software and hardware products "having security implications" that are purchased by government agencies or "Government Licensees" must contain at least 25 percent Indian content by the end of the first year of implementation, and 45 percent by the second year of implementation. Beyond direct government procurement, the rules would force government licensees, including private sector telecommunications service providers, to procure electronic products locally. After facing increased pressure, the Indian government rolled back the proposed private sector requirements in July 2013.
Indonesia-1	May 2009; LCR remains in force	Computer and related services	$22.6 billion in value added for the telecom services industry in 2010	$9.0 billion in computer, communication, and related service imports in 2010	The European Union and the United States requested that Indonesia clarify new measures applicable to investment in Indonesia's broadband telecommunications sector, particularly fair bidding processes between domestic and foreign firms for government-auctioned wireless spectrum (at issue is a LCR of 30 to 50 percent for any bidder).
Indonesia-2	September 2009; LCR remains in force	Electrical utilities		Indonesia enacted its first regulation on the implementation of the new electricity law; this law abolishes the monopoly of state-owned electricity company PT Perusahaan Listrik Negara on the supply and distribution of electricity to end-customers. The law allows private investors, including foreign investors, to generate, transmit, distribute and sell electricity. Indonesia also issued a regulation that specifies the scope of the obligation for foreign investors to divest mining concessions in Indonesia. It requires that within five years of commencing production, 20 percent of the foreign capital must be sold to local parties, including central, provincial, or regional governments, and SOEs.

(continued on next page)

Table A.1 New cases of local content requirements (post-2008) *(continued)*

Country and case number	Date announced; current status	Affected sectors	Size of affected domestic sectors	Estimated affected trade	Description of LCR measure
Indonesia-3	October 2009; LCR remains in force	Transportation and delivery services			Indonesia passed new laws abolishing monopoly power for certain postal services and established specific conditions for foreign providers to cooperate with local service providers, including that the majority of equity participation in joint ventures should be Indonesian and that joint ventures between foreign and domestic providers will be limited to provincial capitals, international airports, and seaports.
Indonesia-4	December 2009; LCR remains in force	Energy			Indonesian regulation PTK No. 007 Revision-1/PTK/IX/2009 requires local and foreign bidders for energy service contracts to use a minimum of 35 percent domestic content in their operations.
Indonesia-5	2010; LCR remains in force	ICT			Indonesia's Negative Investment List (DNI) (Presidential Regulation 36/2010) continues to restrict foreign investment. ICT in particular falls largely under the sensitive area "Communications Services." Maximum foreign capital ownership varies between subsectors, ranging from 49 percent (e.g., for internet service providers) to 95 percent for data communication system service providers. Computer service providers are not specifically identified in the DNI.
Indonesia-6	2011; LCR remains in force	ICT			Article 25 of Indonesia's Undang-undang Informasi dan Transaksi Elektronik states that, "Any provider of Electronic System for public services that operates data center must place the data center and disaster recovery center operations in Indonesia." In 2011 the Ministry of Communications (KOMINFO) required Research in Motion and Google to build server and data centers inside the country and is also approaching other companies like Visa and Mastercard with similar requests.

Indonesia-7	2011; LCR remains in force	Toys	$343.6 million in toys exported in 2010	Indonesia's Directorate General of Manufacturing Industries proposes to enforce in 2012 a new toy safety standard, SNI 8124:2010. The US toy industry is concerned that the safety standard will require redundant in-country testing, as products will have to be tested in Indonesia in addition to whatever safety testing they undergo in their place of manufacturing.
Indonesia-8	January 2011; Rule implementation LCRs being drafted	Government procurement		Article 98 of Presidential Decree 54/2010 gives a public procurement preference to goods and services with a minimum of 25 percent local content (even where the bid is 15 percent higher in price) and applies to bids over $550,000. Article 97 of the decree awards additional preference points to vendors with investments in Indonesia and partnerships with local small and medium-sized enterprises.
Indonesia-9	September 2011; LCR remains in force	ICT		Indonesia issued two decrees: a wireless broadband decree that requires local content of 30 to 50 percent in the wireless sector and a telecommunications decree that requires all service operators spend 35 percent of their capital outlays on domestically made equipment. Currently, at least 40 percent of equipment must be locally sourced, but within 5 years this figure rises to 50 percent.

(continued on next page)

Table A.1   New cases of local content requirements (post-2008) *(continued)*

Country and case number	Date announced; current status	Affected sectors	Size of affected domestic sectors	Estimated affected trade	Description of LCR measure
Indonesia-10	February 2012; LCR remains in force	Mining and minerals	Indonesian mining industry valued at $82.6 billion. 80 percent of mining industry ($66.1 billion) under foreign ownership	$8.8 billion in unprocessed metals and nonmetallic minerals exported in 2010	Indonesia's Ministry of Energy and Mineral Resources (MEMR) Regulation No. 7/2012 implements 2009 law calling for an export ban on unprocessed metals or nonmetallic minerals and restrictions on foreign investment in the mining industry. Effective May 6, 2012, mining firms will be banned from exporting unprocessed metals or nonmetallic minerals, unless they submit a notification to the government indicating their plans for smelter construction. This provision would require firms to locate their mineral processing facilities on-shore in Indonesia. Additionally, implementing regulations created a timetable that requires that 51 percent of shares in operating mining companies must be owned by Indonesian shareholders after 10 years of production. Companies with foreign ownership levels exceeding those outlined in the timetable must divest their shares.
Indonesia-11	June 2012; LCR remains in force	Textiles (other than apparel), leather, footwear, other chemical products, rubber and plastics products, basic metals, fabricated metal products, general and special purpose machinery, electrical machinery, transport machinery			In June 2012, Indonesia's Ministry of Finance implemented Regulation no. 76/PMK.011/2012, which eliminates import tariffs on machinery, goods and materials used in the motorized vehicles assembly and components industries for companies that locally purchase at least 30 percent of the total value of machines. While the LCR is not "mandated," the resolution incentivizes companies to buy local through the use of tariff elimination as a reward.

Indonesia-12	October 2012; LCR remains in force	Retail	In October 2012, Indonesia's Ministry of Trade issued regulation 68/M-DAG/PER/10/2012, which sets a 150 maximum number of outlets that can be directly owned by foreign retailers; to own more than this amount, at least 40 percent must be franchised to other parties. In addition, 80 percent of the goods sold must be locally produced.
Kazakhstan-1	May 2009; LCR remains in force	Public procurement, construction	Kazakhstan adopted changes to its law on public procurement to include a "local clause" in public procurement for goods (20 percent) and services (15 percent). Companies with more than 50 percent foreign shareholding are considered foreign unless they fulfill three criteria for qualifying as a "national producer."
Kazakhstan-2	December 2009; LCR remains in force	Mining and minerals, electricity, refined petroleum products, basic chemicals, rubber and plastics, scraps	Kazakhstan introduced an LCR in the terms of subsoil use contracts. It also tightened legislation with regard to the definition of a domestic company in the subsoil sector, requiring that at least 95 percent of employees be domestic citizens. Existing legal entities may have to reduce the number of foreign personnel.
Kazakhstan-3	May 2010; LCR remains in force	Consumer foodstuffs	Government decree no. 423 introduces a list of common goods that are to be bought from domestic producers, such as bread, pasta, sweets, cereals, milk, milk products, butter, eggs, salt, and nonalcoholic beverages.
Kazakhstan-4	June 2011; LCR no longer remains in force (with respect to Google) as of June 2011	ICT	In 2011, Google was notified of an order issued by Kazakhstan's Ministry of Communications and Information that required all .kz domain names to operate on physical servers within the country's borders. Within a week of Google's protest, the government stated that the order no longer applies to previously registered domains (e.g., google.kz).

(continued on next page)

Table A.1 New cases of local content requirements (post-2008) *(continued)*

Country and case number	Date announced; current status	Affected sectors	Size of affected domestic sectors	Estimated affected trade	Description of LCR measure
Kazakhstan-5	August 2012; LCR remains in force	Land			Kazakhstan introduced new rules (Resolution No. 1028) on local content in the terms of subsoil use contracts. New minimum LCRs are set at 16 percent for goods and 85 percent for works and services.
Kenya-1	July 2009; non-binding LCR recommendation	Crude petroleum and natural gas, stone, metal ores, wood, refined petroleum products, glass products, basic metals		$3.3 billion in products made with raw materials also found in Kenya imported in 2010	The Kenyan Ministry of Industrialization issued a Strategic Plan (2008–12) that aims to increase the use of locally available raw materials by industry to 25 percent by 2012.
Kenya-2	October 2012; LCR remains in force	Coal and lignite, crude petroleum and natural gas, uranium and thorium ores, metal ores, stone, sand and clay, other minerals			In October 2012, Kenya enacted the Mining Act, which requires all foreign investors in the mining sector to maintain a minimum of 35 percent of local shareholders in order to apply for exploration and mining licenses.
Korea-1	October 2011; LCR remains in force	Pharmaceuticals		$3.5 billion in pharmaceutical products imported in 2010	Korea's Special Act on Fostering and Supporting Pharmaceutical Industry provides domestic pharmaceutical companies with information on domestic and overseas pharmaceutical markets and rewards "outstanding" pharmaceutical companies.

Korea-2	2012; LCR under consideration	ICT, financial services		Korea's Financial Services Commission (FSC) is considering regulations that would require insurers to maintain servers for housing company financial data in-country and restricting transfers of such data outside of Korea's borders (the financial data in question do not pertain to policy holders or employees). This is despite provisions in the Korea-US FTA, scheduled to take effect two years from entry into force in 2012, to permit sending data across the border intracompany or to third parties. The data transfer provision in the FTA was intended to establish an innovative precedent in Asia to allow US financial services companies to integrate regional and global operations by using established data processing hubs.
Mexico-1	October 2010; LCR remains in force	Government procurement		In October 2010, Mexico published new regulations to national content for government procurement. These regulations establish a minimum national content of 60 percent in 2011 and 65 percent for 2012 (but included exceptions of 30 to 35 percent for some light manufacturers and automobiles). The federal regulations only apply when federal funds are used, and Mexican states can develop their own rules.
Mongolia-1	May 2012; LCR remains in force	Mining and minerals, banking, telecommunications	Top ten Mongolian mines contain mineral reserves worth $2.75 trillion at current prices. $5 billion in FDI in 2011	The Mongolian parliament passed a law restricting foreign investors from majority control in "strategic industries," unless the deals are approved by parliament. President Tsakhiagiin Elbegdorj and some Mongolian lawmakers indicated that they will revisit the restrictions following parliamentary elections in June 2012 due to a need for balance between encouraging local corruption and protecting the "fundamental interests" of the Mongolian people.

(continued on next page)

183

Table A.1 New cases of local content requirements (post-2008) *(continued)*

Country and case number	Date announced; current status	Affected sectors	Size of affected domestic sectors	Estimated affected trade	Description of LCR measure
Nigeria-1	October 2009; LCR remains in force	Water, beverages, textiles, footwear			Buy-Made-In-Nigeria directed all official catering to be sourced through domestic producers and uniforms and boots of the Nigerian Armed Forces to be sourced locally.
Nigeria-2	April 2010; LCR remains in force	Basic metals, machinery, communication equipment, transport equipment, construction, water transport, financial services		$378.2 million in oil and gas imported in 2010, $75.4 billion exported	The Nigerian Oil and Gas Industry Content Development Act (2010) sets comprehensive and detailed discriminatory requirements for projects in the oil and gas industry. In part, the law increased indigenous participation in the oil and gas industry by prescribing minimum thresholds for the use of local services and materials and to promote the employment of Nigerian staff. Such indigenous or Nigerian companies would be required to have no less than 51 percent of their equity shares held by Nigerians. Additionally, no auxilliary services such as financing and insurance will be affected by the new law.
Paraguay-1	February 2009; LCR remains in force	Glass products, construction, public procurement			Paraguayan public bodies that spend national stimulus funds must give a minimum 70 percent preference to national goods and services.
Russia-1	March 2009; LCR remains in force	Machinery, chemicals		$2.3 billion in agricultural equipment and products imported in 2010	The Russian Ministry of Agriculture introduced order no. 82, which conditions subsidized loans to farmers on the origin of agricultural equipment and primary agricultural products they purchase.
Russia-2	December 2009; LCR remains in force	Transport equipment		$7.8 billion in car parts imported in 2010	Russian government decree no. 533/1018/137H increased an existing import tariff discount (lowering he usual tariff rate of 30 percent to a rate under 5 percent) but restricted eligibility of the discount to auto parts imported by companies which produce all their car models in Russia (i.e., utilizing the full cycle of assembly).

Russia-3	July 2010; LCR remains in force	ICT, manufacturing	$10.5 billion in telecommunications equipment imported in 2010	Russian rules mandate localization rates for telecommunications equipment sold within Russia. The level of localization of manufacturing of such equipment differs between types of equipment and for the first three years of manufacturing. Specifically, the manufacturer has to be a resident of the Russian Federation. The firm should have its own scientific-manufacturing base or cooperation with local enterprises that perform the manufacturing activity.
Russia-4	December 2010; LCR remains in force, but subject to termination by 2018	Transport equipment	$19.1 billion in cars, car engines, and other car parts imported in 2010	Per Joint Order No. 678/1289/184H, effective February 2011, between the Ministry of Economic Development and Ministry of Industry and Trade, automotive component producers qualifying for duty-free import into Russia must make at least 300,000 cars/year (up from 25,000); at least 30 percent of engines must be produced in Russia; and local content of components must amount to 60 percent by 2020. After consultations with the US and the EU, Russia agreed to change the program's termination date from 2020 to 2018.
Russia-5	April 2012; LCR recommended but not backed by law	Automotive manufacturing	$1.4 billion in various vehicles imported by government bodies in 2010	President-elect Vladimir Putin urged all Russian federal and municipal bodies to solely procure vehicles manufactured in Russia, Belarus, and Kazakhstan.
Saudi Arabia-1	October 2012; LCR remains in force	Labor markets; public utilities		In October 2012 the Consultative Assembly of Saudi Arabia (or Shura Council) passed a bill that effectively requires that all operation and maintenance contracts in the public utilities sector employ Saudis. The assistant chairman of the council said that no worker should be employed other than a Saudi unless the job requires a certain specialization or no Saudi workers are available.

(continued on next page)

Table A.1 New cases of local content requirements (post-2008) *(continued)*

Country and case number	Date announced; current status	Affected sectors	Size of affected domestic sectors	Estimated affected trade	Description of LCR measure
South Africa-1	June 2011; LCR remains in force	All industries			South African Regulation Gazette No. 9544 - Regulasieko-erant Vol. 552 - No. 34350 (8 June 2011) revised prefer-ential procurement regulations granting preferences for local products and Broad-Based Black Economic Empow-erment "B-BBEE" scheme effective December 2011.
South Africa-2	March 2010; LCR remains in force	Government pro-curement, trans-port, aviation			South Africa merged its National Industrial Participation Programme (NIPP) with its Competitive Supplier Devel-opment Programme (CSDP), which controls contracting by South Africa's nine state-owned enterprises (SOEs). South African SOEs are now required to demand 30 percent local purchases for any outlay of funds over $10 million, disproportionately affecting government contracts in the energy, rail, and aviation sectors.
South Africa-3	February 2011; LCR remains in force	Retail			The Competition Commission of South Africa issued its recommendation to the Competition Tribunal regard-ing the proposed merger of South African Massmart with US retailer Wal-Mart. The commission approved the merger but cited the sourcing of retail products as a matter of concern. The commission noted that the merging parties had agreed among other things to "source the majority of their products locally."
Switzerland-1	March 2009; LCR remains in force	Foodstuffs, live animals, water, stone, metal ores, uranium ore, crude petroleum and natural gas, forestry			The Swiss Federal Council strengthened protection for Made in Switzerland designations, by increasing both the amount of the raw materials' weight that must come from Switzerland, if the product is promoted as Swiss, from 50 to 80 percent and the extent of the main manufacturing processes that must be done in Switzer-land from 50 to 60 percent.

Switzerland-2	October 2009; LCR remains in force	Consumer foodstuffs	The Swiss Federal Council approved a support package to the agricultural sector that provides price compensation for food manufacturers to buy locally sourced raw materials.
Tanzania-1	June 2009; LCR remains in force	Beverages, tobacco products	Tanzania increased tariffs on beer, wine, and tobacco products that did not meet LCRs of 75 percent.
Turkey-1	December 2008; LCR remains in force	Government Procurement	Turkey's public procurement legislation allows for a 15 percent price preference in favor of domestic suppliers when participating in tenders set aside for Turkish goods and suppliers. A prime minister circular of December 2008 encouraged Turkish contracting authorities to apply those provisions more rigorously.
Turkey-2	December 2010; LCR remains in force	Wind turbines	Turkey implemented local content bonuses for different components of a wind turbine (tower, blade, mechanical, and electrical equipment). The bonuses increase the wind feed-in tariff by up to 50 percent.
Uganda-1	January 2010; LCR rejected	Oil and gas, mining	A version of the Petroleum (Exploration, Development, Production and Value Addition) Act 2010, debated in the Ugandan parliament, contains a local input requirement. The act seeks priority for Ugandan citizens and registered firms owned by Ugandans in the provision of goods and services to the petroleum industry. President Museveni quietly dropped the bill in the run-up to the February 2011 elections due to strong opposition from mining companies over the control that the bill would give to the energy minister.

(continued on next page)

Table A.1   New cases of local content requirements (post-2008) *(continued)*

Country and case number	Date announced; current status	Affected sectors	Size of affected domestic sectors	Estimated affected trade	Description of LCR measure
Ukraine-1	January 2012; LCR remains in force	Electricity derived from renewable sources			Ukraine introduced LCRs for obtaining a specific feed-in tariff for electricity produced from renewables. The law stipulates that government incentives for electricity production from alternative energy sources shall apply on condition that at least 15 percent of the cost of the construction of the respective facility producing electricity must comprise materials, works, and services of Ukrainian origin.
Ukraine-2	November 2012; LCR recommended but pending approval	Glass and non-metallic products, fabricated metal products, general purpose machinery, electricl machinery			In November 2012, Ukraine adopted amendments to the Law of Ukraine on the Electricity Sector, which include LCRs for wind, solar, biomass, and biogas power plants. If approved by the president, the provisions will be effective starting July 2013.
United States-1	April 2009; LCR rejected	Wood products, rubber and plastic products, glass products, basic metals, fabricated metal products, construction, land			The 21st Century Green High Performing Public School Facilities Act (HR 2187) would have subjected $6.4 billion for school renovation and modernization projects for FY2010 to a Buy American clause. The bill was passed in the House but remains in committee in the Senate.
United States-2	June 2009; LCR rejected	Electrical machinery, transport equipment		$3.1 billion in electric car batteries imported in 2010; $1.5 billion exported	The American Clean Energy and Security Act of 2009 (HR 2454) aimed to establish a loan guarantee program to firms that manufacture electric car batteries in the United States. An implicit criteria for local manufacturing was also added to the evaluation of grants for developing plug-in electric vehicles. The bill passed the House but not in the Senate.

United States-3	October 2009; nonbinding recommendation but LCR rejected	Glass products	$82 million contract awarded to Chinese firm for project	The Alliance for American Manufacturing and related groups asked US trade officials to address China's unfair trade practices after the contract for blast-resistant glass for the main tower of the new World Trade Center in New York City was awarded to a Chinese firm. Construction went as planned, with the use of the Chinese-made glass.
United States-4	October 2009; LCR remains in force	Textiles, machinery	$1.3 billion in small arms and small arms parts exported in 2010	The National Defense Authorization Act for FY2010 included Buy American requirements. The proposals related to small arms and uniform procurement and limited the number of foreign workers on construction projects in the relocation of facilities to Guam. Most of these provisions were stripped after reconciliation with the Senate version of the bill, except for a weaker provision relating to procurement of small arms from the "production industrial base."
United States-5	November 2009; nonbinding recommendation, but LCR remains in force	Electrical machinery	$514.2 million in wind turbines imported from China in 2010	Senator Charles Schumer (D-NY) demanded that the Obama administration not use funds from the American Recovery and Reinvestment Act of 2009 (ARRA) to provide funding for the purchase of wind generators produced in China. Eventually, the ARRA did include a Buy American clause that covered renewable energy industries.
United States-6	March 2010; LCR remains in force	Construction		An omnibus spending bill (Public Law 111-147), commonly known as the jobs bill, contained Buy American clauses related to Department of Transportation infrastructure projects.

(continued on next page)

Table A.1　New cases of local content requirements (post-2008) *(continued)*

Country and case number	Date announced; current status	Affected sectors	Size of affected domestic sectors	Estimated affected trade	Description of LCR measure
United States-7	April 2010; LCR remains in force	Basic chemicals		$4.6 billion in biofuels exported in 2010	The US Department of Agriculture published a proposed rule to implement a program to subsidize the production of US biofuels. The subsidies would be available only to biorefineries with at least 51 percent US ownership. This program was initially authorized by Congress in the 2008 Farm Bill, but neither that law nor a predecessor program established citizenship requirements for owners.
United States-8	September 2010; LCR rejected	Textiles			On September 29, 2010, the House of Representatives approved the All-American Flag Act (HR 2853), requiring that all American flags used by any agency of the federal government be made using exclusively US-derived materials and be manufactured in the United States. The bill remains in committee.
United States-9	March 2011; LCR remains in force	Water transport services		$2.7 million in cargo ships and related products imported in 2010; $11.9 million exported	The Department of Energy (DOE) had argued that the cargo preference law did not apply to the DOE's loan guarantee program. The Cargo Preference Act of 1954 requires that US government-financed cargoes be shipped on US flag vessels, provided that such vessels are available at fair and reasonable rates. Preference cargoes are the single most important incentive for US flag operators in the international trades to remain under US registry for international routes. Threatening litigation, the Department of Transportation successfully insisted that the requirements be enforced.

United States-10	March 2011; LCR rejected	Government procurement, stone, apparel, clocks and watches	The Buy American at the Smithsonian Act of 2011 (HR 983) introduced in the US House of Representatives on March 9, 2011 would generally prohibit the Smithsonian Institution from either using non-US materials in construction projects or selling items in its gift shops that are not made in the United States. The bill remains in subcommittee; however, administrators of one Smithsonian gift shop have discontinued purchases of goods not made in the United States.
United States-11	June 2011; LCR rejected	Government procurement	The US House of Representatives passed the Department of Homeland Security Appropriations Act, 2012 (HR 2017) by a vote of 231 to 188 on June 2, 2011. The bill provides $40.6 billion for operations of the Department of Homeland Security in FY2012. In the course of its debate, the House rejected two efforts to attach Buy American provisions to the bill. The bill was signed by the president on November 18, 2011 and became Public Law no. 112-33.
United States-12	October 2011; LCR rejected	Government procurement, live animals, textiles, apparel, office machinery, computer and related services	The House Committee on Homeland Security approved a bill (HR 3116) to authorize appropriations for fiscal year 2012 for the Department of Homeland Security (DHS) that added Buy American provisions related to office equipment and services, uniforms, and narcotics-detection dogs. The amendment (HR 679) was also introduced to the Senate version of the DHS appropriation bill but was not enacted into law.

(continued on next page)

Table A.1 New cases of local content requirements (post-2008) *(continued)*

Country and case number	Date announced; current status	Affected sectors	Size of affected domestic sectors	Estimated affected trade	Description of LCR measure
United States-13	September 2011; LCR remains in force	Investment in aviation sector			The US Congress reauthorized regulations requiring that at least 75 percent of the voting rights in a US airline carrier must be owned by US citizens when it passed the Continuing Appropriations Act of 2012 (Public Law 112-33). This investment restriction was first passed under the Merchant Marine Act of 1920 (also known as the Jones Act) but was set to expire under current law prior to the extension under the Appropriations Act of 2012.
United States-14	2013; LCR pending passing	Steel, iron, and manufactured goods used in water and wastewater projects			The US Congress is expected to introduce a new Buy American amendment in mid-July. The provision will be attached to the 2013 funding bill for the US Environmental Protection Agency and, if passed, would apply to all water and wastewater projects encompassed under the bill, including those at the state level. More than $100 billion is currently available for related infrastructure initiatives; however, the amendment would require all projects use only US-made steel, iron and manufactured goods in the construction or maintenance process.

Note: Blank cells indicate that estimates were not available or difficult to compute.

Sources: LCR measures are from Global Trade Alerts, www.globaltradealert.org, and other sources; size of domestic market and affected trade from authors' calculations based on data extracted from World Bank, World Integrated Trade Solution (WITS) database, United Nations Conference on Trade and Development (UNCTAD) statistics, Organization for Economic Cooperation and Development (OECD) statistics, and Office of the US Trade Representative (USTR). See text for methodology.

References

Balasubramanyam, V. N. 2001. Foreign Direct Investment in Developing Countries: Determinants and Impact. Paper presented at OECD Forum on International Investment, Mexico City, November 26–27. Available at www.oecd.org/daf/inv/investmentstatisticsandanalysis/2407305.pdf.

Baldwin, Robert, and J. David Richardson. 1972. Government Purchasing Policies, Other NTBs, and the International Monetary Crisis. In *Obstacles to Trade in the Pacific Area*, ed. H. English and K. Hay. Ottawa: Carleton School of International Affairs.

Baughman, Laura M., and Joseph F. Francoise. 2009. *Trade Action—or Inaction: The Cost for American Workers and Companies*. Washington: US Chamber of Commerce.

Berkman, Mark, Lisa Cameron, and Judy Chang. 2012. *The Employment Impacts of Proposed Tariffs on Chinese Manufactured Photovoltaic Cells and Modules*. Report prepared for Coalition for Affordable Solar Energy. Washington: Brattle Group. Available at http://coalition4affordablesolar.org/wp-content/uploads/2012/01/TBG_Solar-Trade-Impact-Report.pdf (accessed on January 4, 2013).

Blyde, Juan S., Mauricio M. Moreira, and Christian Volpe. 2011. *Unclogging the Arteries: The Impact of Transport Costs on Latin American and Caribbean Trade*. Special Report on Integration and Trade. Washington: Inter-American Development Bank, and Cambridge, MA: David Rockefeller Center for Latin American Studies, Harvard University.

Botelho, Jose J., Jason Dedrick, Kenneth L. Kraemer, and Paulo B. Tigre. 1999. *From Industry Protection to Industry Promotion: IT Policy in Brazil*. Irvine, CA: Center for Research on Information Technology and Organizations, University of California.

Branco, Fernando. 1994. Favoring Domestic Firms in Procurement Contracts. *Journal of International Economics* 37, no. 1–2: 65–80.

Baziliana, Morgan, Michael Liebreich, Ijeoma Onyejia, Ian MacGill, Jennifer Chase, Jigar Shah, Dolf Gielen, Doug Arent, Doug Landfear, and Shi Zhengrong. 2012. *Re-considering the Economics of Photovoltaic Power*. White Paper (May 16). New York: Bloomberg New Energy

Finance. Available at http://about.bnef.com/white-papers/re-considering-the-economics-of-photovoltaic-power-a-co-authored-white-paper-on-pv-economics.

Bridge to India. 2012. *The India Solar Handbook.* New Delhi. Available at http://bridgetoindia.com/our-reports/the-india-solar-handbook (accessed on December 22, 2012).

CANWEA (Canadian Wind Energy Association). 2008. *WINDVISION 2025: Powering Canada's Future.* Available at www.canwea.ca/images/uploads/File/Windvision_summary_e.pdf.

CBO (Congressional Budget Office). 2010. *Public Spending on Transportation and Water Infrastructure.* Washington. Available at www.cbo.gov/sites/default/files/cbofiles/ftpdocs/119xx/doc11940/11-17-infrastructure.pdf.

CBO (Congressional Budget Office). 2011. Spending and Funding for Highways. *Economic and Budget Issue Brief* (January). Washington. Available at www.cbo.gov/publication/22003.

CEBRI (Centro Brasileiro de Relações Internacionais). 2012. *Domestic Industry Development in the Context of the International Crisis: Evaluating Strategies.* Rio de Janeiro. Available at www.cebri.org/midia/documentos/indenglish.pdf.

Cline, William, and John Williamson. 2010. *Estimates of Fundamental Equilibrium Exchange Rates, May 2010.* Policy Brief 10-15. Washington: Peterson Institute for International Economics.

Copeland, Claudia. 2012. *Water Infrastructure Financing: History of EPA Appropriations.* Congressional Research Service Report to Congress (April 5). Washington: Congressional Research Service. Available at www.fas.org/sgp/crs/misc/96-647.pdf.

Copeland, Claudia, Linda Levine, and William J. Mallett. 2011. *The Role of Public Works Infrastructure in Economic Recovery.* Congressional Research Service Report for Congress (September 21). Washington: Congressional Research Service. Available at www.fas.org/sgp/crs/misc/R42018.pdf.

Deardorff, A. V., and R. M. Stern. 1997. *Measurement of Non-Tariff Barriers.* OECD Economics Department Working Paper 179. Paris: Organization for Economic Cooperation and Development.

Doshi, Viren, Gary Schulman, and Daniel Gabaldon. 2007. *Lights! Water! Motion!* strategy+business, issue 46 (Spring). Booz & Company. Available at www.strategy-business.com/article/07104?pg=all.

EIA (US Energy Information Administration). 2012a. *Annual Energy Outlook.* Washington. Available at www.eia.gov/forecasts/aeo/pdf/0383(2012).pdf.

EIA (US Energy Information Administration). 2012b. *Nigeria Country Analysis* (updated on October 16). Washington. Available at www.eia.gov/countries/cab.cfm?fips=NI.

EPA (Environmental Protection Agency). 2009. *2009 Annual Report: Clean Water State Revolving Fund Programs.* Washington: EPA Office of Water. Available at http://water.epa.gov/grants_funding/cwsrf/upload/2009_CWSRF_AR.pdf.

EPA (Environmental Protection Agency). 2011. *Implementation of the American Recovery and Reinvestment Act of 2009: Clean Water & Drinking Water State Revolving Fund Programs* (May). Washington: EPA Office of Water. Available at http://water.epa.gov/aboutow/eparecovery/upload/epa-WEB-ar-arra-May2011.pdf.

EPA (Environmental Protection Agency). 2013. *American Recovery and Reinvestment Act Quarterly Performance Report: FY 2013 Quarter 1* (January 31). Washington. Available at www.epa.gov/recovery/pdfs/ARRA-FY13-Quarter-1-Performance-Report.pdf.

Evenett, Simon J., ed. 2012. *Débâcle: The 11th GTA Report on Protectionism.* London: Centre for Economic Policy Research. Available at www.iadb.org/intal/intalcdi/PE/2012/10237.pdf.

Evenett, Simon J., and Bernard M. Hoekman. 2002. *Government Procurement: Market Access: Transparency, and Multilateral Trade Rules.* Working Paper. Available at www.wto.org/english/tratop_e/gproc_e/gptran_symp_oct02_pdf_files/symp_oct02_2_hoe_eve_e.pdf.

FHWA (Federal Highway Administration). 2004. Usage Factors for Major Highway Construction Materials and Labor. *Highway Statistics 2003* (October). Washington. Available at www.fhwa. dot.gov/policy/ohim/hs03/htm/pt4.htm (accessed on April 22, 2013).

FHWA (Federal Highway Administration). 2011. A Renewed Focus on Infrastructure. Our Nation's Highways: 2011. Highway Finance Data Collection. Washington: Office of Highway Policy Information. Available at www.fhwa.dot.gov/policyinformation/pubs/hf/pl11028/intro.cfm (accessed on April 22, 2013).

FHWA (Federal Highway Administration). 2013. Weekly List of FHWA Recovery Act Projects, as of March 29. Washington. Available at www.fhwa.dot.gov/economicrecovery/weeklylists. htm (accessed on May 3, 2013).

Frankel, Jeffrey, and David Romer. 1999. Does Trade Cause Growth? *American Economic Review* 3, no. 89: 379–99.

Gangania, Arunabha. 2012. *Governing Clean Energy Subsidies: What, Why, and How Legal? Global Platform on Climate Change, Trade and Sustainable Energy.* Geneva: International Center for Trade and Sustainable Development. Available at http://ictsd.org/i/publications/143945.

GAO (Government Accountability Office). 2008. *Federal-Aid Highways: Federal Requirements for Highways May Influence Funding Decisions and Create Challenges, but Benefits and Costs Are Not Tracked.* Report to Congressional Requesters, GAO-09-36. Washington.

GAO (Government Accountability Office). 2010. *Recovery Act: Project Selection and Starts Are Influenced by Certain Federal Requirements and Other Factors.* Report to the Republican Leader, GAO-10-383. Washington.

GAO (Government Accountability Office). 2011. *Recovery Act: Funding Used for Transportation Infrastructure Projects, but Some Requirements Proved Challenges.* Report to the Congress, GAO-11-600 (June). Washington. Available at www.gao.gov/assets/330/320351.pdf.

Gordon, Kathryn. 2001. *The OECD Guidelines and Other Corporate Responsibility Instruments: A Comparison.* OECD Working Paper on International Investment 2001/5. Paris: Organization for Economic Cooperation and Development.

Government of India. 2009. *Jawaharlal Nehru Solar Mission: Towards Building Solar India.* New Delhi: Ministry of New and Renewable Energy. Available at www.mnre.gov.in/file-manager/User Files/mission_document_JNNSM.pdf.

Government of India. 2011. *Guidelines for Selection of New Grid-Connected Solar Power Projects.* New Delhi: Ministry of New and Renewable Energy. Available at www.mnre.gov.in/solar-mission/jnnsm/introduction-2.

Government of India. 2012. *Commissioning Status of Solar PV Projects under Batch I, Phase I of JNNSM.* New Delhi: Ministry of New and Renewable Energy. Available at http://mnre.gov.in/file-manager/UserFiles/commissioning_status_ spv_batch1_phase1.pdf.

Government of India. 2013. *Commissioning Status of Solar PV Projects under Batch II, Phase I of JNNSM.* New Delhi: Ministry of New and Renewable Energy.

Government of Quebec. 2006. *Using Energy to Build the Quebec of Tomorrow: Quebec Energy Strategy 2006 to 2015.* Quebec: Ministry of Natural Resources and Wildlife. Available at www.mrn. gouv.qc.ca/english/energy/strategy/index.jsp.

Gowlings. 2010. *Wind Energy Law in Canada.* Available at www.gowlings.com/knowledgeCentre/publicationPDFs/Wind%20Energy%20EN.pdf.

Gramlich, Edward. 1990. How Should Public Infrastructure Be Financed? In *Is There a Shortfall in Public Capital Investment? Proceedings of a Conference*, ed. Alicia Munnell. Boston: Federal Reserve Bank of Boston.

Gramlich, Edward. 1994. Infrastructure Investment: A Review Essay. *Journal of Economic Literature* 32, no. 3: 1176–96.

Grossman, G. M. 1981. The Theory of Domestic Content Protection and Content Preference. *Quarterly Journal of Economics* 96, no. 4 (November): 583–603.

Haley, Usha C. V., and George T. Haley. 2013. *Subsidies to Chinese Industry*. Oxford: Oxford University Press.

Heintz, James, Robert Pollin, and Heidi Garrett-Peltier. 2009. *How Infrastructure Investment Supports the U.S. Economy: Employment, Productivity and Growth*. Amherst, MA: Political Economy Research Institute and University of Massachusetts-Amherst.

Hufbauer, Gary Clyde, and Jeffrey J. Schott. 2009. *Buy American: Bad for Jobs, Worse for Reputation*. Policy Brief 09-2. Washington: Peterson Institute for International Economics.

Hufbauer, Gary Clyde, Jeffrey J. Schott, and Woan Foong Wong. 2010. *Figuring Out the Doha Round*. Policy Analyses in International Economics 91. Washington: Peterson Institute for International Economics.

Huld, T., R. Gottschalg, H. G. Beyer, and M. Topic. 2009. Mapping the Performance of PV Modules of Different Types. Paper presented at the 24th European Photovoltaic Solar Energy Conference, Hamburg, Germany September 21–25. Available at www.eupvsec-proceedings.com/proceedings? char=M&paper=5380.

IEA (International Energy Agency). 2012. *World Energy Outlook 2012*. Paris.

IEA (International Energy Agency) and World Bank. 2013. *Global Tracking Framework*. Paris. Available at www.iea.org/newsroomandevents/pressreleases/2013/may/name,38448,en.html (accessed on June 19, 2013).

IMF (International Monetary Fund). 2012. *Nigeria: 2011 Article IV Consultation*. IMF Country Report no. 12/194 (July). Washington. Available at www.imf.org/external/pubs/ft/scr/2012/cr12194.pdf.

IMF (International Monetary Fund). 2013. *Nigeria: 2012 Article IV Consultation*. IMF Country Report no. 13/116 (May). Washington. Available at www.imf.org/external/pubs/ft/scr/2013/cr13116.pdf.

Ihua, Ugwushi Bellema, Chris Ajayi, and Kamdi Nnanna Eloji. 2009. Nigerian Content Policy in the Oil and Gas Industry: Implications for Small to Medium-Sized Oil-Service Companies. In *Repositioning African Business and Development for the 21st Century,* ed. Simon Sigué, Peer-Reviewed Proceedings of the 10th Annual International Conference, Kampala, Uganda, May 19–23. Alberta: International Academy of African Business and Development. Available at http://www.iaabd.org/pdf/IAABD2009Proceedings_Final.pdf.

Jackson, John H. 1969. *World Trade and the Law of the GATT*. Indianapolis: Bobbs-Merrill Company.

JAMA (Japan Automobile Manufacturing Association). 2012. *Automobile Statistics Monthly* 46, no. 3 (June) (in Japanese). Tokyo. Available at www.jama.or.jp/stats/m_report/pdf/2012_06.pdf.

JETRO (Japan External Trade Organization). 2010. *US Business in Brazil: Major Sector Trend* (December) (in Japanese). Tokyo. Available at www.jetro.go.jp/world/cs_america/br/reports/07000499 (accessed on June 30, 2012).

JETRO (Japan External Trade Organization). 2012a. *Medical Device Market and Regulation in Brazil* (March) (in Japanese). Tokyo. Available at www.jetro.go.jp/jfile/report/07000870/br_medi_equi_regulation.pdf (accessed on June 30, 2012).

JETRO (Japan External Trade Organization). 2012b. *Automobile Production and Sales in Major Countries in 2011* (April) (in Japanese). Tokyo. Available at www.jetro.go.jp/world/asia/reports/07000924 (accessed on June 6, 2012).

Jha, Vyomi. 2011. *Cutting Both Ways: Climate, Trade, and the Consistency of India's Domestic Policies*. CEEW Policy Brief. New Delhi: Council on Energy, Environment, and Water.

Johnson, Erik. 2011. *The Price Elasticity of Supply of Renewable Electricity Generation: Evidence from State Renewable Portfolio Standard.* Working Paper WP2011-001. Atlanta, GA: School of Economics, Georgia Institute of Technology.

Johnson, Oliver. 2013. *Exploring the Effectiveness of Local Content Requirements in Promoting Solar PV Manufacturing in India.* Discussion Paper. Bonn: German Development Institute.

Kasteng, Jonas. 2013. *Targeting the Environment: Exploring a New Trend in the EU's Trade Defence Investigations.* Stockholm: Sweden National Board of Trade.

Kowalski, P., Max Büge, and Monika Sztajerowska. 2013. *State-Owned Enterprises: Trade Effects and Policy Implications.* OECD Trade Policy Paper no. 147. Paris: OECD Publishing. Available at www.oecd-ilibrary.org/trade/state-owned-enterprises_5k4869ckqk7l-en.

Krishna, Kala, and Motoshige Itoh. 1988. Content Protection and Oligopolistic Interaction. *Review of Economic Studies* 55: 107–25.

Krueger, Anne O. 1998. Why Trade Liberalization Is Good for Growth. *Economic Journal* 108, no. 450: 1513–22.

Kuntze, Jan-Christoph, and Tom Moerenhout. 2013. *Local Content Requirements and the Renewable Energy Industry: A Good Match?* Geneva: International Centre for Trade and Sustainable Development.

Lahiri, Sajal, and Yoshiyasu Ono. 1998. Foreign Direct Investment, Local Content Requirement, and Profit Taxation. *Economic Journal* 108, no. 447: 444–57.

Levett, Michael, and Ashley Chandler. 2012. *Maximizing Development of Local Content across Industry Sectors in Emerging Markets.* Report of the CSIS Project on US Leadership in Development. Washington: Center for Strategic and International Studies.

Lewis, Joanna I., and Ryan H. Wiser. 2007. Fostering a Renewable Energy Technology Industry: An International Comparison of Wind Industry Policy Support Mechanisms. *Energy Policy* 35: 1844–57.

Limodio, Nicola. 2011. *The Success of Infrastructure Projects in Low-Income Countries and the Role of Selectivity.* World Bank Policy Research Working Paper 5694. Washington: World Bank.

Lin, Justin Y., and Doerte Doemeland. 2012. *Beyond Keynesianism: Global Infrastructure Investments in Times of Crisis.* World Bank Policy Research Working Paper 5940. Washington: World Bank.

Luckey, John R. 2012. *Domestic Content Legislation: The Buy American Act and Complementary Little Buy American Provisions.* Congressional Service Research Report to Congress (April 25). Washington: Congressional Service Research. Available at www.fas.org/sgp/crs/misc/R42501.pdf.

McAfee, R. Preston, and John McMillan. 1989. Government Procurement and International Trade. *Journal of International Economics* 26: 451–60.

Messerlin, Patrick. 2013. *Openness in Public Procurement Markets: Time for a Reality Check.* Policy Brief no. 03/2013. Brussels: European Centre for International Political Economy.

Moran, Theodore H. 1998. *Foreign Direct Investment and Development: The New Policy Agenda for Developing Countries and Economies in Transition.* Washington: Institute for International Economics.

Moran, Theodore H. 2011. *Foreign Direct Investment and Development: Launching a Second Generation of Policy Research.* Washington: Peterson Institute for International Economics.

Mussa, Michael. 1984. *The Economics of Content Protection.* NBER Working Paper 1457. Cambridge, MA: National Bureau of Economic Research.

NRDC (Natural Resources Defense Council). 2012. *Laying the Foundation for a Bright Future: Assessing Progress under Phase 1 of India's National Solar Mission.* New Delhi. Available at www.nrdc.org/international/india/files/layingthefoundation.pdf.

NRTEE (National Round Table on the Environment and the Economy). 2012. *Reality Check: The State of Climate Progress in Canada.* Ottawa.

OECD (Organization for Economic Cooperation and Development). 2003. *Quantitative Assessment of the Benefits of Trade Facilitation.* Paris.

OECD (Organization for Economic Cooperation and Development). 2004. *Employment Outlook.* Paris.

Oliveira, Eduardo Jorge V. 2011. Overview of the Brazilian Industrial Health Complex. Presentation in Brazil, April 11. Available at http://www.vinnova.se/PageFiles/121459189/Eduardo%20Jorge%20Semin%C3%A1rio%20GE%20-%20Ingl%C3%AAs_simplificado.pdf.

Oyejide, Ademola, A. Ogunkola, and A. Bankole. 2005. Import Prohibition as a Trade Policy Instrument: The Nigerian Experience. In *Managing the Challenges of WTO Participation: 45 Case Studies,* ed. Peter Gallagher, Patrick Low, and Andrew L. Stoler. World Trade Organization and Cambridge University Press.

Platzer, Michaela. 2012. *US Solar Photovoltaic Manufacturing: Industry Trends, Global Competition, Federal Support.* Congressional Research Service Report to Congress (June 12). Washington: Congressional Research Service.

PwC (PriceWaterhouseCoopers), World Bank, and IFC (International Finance Corporation). 2011. *Paying Taxes 2012: The Global Picture.* Available at www.doingbusiness.org/˜/media/FPDKM/Doing%20Business/Documents/Special-Reports/Paying-Taxes-2012.pdf.

Richardson, Martin. 1993. Content Protection with Foreign Capital. *Oxford Economic Papers* 45: 103–17.

Rivers, Nic, and Randy Wigle. 2011. *Domestic Content Requirements and Renewable Energy Legislation.* Social Science Research Network.

Romer, Christina, and Jared Bernstein. 2009. *The Job Impact of the American Recovery and Reinvestment Plan* (January 9). Washington. Available at http://otrans.3cdn.net/45593e8ecbd339d074_l3m6bt1te.pdf.

Rosen, Howard. 2005. Labor Market Adjustment Policies and Programs. Peterson Institute for International Economics, Washington. Photocopy.

Schur, Michael, Stephan von Klaudy, Georgina Dellacha, Apurva Sanghi, and Nataliya Pushak. 2008. *The Role of Developing Country Firms in Infrastructure.* Gridlines Note 3. Washington: World Bank Public-Private Infrastructure Advisory Facility.

Stiglitz, Joseph E. 1998. Towards a New Paradigm for Development: Strategies, Policies, and Processes. Prebisch Lecture at United Nations Conference on Trade and Development (UNCTAD), Geneva, October 19.

UNCTC (United Nations Centre on Transnational Corporations). 1991. *The Impact of Trade-Related Investment Measures on Trade and Development: Theory, Evidence and Policy Implications.* New York.

USTR (US Trade Representative). 2011. *The 2011 National Trade Estimate Report on Foreign Trade Barriers.* Washington. Available at www.ustr.gov/webfm_send/2751.

USTR (US Trade Representative). 2012. *The 2012 National Trade Estimate Report on Foreign Trade Barriers.* Washington. Available at www.ustr.gov/sites/default/files/NTE%20Final%20Printed_0.pdf.

Wacziarg, Romain, and Karen Horn Welch. 2008. Trade Liberalization and Growth: New Evidence. *World Bank Economic Review* 22, no. 2: 187–231.

Wells, Jill, and John Hawkins. 2008. *Increasing Local Content in the Procurement of Infrastructure Projects in Low Income Countries,* Briefing Note. London: UK Institution of Civil Engineers and Engineers against Poverty. Available at www.engineersagainstpoverty.org/_db/_documents/Local_content_briefing_note.pdf.

Wilke, Marie. 2011. Getting FIT for the WTO: Canadian Green Energy Support under Scrutiny. *Bridges Trade BioRes Review* 5, no. 1 (April). Available at http://ictsd.org/i/news/bioresreview/103562.

Wilson, John, S., Catherine L. Mann, and Tsunehiro Otsuki. 2003. *Trade Facilitation and Economic Development: Measuring the Impact*. World Bank Policy Research Working Paper 2988. Washington: World Bank.

Wilson, John, S., Catherine L. Mann, and Tsunehiro Otsuki. 2004. *Assessing the Potential Benefit of Trade Facilitation: A Global Perspective*. World Bank Policy Research Working Paper 3224. Washington: World Bank.

World Bank. 2007. *Indonesia: Economic and Social Update* (April). Washington.

World Bank and IFC (International Finance Corporation). 2011. *Doing Business 2012: Doing Business in a More Transparent World*. Washington. Available at www.doingbusiness.org/~/media/fpdkm/doing%20business/documents/annual-reports/ english/db12-fullreport.pdf.

World Economic Forum. 2010. *Positive Infrastructure: A Framework for Revitalizing the Global Economy*. Committee to Improve the State of the World. Geneva.

World Economic Forum. 2013. *Enabling Trade: Valuing Growth Opportunities*. Geneva.

WTO (World Trade Organization) and UNCTAD (United Nations Conference on Trade and Development). 2002. *Trade-Related Investment Measures and Other Performance Requirements*. G/C/W/307 and G/C/W/307/Add.1. Geneva. Available at www.wto.org/english/res_e/booksp_e/analytic_index_e/trims_01_e.htm.

WWEA (World Wind Energy Association). 2012. *World Wind Energy Report 2011* (May). Bonn. Available at www.wwindea.org/webimages/WorldWindEnergyReport2011.pdf (accessed on November 12, 2012).

Index

infant industries
- Brazilian healthcare, 41
- Canadian, 63
- LCRs as support for, 30, 151–52

information and communications technology (ICT) industry
- Brazilian, 43, 44b
- Nigerian, 119

infrastructure
- ARRA-related steel cost increases and, 150t
- Centro Brasileiro de Relações Inernacionais (CEBRI) recommendations on, 44
- EPA funding of wastewater, 142–43
- investment in, as LCR alternative, 30–32, 31t
- jobs created from projects in, 144–45
- as port characteristic, 25, 30
- privately versus publicly owned, 30n
- solar power improvements, 108
- water, 141–42, 141t, 149t

International Energy Agency, 64, 95

investment
- Chinese barriers and incentives to, 85–88
- in infrastructure, as LCR alternative, 30–32
- in Nigerian oil and gas industry, 120–21
- transportation, in Buy American campaigns, 141–42

Japan
- assembled auto imports to, 86
- automobile production capacity in China of, 78–79
- on Canadian FIT scheme as ASCM violation, 69–70
- feed-in tariff (FIT) programs of, 69b
- on Global Harmonization Task Force (GHTF), 53
- imported auto parts to, 85
- medical device and drug lags in, 53, 55
- METI Industrial Statistics Analysis of, 91n
- solar panel costs in, 72
- US water/wastewater equipment and pipe exported to, 142

Jawaharlal Nehru National Solar Mission (JNNSM, India), 13, 93, 95, 99–100, 103t, 107

jobs. See also training expansion
- active labor market programs (ALMPs), 24–25, 25t

- Brazilian fostering of, 45
- Canadian LCRs to create, 63
- domestic creation of, 2
- "first consideration" to Nigerians, 115–16
- Great Recession of 2008–09 losses of, 144
- green, 10, 143
- infrastructure, 31–32, 144–45, 145n
- LCR cost of, 17
- LCR support of, 35, 38–39, 39t, 151–52
- tariffs to create, 152

joint ventures
- China requirement for, 85
- Chinese restrictions on, 77
- in Nigerian oil and gas industry, 111, 112t
- in solar power, 108
- transition to locally fully owned companies, 124

Kazakhstan, LCRs post-2008, 181–82

Kenya, LCRs post-2008, 182

Korea
- assembled auto imports to, 86
- auto parts imports to, 85
- electricity prices in, 64, 66f
- feed-in tariff (FIT) programs and, 69b
- LCRs post-2008, 182–83

labor. See also jobs; training expansion
- active labor market programs (ALMPs), 24–25, 25t
- in Chinese automobile manufacturing, 91
- Nigerian CDA requirements for local, 117–18

Latin American Harmonization Working Party (LAHWP), 54, 61

Latin American Local Content Forum 2012, 4

LCRs (local content requirements), 1–16. See also Buy American/Buy America programs; Nigerian Oil and Gas Content Development Act (CDA)
- average GDPs lower than, 4
- as bad policy, 4–7
- in Brazilian healthcare industry, 54–59
  - alternatives to, 59–61
  - device lags resulting from, 54–56
  - drug lags resulting from, 56–59
- Canadian, 63
- Centro Brasileiro de Relações Inernacionais (CEBRI) recommendations on, 44

characteristics of, 1, 3–4
in Chinese automobile industry, 77
by country, 155–92
delays and cost increases from, 7
drivers of, 2
global screening of, 36
implicit, 45, 51, 59–61
in Indian solar panel industry, 101–107
economies of scale achieved by,
96, 99
as low-cost producer, 93
market share, 107
prices, 102–104
thin film panel advantage, 104–107
jobs affected by, 38–39, 39t
licensing requirements as, 42–43, 45,
50
as local firm percentage of projects or
subsidies, 1
motives behind and effects of, 7–13
in national tariff schedules, 2
OECD country trade negatively affected
by, 38
Ontario FIT program mandates in,
68–69
pushback against, 13–16
in Quebec, 71
rents and surplus shifted by, 9
trade affected by, 37, 37t
weaknesses of, 7
WTO on Ontario, 70
LCRs, alternatives to, 17–34
in Brazilian healthcare industry, 59–61
business-friendly environment as, 17–21
Buy American programs versus, 149–50
for Canadian wind turbine industry, 73
for Chinese automobile industry, 92
corporate social responsibility (CSR) as,
22–23
for Indian solar panel industry, 108
infrastructure investment as, 30–32
logistics improvement as, 25–30
for Nigerian oil and gas industry,
122–24
tariff and subsidy imposition as,
32–34
training expansion as, 23–25
legal challenges to LCRs, in Nigerian oil
and gas industry, 120
licensing requirements
of Brazilian National Health
Surveillance Agency, 44, 50
for local firm preference, 42–43
local capacity building, 22

local content requirements (LCRs). *See* LCRs
(local content requirements)
localizing operations to accelerate
registration approval, 50
local ownership requirements, 2, 35, 77
logistics improvement, as LCR alternative,
25–30
Logistics Performance Index (LPI, World
Bank), 26–27, 28t–29t
low-cost producers, 93–94, 107

Malaysia
on Global Harmonization Task Force
(GHTF), 54
local supplier industrial parks in, 23
solar energy industry in, 99
manufacturing, Chinese state-owned
enterprises (SOEs) in, 80
marine power, 96t–97t, 98f
medical device density, 54–55, 55f
medical devices
in Brazilian healthcare industry, 46t–48t,
48–51
Brazilian LCRs causing lags in, 54–56
Brazilian registration of, 45, 50–51
Brazilian trade in, 42f, 49f, 50t
Mexico
auto parts imports to, 85
electricity prices in, 64, 66f
on Global Harmonization Task Force
(GHTF), 54
LCRs post-2008, 183
US water/wastewater equipment and
pipe exported to, 142
Mongolia, LCRs restricting foreign
investment in mining in, 4, 183
monopoly power, domestic producers
exercising, 8
Morocco, doing business rankings of,
19t–20t
multinational corporations. *See also*
pharmaceuticals
business-friendly environment
encouraging to, 18
corporate social responsibility
guidelines of, 22
manufacturing
of automobiles in China, 80f,
81t–82t
Brazilian environmental licensing
requirements, 50
export processing zones for, 23
local materials purchases of, 22
in Nigerian oil and gas industry, 119

trade-related investment measures (TRIMs), 9
trade remedy cases, 87
trade transaction costs (TTCs), 25–26, 30
training expansion
    in Indian solar power industry, 99, 108
    as LCR alternative, 23–25, 44
    in Nigerian oil and gas industry, 124
Transatlantic Trade and Investment
        Partnership (TTIP), 140–41, 140*n*,
        153
transparency, in classic LCRs, 151–52
Transparency International's Corruption
        Perceptions Index of 2011, 110
transportation investments, 141–42
Turkey, LCRs post-2008, 187

Uganda, LCRs post-2008, 187
Ukraine, LCRs post-2008, 188
unemployment. *See also* jobs; training
        expansion
    infrastructure jobs and, 31–32
    jobs to combat, 4
    training participation and, 24*n*
unemployment insurance, 23
United Arab Emirates, state-owned
        enterprises (SOEs) in, 80
United Kingdom
    assembled auto imports to, 85
    auto parts imports to, 85
    reverse auction subsidies of, 102*n*
    US water/wastewater equipment and
        pipe exported to, 142
United States. *See also* Buy American/Buy
        America programs
    antidumping duties against China, 69*b*
    auto parts imported to, 85
    Brazilian medical device imports from,
        48, 50*t*
    electricity prices in, 64, 66*f*
    employment in infrastructure projects,
        32
    export financing from, 99
    feed-in tariff (FIT) program of, 68
    foreign direct investment in, 85
    on Global Harmonization Task Force
        (GHTF), 53
    India violations of national treatment
        obligation and, 93, 108
    job training financed by, 23
    LCRs post-2008, 188–92
    as Nigerian oil and gas industry
        destination market, 110
    oil field supply exports to Nigeria of,
        112

reverse auction subsidies of, 102*n*
solar electricity prices in, 104
in Transatlantic Trade and Investment
        Partnership (TTIP), 140
wind energy industry in, 63
US Congress, Buy American/Buy America
        programs by, 135
US Environmental Protection Agency, 135,
        140, 141*t*, 143, 148*n*
US Export-Import Bank, 99, 101–102
US Foreign Corrupt Practices Act, 122
US Trade Representative (USTR), 13, 119–21

value-added terms, local content schemes
        for, 8*n*
value chains
    global, 25
    solar electricity, 108
    solar photovoltaic cell, 94*f*
vehicles. *See* automobile industry; China,
        automobile industry in
vertical integration, India's solar energy
        industry's lack of, 99
Vietnam
    on Global Harmonization Task Force
        (GHTF), 54
    on Logistics Performance Index (LPI,
        World Bank), 27
vocational job training programs, 24

Water and Wastewater Equipment
        Manufacturers Association
        (WWEMA), 142, 142*n*
water infrastructure
    Buy American campaigns and, 141–42,
        141*t*
    needs for, 31, 31*t*
    steel imports for, 149*t*
Water Resources Development Act of 2013,
        138
weaknesses of LCRs, 7
wind energy industry. *See also* Canada, wind
        turbines in
    China domestic, 10*n*
    current and projected levels, 96*t*–97*t*
    kilowatts per square kilometer, 75*f*
    LCRs tied to support for, 10
    overnight cost of, 72, 72*f*
    per capita and total capacity, 74*f*
    subsidized and unsubsidized, 98*f*
    top 10 countries in, 64*f*
window dressing, LCRs as, 7
workers, training needs of, 23–25. *See also*
        jobs; training expansion

World Bank
- *Doing Business* report, 18
- Logistics Performance Index (LPI), 26–27, 28t–29t
- Public-Private Infrastructure Advisory Facility, 30

world commerce, trade transaction costs (TTCs) in, 25

World Economic Forum, 26, 30–31

World Trade Organization (WTO)
- Agreement on Subsidies and Countervailing Measures (ASCM), 14, 32, 69–70, 77, 120
- Agreement on Trade-Related Aspects of Intellectual Property Rights (TRIPS), 51
- Agreement on Trade-Related Investment Measures (TRIMs), 14–15, 70, 77, 120
- China in, 77, 86
- Dispute Settlement Body, 13, 15n, 108, 151

World Trade Organization (WTO) *(contd.)*
- Doha Round of negotiations, 26n
- enforcement difficulties, 16
- Government Procurement Agreement (GPA), 3, 14–16, 59, 137, 139, 141, 151
- India violations of national treatment obligation, 93, 108
- LCR analysis by, 153
- LCRs limited by, 13–14, 151
- member-only governments with legal standing to bring a case, 16
- Nigerian LCR policies apart from, 109
- Nigeria violations of national treatment obligation, 120
- on Ontario's LCR, 70
- remedies offering no retroactive relief for the aggrieved firm, 16
- schedule-bound versus applied tariff rates, 32–33, 33t
- Trade Policy Review Mechanism, 153
- two years or more to resolve cases, 16

Other Publications from the
Peterson Institute for International Economics

WORKING PAPERS

Narrowing the U.S. Current Account Deficit*
Alan J. Lenz
June 1992 ISBN 0-88132-103-6

The Economics of Global Warming
William R. Cline
June 1992 ISBN 0-88132-132-X

US Taxation of International Income:
Blueprint for Reform Gary Clyde Hufbauer,
assisted by Joanna M. van Rooij
October 1992 ISBN 0-88132-134-6

Who's Bashing Whom? Trade Conflict in High-
Technology Industries Laura D'Andrea Tyson
November 1992 ISBN 0-88132-106-0

Korea in the World Economy* Il SaKong
January 1993 ISBN 0-88132-183-4

Pacific Dynamism and the International
Economic System* C. Fred Bergsten and
Marcus Noland, eds.
May 1993 ISBN 0-88132-196-6

Economic Consequences of Soviet
Disintegration* John Williamson, ed.
May 1993 ISBN 0-88132-190-7

Reconcilable Differences? United States-Japan
Economic Conflict* C. Fred Bergsten and
Marcus Noland
June 1993 ISBN 0-88132-129-X

Does Foreign Exchange Intervention Work?
Kathryn M. Dominguez and Jeffrey A. Frankel
September 1993 ISBN 0-88132-104-4

Sizing Up U.S. Export Disincentives*
J. David Richardson
September 1993 ISBN 0-88132-107-9

NAFTA: An Assessment Gary Clyde Hufbauer
and Jeffrey J. Schott, *rev. ed.*
October 1993 ISBN 0-88132-199-0

Adjusting to Volatile Energy Prices
Philip K. Verleger, Jr.
November 1993 ISBN 0-88132-069-2

The Political Economy of Policy Reform
John Williamson, ed.
January 1994 ISBN 0-88132-195-8

Measuring the Costs of Protection in the United
States Gary Clyde Hufbauer and
Kimberly Ann Elliott
January 1994 ISBN 0-88132-108-7

The Dynamics of Korean Economic
Development* Cho Soon
March 1994 ISBN 0-88132-162-1

Reviving the European Union*
C. Randall Henning, Eduard Hochreiter, and
Gary Clyde Hufbauer, eds.
April 1994 ISBN 0-88132-208-3

China in the World Economy Nicholas R. Lardy
April 1994 ISBN 0-88132-200-8

Greening the GATT: Trade, Environment,
and the Future Daniel C. Esty
July 1994 ISBN 0-88132-205-9

Western Hemisphere Economic Integration*
Gary Clyde Hufbauer and Jeffrey J. Schott
July 1994 ISBN 0-88132-159-1

Currencies and Politics in the United States,
Germany, and Japan C. Randall Henning
September 1994 ISBN 0-88132-127-3

Estimating Equilibrium Exchange Rates
John Williamson, ed.
September 1994 ISBN 0-88132-076-5

Managing the World Economy: Fifty Years
after Bretton Woods Peter B. Kenen, ed.
September 1994 ISBN 0-88132-212-1

Reciprocity and Retaliation in U.S. Trade Policy
Thomas O. Bayard and Kimberly Ann Elliott
September 1994 ISBN 0-88132-084-6

The Uruguay Round: An Assessment* Jeffrey J.
Schott, assisted by Johanna Buurman
November 1994 ISBN 0-88132-206-7

Measuring the Costs of Protection in Japan*
Yoko Sazanami, Shujiro Urata, and Hiroki Kawai
January 1995 ISBN 0-88132-211-3

Foreign Direct Investment in the United States,
3d ed. Edward M. Graham and Paul R. Krugman
January 1995 ISBN 0-88132-204-0

The Political Economy of Korea-United States
Cooperation* C. Fred Bergsten and
Il SaKong, eds.
February 1995 ISBN 0-88132-213-X

International Debt Reexamined*
William R. Cline
February 1995 ISBN 0-88132-083-8

American Trade Politics, 3d ed. I. M. Destler
April 1995 ISBN 0-88132-215-6

Managing Official Export Credits: The Quest for
a Global Regime* John E. Ray
July 1995 ISBN 0-88132-207-5

Asia Pacific Fusion: Japan's Role in APEC*
Yoichi Funabashi
October 1995 ISBN 0-88132-224-5

Korea-United States Cooperation in the New
World Order* C. Fred Bergsten and
Il SaKong, eds.
February 1996 ISBN 0-88132-226-1

Why Exports Really Matter!*
ISBN 0-88132-221-0

Why Exports Matter More!* ISBN 0-88132-229-6
J. David Richardson and Karin Rindal
July 1995; February 1996

Global Corporations and National Governments
Edward M. Graham
May 1996 ISBN 0-88132-111-7

Global Economic Leadership and the Group of
Seven C. Fred Bergsten and C. Randall Henning
May 1996 ISBN 0-88132-218-0

The Trading System after the Uruguay Round*
John Whalley and Colleen Hamilton
July 1996 ISBN 0-88132-131-1

Private Capital Flows to Emerging Markets after
the Mexican Crisis* Guillermo A. Calvo, Morris
Goldstein, and Eduard Hochreiter
September 1996 ISBN 0-88132-232-6

The Crawling Band as an Exchange Rate
Regime: Lessons from Chile, Colombia, and
Israel John Williamson
September 1996 ISBN 0-88132-231-8

Flying High: Liberalizing Civil Aviation in the
Asia Pacific* Gary Clyde Hufbauer and
Christopher Findlay
November 1996 ISBN 0-88132-227-X

Measuring the Costs of Visible Protection
in Korea* Namdoo Kim
November 1996 ISBN 0-88132-236-9

The World Trading System: Challenges Ahead
Jeffrey J. Schott
December 1996 ISBN 0-88132-235-0

WORKS IN PROGRESS

DISTRIBUTORS OUTSIDE THE UNITED STATES

Australia, New Zealand,
and Papua New Guinea
D. A. Information Services
648 Whitehorse Road
Mitcham, Victoria 3132, Australia
Tel: 61-3-9210-7777
Fax: 61-3-9210-7788
Email: service@dadirect.com.au
www.dadirect.com.au

India, Bangladesh, Nepal, and Sri Lanka
Viva Books Private Limited
Mr. Vinod Vasishtha
4737/23 Ansari Road
Daryaganj, New Delhi 110002
India
Tel: 91-11-4224-2200
Fax: 91-11-4224-2240
Email: viva@vivagroupindia.net
www.vivagroupindia.com

Mexico, Central America, South America,
and Puerto Rico
US PubRep, Inc.
311 Dean Drive
Rockville, MD 20851
Tel: 301-838-9276
Fax: 301-838-9278
Email: c.falk@ieee.org

Asia (*Brunei, Burma, Cambodia, China,*
Hong Kong, Indonesia, Korea, Laos, Malaysia,
Philippines, Singapore, Taiwan, Thailand,
and Vietnam)
East-West Export Books (EWEB)
University of Hawaii Press
2840 Kolowalu Street
Honolulu, Hawaii 96822-1888
Tel: 808-956-8830
Fax: 808-988-6052
Email: eweb@hawaii.edu

Canada
Renouf Bookstore
5369 Canotek Road, Unit 1
Ottawa, Ontario KlJ 9J3, Canada
Tel: 613-745-2665
Fax: 613-745-7660
www.renoufbooks.com

Japan
United Publishers Services Ltd.
1-32-5, Higashi-shinagawa
Shinagawa-ku, Tokyo 140-0002
Japan
Tel: 81-3-5479-7251
Fax: 81-3-5479-7307
Email: purchasing@ups.co.jp
For trade accounts only. Individuals will find
Institute books in leading Tokyo bookstores.

Middle East
MERIC
2 Bahgat Ali Street, El Masry Towers
Tower D, Apt. 24
Zamalek, Cairo
Egypt
Tel. 20-2-7633824
Fax: 20-2-7369355
Email: mahmoud_fouda@mericonline.com
www.mericonline.com

United Kingdom, Europe
(*including Russia and Turkey*)**, Africa,**
and Israel
The Eurospan Group
c/o Turpin Distribution
Pegasus Drive
Stratton Business Park
Biggleswade, Bedfordshire
SG18 8TQ
United Kingdom
Tel: 44 (0) 1767-604972
Fax: 44 (0) 1767-601640
Email: eurospan@turpin-distribution.com
www.eurospangroup.com/bookstore

Visit our website at:
www.piie.com
E-mail orders to:
petersonmail@presswarehouse.com